Ada

Concurrent Programming

Narain Gehani

AT & T Bell Telephone Laboratories, Inc.

PRENTICE-HALL, INC.
Englewood Cliffs, New Jersey 07632

Library of Congress Cataloging in Publication Data

Gehani, Narain (date)
　　Ada : concurrent programming.

　　Includes index.
　　1. Ada (Computer program language)　2. Parallel
programming (Computer science)　I. Title.
QA76.73.A35G433　1984　　001.64'24　　84-4
ISBN 0-13-004011-8

To Sweets

**Prentice-Hall Software Series
Brian W. Kernighan, advisor**

Editorial/production supervision: Nancy Milnamow
Cover design: Lundgren Graphics
Manufacturing buyer: Gordon Osbourne

Printed in the United States of America

10　9　8　7　6　5　4　3　2

ISBN　0-13-004011-8

Prentice-Hall International, Inc., *London*
Prentice-Hall of Australia Pty. Limited, *Sydney*
Editora Prentice-Hall do Brasil, Ltda., *Rio de Janeiro*
Prentice-Hall Canada Inc., *Toronto*
Prentice-Hall of India Private Limited, *New Delhi*
Prentice-Hall of Japan, Inc., *Tokyo*
Prentice-Hall of Southeast Asia Pte. Ltd., *Singapore*
Whitehall Books Limited, *Wellington, New Zealand*

Contents

Preface

1. Advantages of Concurrent Programming Facilities

Concurrent algorithms occur in many application areas; operating systems, databases, simulation, weather prediction, real-time system design, scientific programming, artificial intelligence and robotics all need concurrent programming facilities. The presence of such facilities in a programming language allows the natural expression of these algorithms as concurrent programs—a distinct advantage if the underlying computer offers parallelism. On the other hand, the lack of concurrent programming facilities forces these concurrent algorithms to be written as sequential programs, destroying the structure of the algorithms and making them hard to understand and analyze. It is usually difficult, if not impossible, for a compiler to extract the concurrency from a concurrent algorithm expressed as a sequential program. Consequently, sequential programs representing concurrent algorithms cannot be executed efficiently on computers offering genuine parallelism. By exploiting the fact that peripheral devices can operate in parallel with the processor, concurrent programs can be more efficiently executed even on a single processor.

2. Reasons for the Renewed Interest in Concurrent Programming

Initial interest in concurrent programming, not withstanding the fact that early computers did not offer genuine parallelism, resulted from two needs—the desire to exploit the ability of the peripherals and the CPU to operate in parallel, and the desire to express concurrent algorithms easily. Much vigor has been injected into concurrent programming research by recent developments in computer architectures and economics of computer manufacturing, which have made it feasible to construct networks of computers-on-a-chip that rival the power of big computers at a fraction of their cost. There is one problem with these computer networks. How can programs be written so that different program components can be efficiently executed on different component computers of the computer network—the components communicating using messages or using shared memory?

3. Debate: How Should Concurrency Be Provided?

Traditional and widely used programming languages, such as Pascal, Fortran and C, do not provide any facilities for concurrent programming. Providing such facilities has been considered by many to be the domain of the underlying operating system. Concurrent execution of a program is achieved by means of ad hoc operating system calls with no clear or precisely defined semantics. This exacerbates the problems of program understanding, portability and correctness. To this day, some computer scientists believe that concurrent programming facilities should not be provided by a programming language, but instead should be made available to programs by the operating system.

Writing concurrent programs is harder than writing sequential programs, especially if the underlying computer architecture consists of a network of hundreds or thousands of computers. Consequently, another group of computer scientists believes that instead of designing concurrent programming facilities, language designers should focus on programming languages that will allow a compiler to extract concurrency from sequential programs.

I shall discuss the pros and cons of providing concurrent programming facilities in programming languages in this book.

Sequential programming is now reaching a stage of maturity. After over 25 years of experience in writing sequential programs in a high-level programming language (since the design of Fortran), there has now emerged a general consensus on the facilities that should be provided for sequential programming. For example, it is now generally agreed that a programming language should provide statements for sequential composition, selection and loops, type checking, facilities for modular program construction, separate compilation and so on. However, despite this consensus, there is still some debate on the specifics. For example, although it is agreed that strong typing is good, because it leads to better error checking and because it allows a compiler to generate good code, there is disagreement on how strongly a programming language should enforce its typing rules. Strong-typing proponents argue that strict enforcement of typing leads to maximum error detection; its opponents argue that it leads to inflexibility and hinders the writing of programs.

In the case of concurrent programming, as yet there is not much experience in using high-level concurrent programming facilities—especially in writing production quality software. Consequently, computer scientists have not been able to arrive at a consensus on appropriate high-level facilities for concurrent programming.

I expect that the inclusion of concurrent programming facilities in the Ada language will have a major influence on the eventual consensus on high-level concurrent programming facilities. Concurrent programming in the Ada language is easy and straightforward, because its facilities, although novel and extensive, are simple to understand and use.

4. Concurrency in Ada

Earlier programming languages, such as PL/I and Algol 68, provided rudimentary facilities for concurrent programming. Recognition of the importance of concurrency has led to the design of several new languages, such as Concurrent Pascal (and other variants of Pascal with concurrent facilities), Modula, Modula-2, Concurrent Euclid and now Ada with high-level facilities for concurrent programming.

From a programming language viewpoint, a major advance was a proposal by Hoare [HOA78b] in which he advocated the use of the *rendezvous* concept as the basis for concurrent programming. Hoare defined a concurrent program a collection of sequential programs executing in parallel—all cooperating to implement one common goal. These sequential programs, i.e., processes, interact by first synchronizing and then exchanging information; individual activities are resumed upon completion of the interaction. Synchronization and communication are viewed as an integral activity, which is called the *rendezvous*. Ada's concurrent programming facilities are based on Hoare's ideas with modifications and additions to deal with realities of hardware and with other practical needs, such as the ability to write program libraries and the ability to respond to errors and failures.

Ada is the first major general purpose programming language to provide high-level concurrent programming facilities based on the rendezvous concept. Although these facilities seem to be elegant and easy to use, they are as yet essentially untried and untested in the field. Only time and experience will lead to their useful evaluation. Consequently, it is natural to expect the discovery of problems and limitations. For example, although these facilities seem quite elegant and appropriate for many kinds of concurrent programming applications, such as operating systems, real-time programming and device drivers, they do not seem to be very appropriate for some application areas, e.g., numerical analysis, where concurrent programming involves writing parallel vector and matrix operations.

5. Goals of This Book

In this book, I will explain the concurrent programming facilities in Ada and show how to use them effectively in writing concurrent programs. I will also briefly survey concurrent programming facilities in other languages, discuss some issues specific to concurrent programming and, finally, discuss some limitations of the concurrent programming facilities in Ada.

6. About This Book

This book is aimed at readers with a good knowledge of a high-level sequential programming language such as C, Pascal, PL/I, Fortran, Algol 60 or the sequential part of Ada. Familiarity with concurrent facilities in languages such as PL/I or Algol 68, Concurrent Pascal, Concurrent Euclid, Modula or Modula-2, or with concurrent programming concepts such as *communicating sequential processes* and *monitors*, will make it easier to understand Ada's concurrent programming facilities.

Most published concurrent programming examples are drawn from the realm of operating systems. As mentioned earlier, the need for concurrent programming arises in many other application areas. To rectify this bias, this book contains many examples from other application areas, such as simulation, real-time programming and device control.

This book was written using, as the basis, a major portion of the chapter on concurrency in *Ada: An Advanced Introduction* [GEH83a]. Some examples have also been taken from that book. A considerable amount of new material has been added, along with many new examples. Chapters in this book focus on the following topics:

- An introduction to concurrent programming—the concurrent programming model in Ada and a historical view of other concurrent programming models.

- Tasking, i.e., concurrent programming, facilities in Ada.

- Task types.

- Exceptions and tasking.

- Device drivers.

- Real-time programming.

- Topics related to concurrent programming.

- More examples of concurrent programming.

In addition to Chapter 8, which contains only examples, each chapter contains several complete examples. These were tested using the New York University's Ada compiler, the first validated Ada compiler. This compiler, which is written in SETL, requires an enormous amount of memory to run and is very slow. Consequently, only limited program testing was possible. Moreover, some programs had to be tested in a simulated environment since the NYU compiler does not support *representation* specifications which allow an Ada program to interface with the hardware.

The examples given in the book are developed using stepwise refinement [WIR71, GEH81] to help the reader in understanding the structure of the solution.

For the benefit of the reader not familiar with the Ada language, the sequential part of Ada is summarized in the Appendix. This summary is essentially a condensation of the seven chapters in *Ada: An Advanced Introduction* which focus on the sequential aspects of Ada.

Throughout the book, references to the appropriate section of the *Ada Reference Manual* [DOD83] are provided (numbers in brackets, e.g. [5.2]) as an aid in looking up additional details. These references appear in chapter and section headings and in the text.

Finally, the book contains an annotated bibliography of many articles and books related to the Ada language (especially those dealing with its concurrent programming facilities) and to concurrent programming in general. Readers are urged to scan the bibliography, since this may whet their appetite for concurrent programming and lead them to read some of the papers or books—many of which are excellent.

7. Preparation of the Book

This book was prepared using the extensive document preparation tools such as *pic* (preprocessor for drawing figures), *tbl* (preprocessor for making tables), *eqn* (preprocessor for formatting equations), *mm* (collection of TROFF macros for page layout) and *troff* (formatter) which are available on the Unix^{TM} operating system.

The Unix operating system encourages the use of concurrency by providing facilities that allow the convenient specification of concurrent processes and a limited form of interaction between them. For example, the concurrent execution of processes P_1, P_2, P_3, $\cdots$ P_n is specified as

$$P_1 \mid P_2 \mid P_3 \mid \cdots \mid P_n$$

The output of P_1 is *piped* to P_2, the output of P_2 is piped to P_3 and so on.

Concurrent execution of the above tools was used to phototypeset this book (of course!). A simplified version of the command used for typesetting is

$$\text{pic} \mid \text{tbl} \mid \text{eqn} \mid \text{troff} -\text{mm} - \mid \text{apsend}$$

The program *apsend* takes the output of the formatter, *troff*, and sends it to the typesetter to produce the galleys.

Murray Hill, N. J.   Narain Gehani

Acknowledgements

Without the active support of my current and past management, A. N. Netravali, R. W. Lucky, J. O. Limb and H. G. Alles, this book might not have seen the light of day. I am grateful to them for their understanding and encouragement.

I have benefited immensely from the comments and criticism that my friends and colleagues have so generously provided. I must thank R. B. Allen, A. R. Feuer, R. E. Fritz, D. Gay, D. Gries, B. W. Kernighan, J. P. Linderman, J. C. McGraw, A. N. McGettrick, W. D. Roome, E. Schonberg and C. S. Wetherell for their assistance. In particular, I very grateful to Bob Allen, David Gay, David Gries, John Linderman and Bill Roome for their extremely detailed comments and suggestions. I am also grateful to J. P. Fishburn for helping me understand various versions of the alpha-beta algorithm.

R. L. Drechsler has helped me beyond the call of duty with various kinds of typesetting problems; for this help I am very grateful to him. I must also thank Phyllis Policastro of Reprographic Services at Bell Labs for always cheerfully agreeing to my requests for quick service.

Finally, testing of the examples in this book was made possible by the NYU Ada Compiler, which was provided to me by Professor E. Schonberg and D. Shields of New York University.

Chapter 1: **Concurrent Programming: A Quick Survey** [9]

1. Introduction

The Ada programming language, like PL/I and Algol 68 but unlike most other major programming languages, such as Algol 60, Pascal, Cobol, Fortran or C, provides facilities for concurrent programming. A programming language that does not provide such facilities discourages programmers from inventing concurrent solutions for their problems—Ludwig Wittgenstein's famous statement is quite appropriate here:

> The limits of my language mean the limits of my world.

The ability to write *concurrent programs*, i.e., programs with components that can be executed in parallel, is desirable for many reasons [HOA78a, GEH83a]:

- It leads to notational convenience and conceptual elegance in writing operating systems, real-time systems, database systems and simulation programs, all of which may have many events occurring concurrently.

- Inherently concurrent algorithms are best expressed with the concurrency explicitly stated; otherwise the structure of the algorithm may be lost.

- It can reduce program execution time, because genuine multiprocessing hardware can be used to execute different parts of a program in parallel.

- Even on single CPU (central processing unit) computers concurrent programming can reduce program execution time because lengthy input/output operations and the CPU operation can proceed in parallel.

PL/I and Algol 68 were two of the first programming languages to provide concurrent programming facilities. However, these facilities were rather rudimentary. For example, PL/I provided low-level facilities for task (i.e., parallel process) creation and an inter-task signaling mechanism. These facilities were not widely used because they were low-level in nature and they did not blend well with the rest of PL/I. Newer languages, such as Concurrent Pascal, Concurrent Euclid, Modula-2 and Ada, provide high-level concurrent programming facilities that are well integrated with the rest of the language. Consequently, these languages are preferred over PL/I and Algol 68 for concurrent programming.

The initial desire to use concurrent programming languages stemmed from attempts to write conceptually elegant programs that reflected the structure of an algorithm. However, current interest is motivated largely by the desire to take advantage of recent developments (in computer economics and architectures) that have made the construction of networks of computers-on-a-chip feasible. These network computers have computing capabilities which compare favorably with those of large computers; they are more reliable and cheaper than maxicomputers. Intercomputer communication on these network computers occurs by means of message passing or using shared memory.

How can efficient and reliable programs be written so their components can be executed in parallel on different computers that form the network computer? The search for an answer has renewed vigorous interest in concurrent programming and has been the inspiration for much recent research [AND83].

1.1 Should the Programming Language Provide Concurrent Programming Facilities?

Although the Ada language provides explicit concurrent programming facilities, many computer scientists argue that it is not the role of a programming language to provide concurrency. Some of them believe that concurrent programming facilities should be provided by means of library subprograms; others believe that *dataflow* programming is a much better approach.

1.1.1 Concurrent Programming Facilities Provided by Library Subprograms: Some of the first applications of concurrent programming were in the design of operating systems. One school of thought favors providing concurrency by means of library subprograms that call appropriate primitives of the underlying operating system. It can be argued that providing concurrent programming facilities in a programming language is inappropriate, since it makes the hard task of language design even more difficult [RIT78]; also, such facilities tend to make strong assumptions about the underlying operating system, when in actual practice there may be a very poor match between these facilities and the operating system [RIT78]. On the other hand, the availability of appropriate concurrent programming facilities in the programming language used to implement an operating system can actually simplify the complex task of writing an operating system—an inherently concurrent program.

Using library subprograms for concurrency in an otherwise sequential programming language may also lead to additional disadvantages:

1. The sequential programming language may not have appropriate control statements to support the concurrent programming facilities, since these facilities are provided as an afterthought to an otherwise sequential programming language. Consequently, it may not be easy to specify clearly and precisely some concurrent programming concepts.

2. The semantics of these subprograms and the interaction of concurrency with the facilities in the rest of the programming language may not be clearly or precisely defined.

3. The subprograms providing concurrency are often local and ad hoc extensions to the sequential programming language, resulting in programs that are difficult, if not impossible, to port.

4. A compiler may not be easily able to optimize concurrent programs well, since it will be tuned to optimizing sequential programs [PRA83].

5. It will be necessary to use assembly language to implement these library subprograms because the sequential language does not have facilities to express parallelism. Use of assembly language violates the assumption that a library is a true extension of the language because all the subprograms in the library could have been written in the language [PRA83].

1.1.2 Dataflow Programming: Another group of computer scientists, representing the *dataflow* school of thought, feel that programming languages should not provide explicit concurrent programming faciltities. Instead, they advocate that languages be designed to allow writing of apparently sequential programs in a way that lets a compiler easily extract the implicit concurrency inherent in the programs. For example, implicit concurrency in programs written in the dataflow language VAL [MCG82b] is encouraged by providing array operations and by not allowing side effects in expressions.

Dataflow programming advocates feel that writing sequential programs is easier than writing concurrent programs (rightly so!) and that a compiler can do a better job of extracting the concurrency than the average programmer in transforming sequential programs to concurrent programs. However, one problem with dataflow programs is that they cannot be executed efficiently on conventional computer architectures.

Dataflow programming proponents argue that conventional computer architectures are obsolete, since physical constraints, such as the speed of light and power-cooling ratios, may soon limit the speed achievable by a single processor [MCG82b]. As an alternative, they propose radically different computer architectures called *dataflow* machines, which consist of hundreds, even thousands, of cooperating processors. It is for such computers that dataflow programming languages will be advantageous, since the explicit specification of concurrency to harness the numerous processors will be a monumental, if not impossible, task.

Dataflow programming suffers from two important disadvantages:

1. It offers parallelism at the "micro-level", i.e., at the level of basic operations, such as addition and subtraction; it does not offer parallelism at the "macro-level", i.e., at the subprogram level. Consequently, dataflow programming seems suitable primarily for computation-intensive programs that perform operations on large arrays, e.g., programs for

weather prediction. Dataflow programming languages, such as VAL, make it easy for new array values to be computed in parallel instead of one element at a time [MCG82b].

2. No realistic dataflow machines have been constructed.

1.2 Interaction Between Parallel Processes

An important facet of concurrent programming is process interaction. Interaction between processes consists of information exchange and synchronization. Processes need to interact with each other for several reasons:

1. *Cooperative Computing or Information Exchange*: A program may be designed as a collection of several processes with each process responsible for a portion of the computation. These processes may have to interact with each other to exchange information.

2. *Activity Synchronization*: Processes execute in parallel with independent speeds, i.e., asynchronously. To coordinate their activities, processes may need to synchronize with each other.

3. *Sharing a Limited Resource in Mutual Exclusion*: A process may require exclusive access to (i.e., use of) a shared resource, such as a line printer [HOA78a] or a portion of a database. To get exclusive access to a resource, a process must interact with other processes competing for the shared resource. This interaction may be direct or indirect by means of a process that manages the resource.

2. Concurrency in Ada

Ada provides high-level facilities for expressing concurrent algorithms. The model of concurrency in Ada is based on Hoare's "Communicating Sequential Processes" [HOA78b], in which parallel processes synchronize and communicate by means of input and output statements. This model was also influenced by Brinch Hansen's "Distributed Processes" [BRI78a].

An Ada implementation may provide true concurrency if the underlying computer is a multicomputer or a multiprocessor, or it may simulate concurrency by multiprogramming (i.e., interleaved execution). Whether the concurrency is real or simulated will not affect the result of program execution, *provided* that the program does not rely on the underlying hardware configuration or on the hardware timing characteristics.

2.1 Rendezvous—The Basis of Concurrent Facilities in Ada [9.5]

An important notion in process interaction arises from viewing process synchronization and communication as inseparable activities [DOD79b, CON63]. Two processes interact by first synchronizing, then exchanging information and, finally, by continuing their individual activities. This synchronization or meeting to exchange information is called the *rendezvous*. The rendezvous concept unifies the concepts of synchronization and communication between processes.

Ada is the first programming language to use the rendezvous as the basis of its concurrent programming facilities. Consequently, only experience in using these facilities will prove their appropriateness and suitability for a variety of programming domains.

Processes are called *tasks* in Ada. Tasks, along with subprograms, packages and generic units, constitute the four kinds of program units from which programs are composed. Tasks contain synchronization and communication points called *entries*, which may be called by other tasks. An entry call is very similar to a procedure call—the similarity is more syntactic than semantic. Synchronization between two tasks occurs when the task *issuing* an *entry call* and the task *accepting* an entry call establish a rendezvous.

Ada's rendezvous can be explained in terms of two tasks A and B that need to synchronize or exchange information. Task A, which calls an entry of B, will have to wait if B is not ready to accept the entry call. If A does not want to wait for B, then it has the option of doing something else and issuing the entry call again at some later time (i.e., A can *poll* B to see if B is ready to rendezvous). A can alternatively elect to wait a specified period for B to accept the call before giving up (i.e., A can *time-out*) and possibly try again later. If A waits for B, then when B gets ready, a rendezvous is established between A and B.

If several tasks call the same entry of a task, then the calling tasks will rendezvous with the called task in first-in first-out (FIFO) order. During the rendezvous, execution of the calling task is suspended while the accepting task executes statements necessary for exchanging information. After the rendezvous is complete, both tasks resume execution in parallel.

The rendezvous concept is explained pictorially in Figure 1.1 where three situations involving task A calling task B are illustrated:

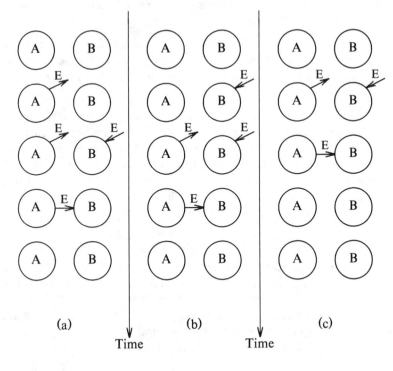

(a)   (b)   (c)

Time   Time

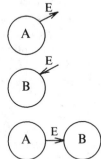

Task A has issued an entry call E to task B

Task B is ready to accept a call to entry E

Task A and B rendezvous at entry E

Figure 1.1: Rendezvous

In case (a), task A issues a call to entry E of B before task B is ready to accept it. Task A waits (i.e., its execution is suspended) until task B is ready to rendezvous. In case (b), task B is ready to accept the entry call before A is ready to issue one. This time task B waits for task A. Finally, in case (c), task A issues the entry call at exactly the same moment that B becomes ready to accept it.

Having established the rendezvous, i.e., having synchronized, the two tasks, if necessary, exchange information. After the rendezvous is completed, both tasks resume execution.

Communication between two tasks can occur during a rendezvous. Communication may be bidirectional and can take place using actual parameters in the entry call and the corresponding formal parameters in the *accept* statement corresponding to the entry call. The rendezvous mechanism is the primary means of communication between tasks.[1]

2.2 A Vending Machine—An Example [BRI78a]

The flavor of tasking in Ada is illustrated by giving details of one task, named VENDING_MACHINE. This task is used to control a vending machine that accepts coins one at a time (see Figure 1.2):

Figure 1.2: The vending machine

---

1. Tasks can also communicate using global variables—synchronization must then be done explicitly.

When the only button on the vending machine is pressed, the machine delivers an item—provided the item supply has not been exhausted and the coins deposited by the customer cover the cost of the item; otherwise all the money deposited by the customer is returned. Customers can either insert coins or press the button, but cannot do both at the same time.

Task VENDING_MACHINE interacts with two tasks: MONEY and SUPPLIES (see Figure 1.3):

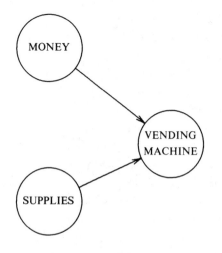

Figure 1.3: Tasks controlling the vending machine

When the customer inserts a coin into the machine, task MONEY (the interface to the *coin acceptor* mechanism) calls entry INSERT of VENDING_MACHINE with the amount of money inserted. When the customer presses the button, task SUPPLIES (the interface to the button, and the item release and change return mechanisms) calls entry PUSH of VENDING MACHINE to find out how much change is to be returned and whether or not an item is to be supplied to the customer.

All three tasks execute concurrently—each task can be executed by a dedicated computer or, alternatively, all three tasks can be executed on the same computer by means of interleaved execution.

Like subprograms and packages in Ada, a task has two parts—a specification and a body. Only information given in a task specification is accessible by other tasks. The specification of task VENDING_MACHINE is[2]

```
task VENDING_MACHINE is
   entry INSERT(COIN: in INTEGER);
   entry PUSH(CHANGE, GOODS: out INTEGER);
end VENDING_MACHINE;
```

Task VENDING_MACHINE has two entries—INSERT and PUSH. Entry INSERT is called by task MONEY to inform task VENDING_MACHINE about the amount of money deposited by the customer. Entry PUSH is called by task SUPPLIES to find out whether or not an item is to be given to the customer and how much change is to be returned to the customer.

The body, i.e., the implementation, of VENDING_MACHINE is

```
task body VENDING_MACHINE is
   ITEMS: INTEGER := 50;
   PRICE: INTEGER := 25;
   PAID: INTEGER := 0;
begin
loop    ——forever
   select    ——one of INSERT or PUSH
      accept INSERT(COIN: in INTEGER) do
         PAID := PAID + COIN;
      end INSERT;    ——calling task is free to resume execution now
   or
      accept PUSH(CHANGE, GOODS: out INTEGER) do
         if ITEMS > 0 and PAID >= PRICE then
            CHANGE := PAID - PRICE;
            GOODS := 1; ITEMS := ITEMS - 1;
         else
            CHANGE := PAID; GOODS := 0;
         end if;
      end PUSH;    ——calling task is free to resume execution now
      PAID := 0;
   end select;
end loop;
end VENDING_MACHINE;
```

---

2. Ada identifiers that are designated as *reserved words* will be printed in boldface in the text to distinguish them from other identifiers.

Task VENDING_MACHINE never terminates—it loops forever, accepting calls to either entry INSERT or entry PUSH. It is aborted when the computer is halted, as it might be for replenishing supplies.

The *select* statement has two alternatives—one for each of the two entries INSERT and PUSH. Execution of the *select* statement occurs as follows:

1. If there is no call pending to either entry INSERT or entry PUSH, then execution is delayed until such an entry call is issued.

2. If there is only one entry call pending (to either entry) then that entry call is accepted.

3. If there are several calls pending to only one entry, say to INSERT as a result of a customer being extremely fast and adroit at putting coins in the machine, then the first call is accepted.

4. If calls to both entries are pending, then the first call to one of INSERT or PUSH (nondeterministic, i.e., random, selection is used here) is accepted.

An *accept* statement is executed in sequence, just like any other statement. Execution of an *accept* statement is delayed until a matching entry call has been made by another task, i.e., when a rendezvous is possible. Acceptance of an entry call means that the corresponding *accept* statement is executed.

Examples of calls to entries INSERT and PUSH, issued say from tasks MONEY and SUPPLIES, respectively, are

```
VENDING_MACHINE.INSERT(AMOUNT);
VENDING_MACHINE.PUSH(RETURN_MONEY, QUANTITY);
```

When a rendezvous occurs, the corresponding *accept* statement is executed. Syntactically, entry calls are similar to procedure calls, but they must be qualified by the name of the task containing the entry. In this example, entry calls are semantically similar to procedure calls. Semantic differences between entry and procedure calls will become clear in later chapters when the semantics of entry calls are explained. The rendezvous is terminated upon completion of the *accept* statement.

Only the skeletons of the bodies of the tasks MONEY and SUPPLIES are given, so as to avoid getting into details of how tasks interface with the hardware, e.g., the coin acceptor mechanism (interfacing with the hardware is discussed in Chapter 5 on *Device Drivers*).

The body of task MONEY has the form

```
task body MONEY is
    ⋮
begin
    loop    ——forever
        Wait until a coin is deposited
        ⋮
        VENDING_MACHINE.INSERT(AMOUNT);
        ⋮
    end loop;
end MONEY;
```

The body of task SUPPLIES has the form

```
task body SUPPLIES is
    ⋮
begin
    loop    ——forever
        VENDING_MACHINE.PUSH(RETURN_MONEY, QUANTITY);
        if RETURN_MONEY /= 0 then
            Return change RETURN_MONEY;
        end if;
        if QUANTITY /= 0 then
            Supply QUANTITY items to customer;
        end if;
    end loop;
end SUPPLIES;
```

There are significant differences between Ada's tasking facilities and the concurrent programming facilities found in other languages or language proposals. For later illustration of some of these differences, note the following two aspects of the task VENDING_MACHINE:

1. *Internal Bookkeeping*: The statement

    PAID := 0;

    which represents internal bookkeeping (a very small portion of the task in this example), is not contained in the *accept* statement for the entry PUSH. It may be executed in parallel with task SUPPLIES after the rendezvous at entry PUSH has been completed. SUPPLIES is not held up unnecessarily while this statement is being executed. Had this internal bookkeeping been done inside the *accept* statement for PUSH, then resumption of SUPPLIES would have to wait for the completion of the bookkeeping.

    Since the internal bookkeeping is minimal in this example, parallel execution of the internal bookkeeping does not represent a big gain of concurrency here. However, in cases where the internal bookkeeping represents a significant portion of the execution of a task, a *substantial gain* in concurrency will be achieved by ensuring that the internal bookkeeping is done outside the *accept* statement, i.e., in parallel with the calling task.

2. *Synchronization Constraints*: The flow of execution in a task can be used to ensure that entry calls are accepted in some desired order. Suppose that every call to INSERT is to be followed by a call to PUSH. This constraint can be easily implemented by modifying the flow of execution in VENDING_MACHINE—by removing the *select* statement:

```
loop
    accept INSERT(COIN: in INTEGER) do
        .
        .
    end INSERT;
    accept PUSH(CHANGE, GOODS: out INTEGER) do
        .
        .
    end PUSH;
    PAID := 0;
end loop;
```

Every rendezvous at INSERT must now be followed by a rendezvous at PUSH and vice versa.

2.3 Naming Asymmetry

The naming scheme used for the rendezvous is asymmetric; the caller (entry call issuer) is required to specify the name of the called task (entry call acceptor), while the called task does not specify the name of the caller. For example, in the case of the task VENDING_MACHINE, any task could call its entries INSERT and PUSH. On the other hand, when calling entries INSERT and PUSH, the name of the task containing them, i.e., VENDING_MACHINE, must be specified.

This asymmetry was introduced in Ada to allow the development of libraries containing *server* tasks. However, one consequence of this asymmetry is that the task containing an entry cannot restrict calling of the entry to certain tasks.

2.4 Mutual Exclusion

As mentioned earlier, a special case of synchronization is *mutual exclusion* [ROU80] by which a task gets exclusive access to a shared resource, e.g., a line printer, a variable, a portion of a database or a tape drive. Exclusive access is required for meaningful operations in many situations. For example, suppose that several tasks want to use a line printer. If these tasks do not get exclusive access to the printer, then the output of these tasks may be intermingled, resulting in garbage output.

Exclusive use of a resource can be provided in Ada by using a task to control the resource and by having other tasks access the resource via the controlling task. Requests (entry calls) for the resource are accepted and honored one at a time by the controlling task. A requesting task has exclusive use of the resource while it is in rendezvous with the controlling task, since the controlling task will rendezvous with only one task at a time (no nested rendezvous). The controlling task executes requests to use the resource on behalf of the requesting tasks.

An alternative way of providing mutual exclusion is by using a task to simulate a *semaphore*, which is a low-level, but very versatile, synchronization facility (see section 3.1 of this chapter). For example, the mutual exclusion provided by a task controlling a resource cannot be used directly to implement a solution of the *multiple reader single writer* problem (i.e., simultaneous reading of shared data by many tasks, but data updates by only one task at a time; this is discussed in Chapter 2 on *Tasking Facilities*). This problem can be solved by using semaphores.

3. Synchronization and Communication—A Historical Perspective

Over the years, several concurrent programming mechanisms have been proposed each focusing on a different aspect of task interaction, i.e., information exchange, synchronization or mutual exclusion. Experience and better understanding have lead to an evolution of mechanisms for concurrent programming with emphasis on goals such as ease of use, program readability, understandability, reliability and verifiability, and error detection.[3]

To give a flavor of concurrent programming mechanisms found in other programming languages, the semaphore will be discussed in detail and some other mechanisms will be discussed briefly. Semaphores are a versatile tool and can be used in a variety of ways. But, because they are a low-level synchronization tool, their use leads to many problems.

Many higher level alternatives have been proposed that avoid the problems associated with semaphores. All these mechanisms are equivalent because they can all be used for implementing task communication, task synchronization and mutual exclusion. However, these mechanisms have been most successful in eliminating problems only in the aspect of concurrency on which they focus.

---

3. Readers interested only in Ada's concurrent programming facilities can skip the remainder of this chapter, which describes some other concurrent programming facilities. These facilities are also briefly compared with the facilities in Ada. The vending machine example is used to illustrate some of the differences.

For example, path expressions [CAM74] focus on synchronization, message schemes and pipes [THO74] focus on communication, and critical regions and monitors focus on mutual exclusion. None of these mechanisms provides an elegant way to support all three aspects of task interaction: communication, synchronization and mutual exclusion. Hoare's recent concurrent programming proposal, "Communicating Sequential Processes" [HOA78b], represents the first suggestion to support all three aspects of task interaction.

3.1 Semaphores

The *semaphore*, one of the earliest synchronization tools, was invented by E. W. Dijkstra [DIJ68]. A semaphore[4] is a variable that is used to exchange timing signals between concurrent processes by means of the operations P (wait) and V (signal),[5] which have the following semantics [BRI73]:

P(S)   If the semaphore S has the value TRUE, then suspend the calling task; otherwise, set S to TRUE and let the task continue execution.

V(S)   If there are tasks waiting, suspended as a result of executing a P operation on S, then allow one such task to proceed; otherwise set the semaphore S to FALSE.

The P and V operations are *atomic*, i.e., indivisible, and are mutually exclusive on the same semaphore. Semaphores are assumed to be FALSE initially.

The use of a semaphore as a synchronization facility is illustrated by the following paradigm in which task A waits for a signal from task B:

---

4. According to the *Webster's New Collegiate Dictionary*, a *semaphore* is an apparatus for visual signaling. The version of the semaphore discussed in this section is also called the *binary* semaphore, because it can have only one of two values—TRUE or FALSE. Another version of the semaphore, called the *integer* or the *general* semaphore [AND83], can be assigned any nonnegative integer value.

5. P and V were originally selected to represent the Dutch words *passeren* and *vrygeven*, which mean *to pass* and *to release*, respectively. Reflections on the definitions of P and V led Dijkstra and his colleagues to consider P as representing the word *prolagen* formed by combining the two Dutch words *proberen* and *verlagen*, which mean *to try* and *to decrease*, respectively, and V as representing the Dutch word *verhogen*, which means *to increase* [AND83].

P(S), i.e., wait for B   V(S), i.e., signal A

(in task A)   (in task B)

Using semaphores, mutual exclusion is easily implemented by requiring all tasks to execute the P operation before accessing the shared data (or using the shared resource) and the V operation after completing access (or use):

```
P(S);                P(S);
access shared data   access shared data
V(S);                V(S);


task A               task B
```

Exclusive access to the shared data is guaranteed if every task sharing the data uses the above paradigm to access the shared data [DOD79b]. A task executing the P operation is delayed if another task is in the midst of accessing the shared data. In this case the delayed task will be allowed to continue only after the task accessing the shared data has completed its access and executed a V operation.

Several tasks may be waiting as a result of executing the P operation. Which waiting task is to be allowed to resume execution when a V operation is performed? Any reasonable scheduling discipline may be used in the implementation of the V operation to select the next task that will be allowed to resume execution. For example, an implementation of the V operation may use the FIFO scheduling discipline' to select the next task that will be allowed to resume execution. Alternatively, a priority scheduling discipline can be used in the implementation of the V operation, but this will require modification of the P operation to allow the specification of a resumption priority. The V operation can then be implemented to allow the task with the highest priority to resume execution; if there is more than one task with the highest priority, then the task that has waited the longest could be allowed to resume execution.

As discussed above, semaphores can be used for both mutual exclusion and synchronization. Although semaphores are simple and easy to use, they are a low-level tool and must be used with care. They do not directly express the concepts of concurrent programming, e.g., mutual exclusion, and must be used to the express high-level concepts just as assembly language instructions are used to express higher-level programming constructs. Like programs that use *gotos*, programs that use the semaphore are hard to understand, difficult to prove correct and error prone. These problems arise because [DOD79b]

- it is possible to bypass semaphore operations by jumping around them,
- forgetting to use the P operation before accessing shared data will allow more than one task to update the shared data simultaneously, resulting in data inconsistency; using them in the wrong order also causes similar problems,
- forgetting to use the V operation after accessing the shared data can lead to a task waiting forever,
- it is not possible to perform an alternative action if a semaphore is busy (i.e., TRUE),
- it is not possible to wait for more than one semaphore and
- semaphores are visible to tasks that do not need them.

3.1.1 The Vending Machine Example Using Semaphores: The vending machine is represented by two integer variables ITEMS and PAID and the two tasks MONEY and SUPPLIES that access these variables. These two tasks synchronize accesses to ITEMS and PAID by means of P and V operations on a semaphore S (see Chapter 4 on *Task Types* for an example illustrating how semaphores are simulated using tasks).

The above variables and the semaphore are declared as

        ITEMS, PRICE, PAID: INTEGER;
        S: SEMAPHORE;   ——initially FALSE

Unlike the Ada version (see section 2.3 of this chapter) where the state of the vending machine, represented by the variables ITEMS and PAID, was encapsulated in the task VENDING_MACHINE, which had its own flow of control, there will be no such task in the semaphore version. The state variables will be global to the tasks MONEY and SUPPLIES, since they must be accessible to both tasks. These variables will have to be initialized by one of the tasks MONEY or SUPPLIES, or by a task created especially for this purpose, by executing the following statements:

        ITEMS := 50; PRICE := 25; PAID := 0;

The variables must, of course, be initialized before the actions of the first customer are processed by task MONEY or task SUPPLIES.

Task MONEY updates variable PAID to reflect the amount of money inserted by the customer by executing the following statements:

```
P(S);
PAID := PAID + COIN;
V(S);
```

When the customer pushes the button, task SUPPLIES computes the amount of change to be returned and the number of items to be delivered, and updates the two variables PAID and ITEMS appropriately:

```
P(S);
if ITEMS > 0 and PAID >= PRICE then
    CHANGE := PAID − PRICE;
    GOODS := 1; ITEMS := ITEMS − 1;
else
    CHANGE := PAID; GOODS := 0;
end if;
PAID := 0;
V(S);
```

Any omission or erroneous use of the P and V operations will lead to errors.

In the Ada version, the state of the vending machine was updated by task VENDING_MACHINE whenever it accepted an entry call from tasks MONEY and SUPPLIES. Moreover, VENDING_MACHINE did its internal bookkeeping in parallel with SUPPLIES. In the semaphore version, the state of the vending machine is updated by tasks MONEY and SUPPLIES executing appropriate statements. The internal bookkeeping, i.e., executing

```
PAID := 0;
```

is now done by SUPPLIES, thus reducing the amount of parallelism in the vending machine. Moreover, conceptually the internal bookkeeping is not the responsibility of task SUPPLIES.

Enforcing the constraint that each insertion of a coin be followed by a button push will require using an additional signaling mechanism. For example, this signaling mechanism can be implemented by using two semaphores X and Y declared as

```
X, Y: SEMAPHORE;
```

Semaphores X and Y will be used by tasks MONEY and SUPPLIES to determine if they can accept a coin from the customer and respond to the pushing of the button, respectively. Since task SUPPLIES must wait until the customer has deposited a coin, semaphore Y will be initialized to TRUE. The vending machine variables are initialized as

```
ITEMS := 50; PRICE := 25; PAID := 0; Y := TRUE;
```

The code executed by task MONEY is modified as follows:

    P(X);   −−after the first execution, MONEY must wait until SUPPLIES
            −−allows it to proceed

    PAID := PAID + COIN;

    V(Y);   −−allow SUPPLIES to proceed

The code executed by task SUPPLIES is modified as follows:

    P(Y);   −−SUPPLIES must wait until MONEY allows it to proceed

    if ITEMS > 0 and PAID >= PRICE then
        CHANGE := PAID − PRICE;
        GOODS := 1; ITEMS := ITEMS − 1;
    else
        CHANGE := PAID; GOODS := 0;
    end if;
    PAID := 0;

    V(X);   −−allow MONEY to proceed

3.2 Critical Regions

The possibility of errors such as the inadvertent omission of the P and V
operations or their use in the wrong order can be eliminated by using the
critical region−a syntactic abbreviation equivalent to the use of the P and V
pair to implement mutual exclusion [BRI72, BRI73b, HOA78a, DOD79b].
The *critical region* statement

    region SD **do** S

specifies that when statement S is executed, it will have exclusive access to the
shared variable SD. Execution of S will be delayed if some other task is in the
process of accessing SD.

An extension of the *critical region* statement, the *conditional critical region*
[BRI72] statement, allows the specification of a synchronization condition with
the shared variable. Execution of the *conditional critical region* statement

    region SD **when** B **do** S

is delayed until the synchronization condition B is true and exclusive access to
SD can be guaranteed. The value of B is determined by repeated checking,
i.e., *busy waiting*.

Critical regions and conditional critical regions represent only a partial solution
to the problems of task interaction. They solve the mutual exclusion problem;

the conditional critical regions also solve the synchronization problem, but CPU time is wasted in busy waiting [BRI72].

Implementation of the vending machine using critical regions is similar to its implementation using semaphores.

3.3 Monitors

A *monitor* is a shared data structure that is accessed using associated operations called *monitor operations.* Monitor operations are performed in mutual exclusion. Simultaneous requests for the execution of monitor operations are serialized by the monitor and executed, in some unspecified order, one at a time. The significance of the monitor concept is that all operations for task synchronization and communication are encapsulated in one place—the monitor [BRI81b]. Concurrent Pascal, designed by Brinch Hansen [BRI75], was the first language to be based on the monitor concept.

Although the monitor is a high-level concurrent programming mechanism, it suffers from several disadvantages. It must be complemented by a low-level synchronization mechanism such as the semaphore. Consequently, concurrent programming facilities based on the monitor are a combination of high-level and low-level concepts and they therefore suffer from some of the same problems associated with semaphores. Moreover, the whole monitor concept is a very intricate combination of shared variables, procedures, task scheduling and modularity [BRI81b].

Unlike an Ada task, a monitor is a passive object. A task executes in parallel with other tasks in the program—each task executes on its own. A monitor, on the other hand, waits for a task to request execution of one of its operations—a monitor operation is executed using the flow of control of the requesting task (requesting execution of a monitor operation is similar to a procedure call).

3.3.1 The Vending Machine Example Using a Monitor: The variables representing the state of the vending machine are encapsulated in a monitor, called VENDING_MACHINE. Monitor operations INSERT and PUSH are called by tasks MONEY and SUPPLIES, respectively, to update the amount of money inserted by the customer and to determine the number of items and change to be given to the customer:

```
monitor VENDING_MACHINE is
ITEMS, PRICE, PAID: INTEGER;

procedure INSERT(COIN: in INTEGER) is
begin
    PAID := PAID + COIN;
end;

procedure PUSH(CHANGE, GOODS: out INTEGER) is
begin
    if ITEMS > 0 and PAID >= PRICE then
        CHANGE := PAID − PRICE;
        GOODS := 1; ITEMS := ITEMS − 1;
    else
        CHANGE := PAID; GOODS := 0;
    end if;
    PAID := 0;
end;
begin
    ITEMS := 50; PRICE := 25; PAID := 0;    −−initial statements
end;
```

The initial statements of a monitor are executed when the declaration of the monitor is processed—prior to accepting any requests to execute the monitor operations.

As in the semaphore version, the internal bookkeeping is not done in parallel with the execution of the task SUPPLIES, since the monitor is a passive object with no flow of control of its own. Moreover, implementation of the synchronization constraint requiring that a call to INSERT (inserting a coin) must be followed by a call to PUSH (pushing of the button) requires the use of a semaphore. Unlike the semaphore version, access to variables ITEMS and PAID is not direct and is possible only by using the monitor operations.

3.4 Message-Based Systems

Several varieties of message-based systems have been proposed and implemented. Basically, in all these systems, a task can send a message to or receive a message from another task. Message sending can be *blocking* or *nonblocking*. In the case of a blocking send, the sender is forced to wait until the message has been accepted by the receiver; in the case of a nonblocking send, the sender is free to continue execution regardless of whether or not the message has been accepted by the receiver—the message is buffered if the receiver is not ready.

Some computer scientists believe that concurrent programming based on message passing schemes is naturally appealing and leads to programs with a high degree of concurrency and efficient resource utilization [GEN81]. However, message-based systems do have some significant disadvantages. For example, a sizable message controller is needed and message-based systems seem to adopt ad hoc conventions for the message format. Moreover, it is usually not possible to implement mutual exclusion efficiently [DOD79b].

3.4.1 The Vending Machine Example Using Messages: The message passing primitives used to implement the vending machine are simplified versions of the primitives in Thoth, a message-based real-time operating system [GEN81].

As in the Ada version (see section 2.3 of this chapter), the vending machine is implemented as three tasks—VENDING_MACHINE, MONEY and SUPPLIES. However, instead of calling entries, these tasks communicate and synchronize using the message passing primitives. Tasks MONEY and SUPPLIES send messages of type ACTION to task VENDING_MACHINE, indicating that the value of the coin deposited by the customer and that the customer has pressed the button, respectively. Message type ACTION is defined as

```
type ACTION is
  record
     OPERATION: OPCODE;
     COIN: INTEGER;   --ignored for PUSH
  end record;
```

where OPCODE is defined as

```
type OPCODE is (INSERT, PUSH);
```

Task VENDING_MACHINE sends a message of type DELIVER to task SUPPLIES indicating the amount of change to be returned to the customer and the number of items to be supplied to the customer:

```
type DELIVER is
  record
     CHANGE, GOODS: INTEGER;
  end record;
```

A message of record type T, with fields f_1, f_2, ..., f_n, is written as

$$T(v_1, v_2, ..., v_n)$$

where v_i is the value for the record field f_i. For example,

```
ACTION(INSERT, 25)
```

is a message of type ACTION with fields OPERATION and COIN having the values INSERT and 25, respectively.

A task sends a message M to a task T by executing the *blocking send* command

    send(T, M);

The task sending the message is blocked (i.e., delayed) until the message is accepted by the task T. A task receives a message M from another task by executing the *receive* command:

    S := **receive**(M);

The name of the task sending the message is stored in variable S. The task executing the command is blocked until it receives a message from some other task.

Task VENDING_MACHINE is declared as

```
task body VENDING_MACHINE is
   ITEMS: INTEGER := 50;
   PRICE: INTEGER := 25;
   PAID: INTEGER := 0;
   REQUESTER: TASK_NAME;
   M: ACTION;
begin
   loop
      REQUESTER := receive(M);
      if M.OPERATION = INSERT then
         PAID := PAID + M.COIN;
      elsif M.OPERATION = PUSH then
         if ITEMS > 0 and PAID >= PRICE then
            CHANGE := PAID − PRICE; GOODS := 1;
            ITEMS := ITEMS − 1;
         else
            CHANGE := PAID; GOODS := 0;
         end if;
         send(REQUESTER, DELIVER(CHANGE, GOODS));
         PAID := 0;
      end if;
   end loop;
end VENDING_MACHINE;
```

When the customer puts coins into the vending machine, task MONEY sends a message to VENDING_MACHINE, e.g.,

    send (VENDING_MACHINE, ACTION(INSERT, AMOUNT));

When the customer presses the button on the vending machine, task SUPPLIES sends an appropriate message to VENDING_MACHINE and then waits for an answering message, e.g.,

> **send** (VENDING_MACHINE, ACTION(PUSH, 0));
> S := **receive** (M);

The message-based version of the vending machine is similar to the Ada version, but there are some differences. For example, VENDING_MACHINE must explicitly send an answering message to SUPPLIES after receiving a message indicating that the customer has pushed the button. SUPPLIES is free to resume execution after sending the message to VENDING_MACHINE, but it follows this action by waiting for an answering message from VENDING_MACHINE. Failure to do so will cause VENDING_MACHINE to be blocked attempting to send an answer to SUPPLIES. (Of course, this blocking would not occur if the message-sending facility in the language were nonblocking.) On the other hand, in the Ada version, task SUPPLIES is suspended while VENDING_MACHINE prepares the information to be given to SUPPLIES. Only one rendezvous is necessary because the called task can send information to the caller during the rendezvous; in the message-based version, two messages must be exchanged.

As in the Ada version, the internal bookkeeping is done in parallel with task SUPPLIES. Implementation of the synchronization constraint requiring that an insertion of a coin be followed by button depression is more complicated than in the Ada version. The message-based version of task VENDING_MACHINE can determine the customer's action only after receiving messages from SUPPLIES and MONEY, while in the Ada version this determination is done prior to accepting the messages (by using different entries for the two actions). Consequently, implementing the synchronization constraint requires explicit internal buffering of the extra INSERT operations until the requisite number of PUSH operations have arrived.

3.5 Communicating Sequential Processes

In 1978, Hoare proposed a novel approach to concurrent programming [HOA78b], called "Communicating Sequential Processes" (CSP). CSP has had a major impact on concurrent programming ideas and research because of its conceptual simplicity and potential for efficient implementation.

CSP unifies the concepts of synchronization and communication. Processes in CSP synchronize and communicate by means of *input* and *output* statements. A rendezvous must be established between two tasks before they can synchronize or communicate with each other. A rendezvous is established when one task is ready to execute an *input* statement and the second task is ready to execute the corresponding *output* statement. If either task is not ready, then the other task is forced to wait. Specification of task synchronization conditions is straightforward, since input statements can be prefixed with synchronization conditions.

As mentioned earlier, Ada's tasking is based on CSP. CSP's *input* and *output* statements correspond to Ada's *accept* statements and entry calls, respectively. There are some important differences:

1. Information transfer in CSP is unidirectional—from the task executing the *output* statement to the task executing the *input* statement. Consequently, two rendezvous are required for bidirectional communication.

2. A CSP rendezvous allows only parameter copying, whereas in an Ada rendezvous, in addition to parameter copying, the called task can execute statements and return results to the calling task—the calling task is suspended for this period.

3. CSP requires that process names be specified in both the *input* and *output* statements. As a consequence of this requirement, it is not possible to implement task libraries in CSP [HOA78b].

As in Ada, exclusive access to data or a resource encapsulated in a task is automatically provided in CSP, because a task can interact with only one other task at a time. Communication in CSP is explicit, requiring no shared variables. CSP is therefore suitable for distributed computer architectures where the component computers do not share memory.

The CSP *input* statement has the form

$$P ? id(x)$$

specifying that a value is to be received from task P and is to be assigned to the variable x; identifier *id* is used to classify communications from other tasks into different categories. For multiple values, the form

$$P ? id(x_1, x_2, ..., x_n)$$

is used.

The CSP *output* statement has the form

$$P ! id(e)$$

specifying that expression e is to be output to task P. For multiple values, the form

$$P ! id(e_1, e_2, ..., e_n)$$

is used.

3.5.1 CSP Version of the Vending Machine Example: The vending machine example written in CSP (adapted from WEL80) is

```
process VENDING_MACHINE is
   ITEMS, PRICE, COIN, PAID: INTEGER;
   ITEMS := 50; PRICE := 25; PAID := 0;
loop
   select
      MONEY ? DEPOSIT(COIN) →
         PAID := PAID + COIN;
   or
      SUPPLIES ? PUSH() →
                        --signal PUSH is sent by SUPPLIES to indicate
                        --that the customer has pressed the button and
                        --that it wants information about the change to
                        --be returned to the customer and the number
                        --of items to be supplied
         if ITEMS > 0 and PAID >= PRICE then
            SUPPLIES! (PAID-PRICE, 1);
            ITEMS := ITEMS - 1;
         else
            SUPPLIES! (PAID, 0);
         end if;
         PAID := 0;
   end select;
end loop;
end;
```

Task MONEY informs VENDING_MACHINE about the amount of money deposited by the customer by using an *output* statement of the form

VENDING_MACHINE!DEPOSIT(AMOUNT);

The corresponding *input* statement in VENDING_MACHINE is

MONEY ? DEPOSIT(COIN)

A rendezvous between MONEY and VENDING_MACHINE involving execution of the above two statements results in the assignment

COIN := AMOUNT;

Task SUPPLIES informs VENDING_MACHINE, by means of the *output* statement, that the customer has pressed the button

VENDING_MACHINE!PUSH();

This *output* statement transmits a value of type *signal* to VENDING_MACHINE, since no arguments are associated with PUSH(). Signals are used for synchronizing tasks. The corresponding *input* statement in VENDING_MACHINE is

SUPPLIES ? PUSH ( )

The CSP version is very similar to the Ada version, but there are some important differences. As mentioned earlier, process names must be specified in both the *input* and *output* statements. Moreover, since communication in CSP is unidirectional, information exchange between the processes SUPPLIES and VENDING_MACHINE requires two rendezvous:

1. SUPPLIES informs VENDING_MACHINE that the customer has pressed the button by means of the signal PUSH ( ) and it then waits to receive the necessary information from VENDING_MACHINE.

2. After receiving the signal PUSH ( ), VENDING_MACHINE supplies the appropriate information to task SUPPLIES by means of one of the two output statements

   SUPPLIES ! (PAID−PRICE, 1);
   SUPPLIES ! (PAID, 0);

   to return the appropriate information to SUPPLIES.

As in the Ada version, the internal bookkeeping occurs in parallel with the execution of SUPPLIES; requiring the customer to press the button after every insertion of a coin is straightforward.

3.6 Distributed Processes

Brinch Hansen's recent proposal for concurrent programming [BRI78a], called "Distributed Processes" (DP), suggests that tasks communicate and synchronize by calling procedures in other tasks. Although DP has been an influence on the concurrent programming facilities in the present version of Ada [DOD83], it was a dominant factor in the design of the concurrent facilities in Preliminary Ada [DOD79a, WEL81]. Both entry and procedure calls were used for task communication and synchronization in Preliminary Ada. However, procedure calls were dropped in an effort to simplify Ada [DOD83].

A DP process provides procedures that are called by other processes for synchronization and communication. Calls to these procedures are called *external requests*. A process performs two kinds of operations—execution of the initial statement and execution of external requests. A process begins by executing its initial statement. This initial statement is executed until it terminates or until further execution is not immediately possible because some condition is false—execution can be resumed only when this condition becomes true. At this time, another operation (external request), if pending, is started. When this operation terminates or is suspended, because some condition cannot be immediately satisfied, execution of another operation is resumed or started, or the execution of the initial statement resumed.

3.6.1 The Vending Machine Example Written in DP: Brinch Hansen's version of the vending machine [BRI78a, WEL80, WEL81] written in an Ada-like notation is

```
process VENDING_MACHINE is
    ITEMS, PRICE, PAID: INTEGER;

    procedure INSERT(COIN: in INTEGER) is
    begin
        PAID := PAID + COIN;
    end;

    procedure PUSH(CHANGE, GOODS: out INTEGER) is
    begin
        if ITEMS > 0 and PAID >= PRICE then
            CHANGE := PAID − PRICE;
            GOODS := 1; ITEMS := ITEMS − 1;
        else
            CHANGE := PAID; GOODS := 0;
        end if;
        PAID := 0;
    end;
begin
    ITEMS := 50; PRICE := 25; PAID := 0;    −−initial statement
end;
```

There are many differences between the Ada (see section 2.3 of this chapter) and DP versions of the vending machine. For example, in Ada, the *accept* statement corresponding to an entry call must be executed in full before another entry call can be accepted (assuming *accept* statements are not nested). However, in DP another external request may be executed if a currently executing operation is forced to wait for a condition to become true—execution of the external requests and the initial statement is interleaved. In Ada, unlike DP, it is possible to specify that an entry call is to be accepted only when some synchronization condition has been satisfied.

Unlike in the Ada version, the internal bookkeeping statement

```
PAID := 0;
```

is not executed in parallel with the process making the external request PUSH. Instead, the requesting process is made to wait until the bookkeeping is completed. Execution of this statement in parallel with the requesting task requires program modification and the addition of more logic to the program.

Similarly, changing the program to require that a call to INSERT is followed by a call to PUSH is not straightforward. Since there is no flow of control relating the calls to procedures PUSH and INSERT, additional variables and logic must be introduced to implement this synchronization constraint.

3.7 Some Comments

Task communication mechanisms can be classified as direct and indirect. Direct communication occurs when tasks send messages to each other directly without the use of intermediaries. Indirect communication occurs when tasks exchange information by reading and writing shared variables. Similarly, synchronization mechanisms can also be classified as direct and indirect. Direct synchronization involves explicit signaling between the synchronizing tasks. Indirect synchronization is accomplished by testing and setting shared variables [AND81].

Ada's rendezvous is a high-level concept that unifies the concepts of synchronization and communication. Concurrency mechanisms, such as semaphores, events, and signals, were rejected by the designers of Ada because they are low-level mechanisms. Monitors were rejected because they are not always easy to understand and because their associated signals are low-level in nature. Message systems were rejected because they require a sizable message controller [DOD79b].

Although most of the above proposals, like CSP, DP and programming languages such as Concurrent Pascal, have simple and elegant high-level facilities for concurrent programming, it is worth remembering that the rendezvous mechanism and related facilities in Ada represent a first attempt to provide high-level concurrent programming facilities in a general purpose programming language designed for wide usage. Ada's concurrent programming facilities are far more elaborate than those of CSP, because Ada is designed to address real and pragmatic issues while CSP represents an idealized concurrent programming model. For example, Ada provides facilities for the construction of task libraries, time-outs, interfacing with hardware, error handling and abortion of tasks—important facilities for the construction of large real-time programs. Not one of these facilities is provided in CSP.

Chapter 2: **Tasking Facilities** [9]

There is as yet no consensus on what constitutes a good or an appropriate set of concurrent programming facilities. However, it is agreed that the following properties are desirable [HOA78a]:

1. *Security from Error*: Concurrency adds, to the already hard task of writing correct sequential programs, another dimension of complexity —that of time-dependent errors. Detection of time dependent errors is harder than the detection of other kinds of errors because these errors are not always easily reproducible. Moreover, in many concurrent programming applications the cost of a programming error is very high. Consequently, it is extremely important that concurrent programming facilities should allow for maximum amount of error checking at compile-time. Needless to say, the introduction of concurrency in programs also exacerbates the hard problem of proving the correctness of programs.

2. *Conceptual Simplicity*: Concurrent programming facilities should be simple and elegant to use, should guide the programmer toward good program structure and should lead to programs that are easily understandable.

3. *Efficiency*: Many concurrent programming applications have severe timing and storage constraints. Consequently it is important that high-level concurrent programming facilities be efficient—otherwise programmers will resort to writing in assembly language.

4. *Breadth of Application*: Concurrent programming facilities should be suitable for programming a wide variety of applications. These facilities should include logically distinct high-level facilities for interfacing with the hardware registers and interrupts so that device drivers can be written easily—device drivers are an important component of real-time programs.

The concurrency in Ada has been designed taking these concerns into account [DOD79b].

The concurrent programming facilities in Ada will now be discussed in detail. In the initial portion of the next section, there may be some repetition of the material that was discussed informally in Chapter 1, in order to make the detailed discussion of the Ada's concurrent facilities self-contained.

1. Task Specification and Body [9.1]

Components of a program that execute in parallel are called *tasks*. Tasks, subprograms, packages and generic units are the four program components in Ada which are used to compose programs. Like the other program components, a task consists of two parts: a specification and a body. Interaction with a task requires knowledge only of its specification. Details of the task implementation, represented by the task body, are inaccessible from outside the task body.

A task specification has either the form

  task identifier;

or the form

  task identifier **is**
   entry declarations
   representation clauses
  end identifier;

The first form is used for a task that does not have any entries—such a task cannot be called by other tasks for a rendezvous. The *representation clauses* in a task specification allow hardware interrupts to be treated as entry calls (see Chapter 5 on *Device Drivers*).

A task body has the form[6]

  task body identifier **is**
   declarations
  begin
   sequence_of_statements
  [exception
   exception handlers**]**
  end identifier;

---

6. Extended BNF notation, as used in the *Ada Reference Manual*, is used in defining the syntax:
- **[** a **]** specifies the optional occurrence of item a
- **{** a **}** specifies 0 or more occurrences of item a
- a **|** b specifies either item a or item b

Bold and bigger characters will be used for the BNF meta symbols **[ ]**, **{ }** and **|** to distinguish them from the Ada characters [ ], {} and |.

1.1 An Example

Consider a task PRODUCER that reads text from the standard input file and sends it to another task, CONSUMER (see Figure 2.1). CONSUMER converts lower case characters to upper case and then writes them on the standard output file.

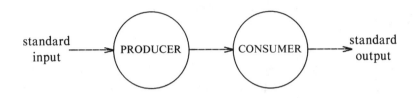

Figure 2.1: Tasks PRODUCER and CONSUMER

The specifications of the two tasks are

```
task PRODUCER;

task CONSUMER is
    entry RECEIVE(C: in CHARACTER);
            --C is a formal parameter, just as in a subprogram
end CONSUMER;
```

PRODUCER reads characters, one at a time, from the standard input and sends them to CONSUMER by calling entry CONSUMER.RECEIVE:

```
task body PRODUCER is
    C: CHARACTER;
begin
    while not END_OF_FILE(STANDARD_INPUT) loop
       GET(C);
       CONSUMER.RECEIVE(C);
    end loop;
end PRODUCER;
```

Entry calls are similar to procedure calls but include the name of the task that contains the entry, e.g., CONSUMER.RECEIVE(C).

CONSUMER accepts characters from PRODUCER, converts lower case characters to upper case, and prints the characters on the standard output file:

```
task body CONSUMER is
  X: CHARACTER;
begin
  loop
    accept RECEIVE(C: in CHARACTER) do
        --the names of the calling tasks are not specified
      X := C;
          --X is needed to record the value of C for use
          --outside the accept statement, since C is local
          --to the accept statement
    end RECEIVE;
    PUT(UPPER(X));
          --output the upper-case form. The PUT statement
          --has been placed outside the accept statement
          --so that the caller is not delayed while the
          --PUT statement is being executed.
  end loop;
end CONSUMER;
```

The two tasks rendezvous when PRODUCER has issued the entry call CONSUMER.RECEIVE and CONSUMER is ready to accept it. If PRODUCER (CONSUMER) reaches the rendezvous point RECEIVE before CONSUMER (PRODUCER), then it is forced to wait for CONSUMER (PRODUCER). Both tasks synchronize at the entry RECEIVE. Execution of CONSUMER.RECEIVE terminates when execution of the corresponding *accept* statement in CONSUMER terminates.

As mentioned before, PRODUCER will terminate upon reaching the end of its body. However, CONSUMER will not terminate, because it has an endless loop and it will continue waiting at the *accept* statement, indicating its willingness to accept another entry call and rendezvous.

Tasks must occur textually within a subprogram or a package. Tasks PRODUCER and CONSUMER, along with function UPPER, are therefore put into procedure CONVERT_TO_UPPER_CASE to form a main program:

```
with TEXT_IO; use TEXT_IO;
     --package TEXT_IO contains the input and output
     --procedures GET and PUT and functions
     --END_OF_FILE and STANDARD_INPUT

procedure CONVERT_TO_UPPER_CASE is

  task PRODUCER;

  task CONSUMER is
    entry RECEIVE(C: in CHARACTER);
  end CONSUMER;

  --insert function UPPER here
  --(details of UPPER are not given in this book)

  task body PRODUCER is
    C: CHARACTER;
  begin
    while not END_OF_FILE(STANDARD_INPUT) loop
      GET(C);
      CONSUMER.RECEIVE(C);
    end loop;
  end PRODUCER;

  task body CONSUMER is
    X: CHARACTER;
  begin
    loop
      accept RECEIVE(C: in CHARACTER) do
        X := C;
      end RECEIVE;
      PUT(UPPER(X));
    end loop;
  end CONSUMER;

begin     --PRODUCER and CONSUMER become active
  null;
        --according to the syntax, a subprogram body must
        --have at least one statement even if it is the
        --null statement
end CONVERT_TO_UPPER_CASE;
```

The two tasks become active immediately before the executable part of the procedure CONVERT_TO_UPPER_CASE is executed.[7]

1.2 Queuing of Entry Calls [9.5]

Several tasks can issue calls to the same entry of another task. These entry calls are put in a queue associated with the entry and accepted in first-in first-out (FIFO) order. The number of tasks waiting at an entry E is given by the attribute E'COUNT. At any time, a task can be in at most one entry queue.

Figure 2.2 illustrates acceptance of entry calls in FIFO order. Tasks A and B are both interested in rendezvousing with task C at entry E. Tasks A and B issue entry calls before task C has indicated its readiness to accept an entry call. Task C establishes a rendezvous first with task B, because it issued an entry call before task A:

----

7. The loop in the body of PRODUCER could have been written simply as
    loop
        GET(C);
        CONSUMER.RECEIVE(C);
    end loop;
    On reaching the end of the file, an execution of GET will raise an exception, which will cause termination of the task, because no exception handler has been provided (see the section on exceptions in the Appendix).

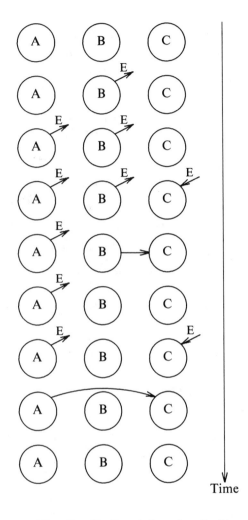

First B calls C and then A calls C
C services B first and then A

Figure 2.2: Queuing of Entry Calls

2. Nested Rendezvous

Generally, a task will complete a rendezvous with another task before engaging
in a rendezvous with a third task. However, there are situations where two

tasks rendezvousing with each other need to interact with a third task before completing their rendezvous. Suppose task A calls task B for some information and that task B can supply this information, but only after interacting with task C. For this to happen, it must be possible for the task accepting an entry call to interact, during a rendezvous, with other tasks. This interaction is depicted diagrammatically as shown in Figure 2.3:

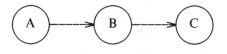

Figure 2.3: Task B in rendezvous with tasks A and C

In this situation, task B must complete its rendezvous with task C before ending its rendezvous with task A.

Alternatively, task B can accept an entry call from task T_1 in the middle of its rendezvous with task A. While communicating with T_1 it can accept another entry call from task T_2, and so on in a similar fashion with the additional tasks T_3, ..., T_{n-1}, T_n, as shown in Figure 2.4:

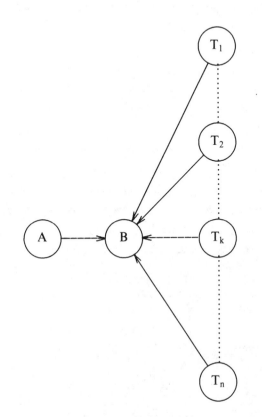

Figure 2.4: Task B in rendezvous with tasks A, T_1, T_2,..., T_n

Task B must complete its rendezvous with the tasks in the reverse of the order in which they were established, i.e., T_n, ..., T_1 and A.

3. Entries and Accept Statements [9.5]

Entry declarations and calls are syntactically similar to procedure declarations and calls. Entry declarations can occur only in the specification of a task. The corresponding *accept* statements are given in the body of the task. More than one *accept* statement can be given for an entry declaration. Communication between two tasks takes place, when they rendezvous, through the actual parameters in the entry call and the formal parameters in the corresponding *accept* statement.

The task accepting the entry call causes suspension of the calling task until information is exchanged; the suspension lasts until execution of the *accept* statement (in the called task) is completed. Under no circumstances can the calling task suspend execution of the called task. This one-sided suspension of execution is another asymmetry (the asymmetry discussed in the previous chapter was the naming asymmetry) in Ada's tasking mechanism. Tasks can also wait to accept entry calls from more than one task and can issue calls for an immediate rendezvous or one within some specified time period.

If a task calls its own entry, *deadlock* occurs, i.e., although the task has not *completed* or *terminated*, it will not be able to continue execution. (Task completion and termination are discussed later in section 6 of this chapter; deadlock is discussed in Chapter 7 titled *Some Issues in Concurrent Programming*.) Such calls are not prohibited in Ada, but an implementation may not allow then or it may warn the user of their consequences.

As an example of the ability of the called task to suspend the calling task, consider a task A interacting with a task DATABASE that manages a database. When A establishes rendezvous with DATABASE to add information to the database, DATABASE delays A only as long as is necessary to get the information from A. Task A is then allowed to proceed while DATABASE converts the information into the proper format and inserts it into the database. On the other hand, when A establishes a rendezvous with DATABASE to retrieve information from the database, A is delayed while DATABASE actually retrieves the requested information.

An attempt to call an entry of a task that has completed, terminated or become *abnormal* (discussed later in section 7 of this chapter) results in an error (the exception TASKING_ERROR is raised). Attribute T'CALLABLE (of type BOOLEAN) of a task T can be used to determine whether a task T has completed, terminated or become abnormal.[8]

3.1 Syntax

Examples will be used to illustrate the syntax of entry declarations, entry calls and *accept* statements. Parameters are used in entries for an exchange of information between the task containing the entry and the task calling the entry. An entry without parameters is used just for synchronization. Some examples of entry declarations are

---

8. A task is said to have *completed* upon finishing execution of its body. Subject to some conditions being satisfied, it then *terminates*. See section 6 of this chapter for more details.

> **entry** SIGNAL;   −−no parameters
> **entry** SET(T: **in** DURATION);
> **entry** READ(C: **out** CHARACTER);
> **entry** WRITE(C: **in** CHARACTER);

A family of entries (i.e., an array of entries) can also be declared:

> **entry** D_WRITE(1..5)(B: **in** BLOCK);   −−for 5 disks
> **entry** REGISTER_REQUEST(ID)(D: **in out** DATA);
>   −−register request for service; one entry for each element of
>   −−the discrete type ID

Some examples of entry calls are

> ALARM.SET(NEXT_MOVE_TIME);
> BUFFER.READ(C);
> DISKS.D_WRITE(J)(B);   −−write block B on disk J

An *accept* statement must have statements associated with it if information is to be exchanged with the calling task. Information is received from the calling task by recording values of the parameters of the *accept* statement; information is supplied to the calling task by assigning values to the parameters. Examples of *accept* statements are

> **accept** SIGNAL;
>
> **accept** SET(T : **in** DURATION) **do**
>   PERIOD := T;
>   −−calling task suspended while this assignment is executed
> **end** SET;
>
> **accept** READ(C: **out** CHARACTER) **do**
>   C := Q(INB **mod** N + 1);
> **end** READ;
>
> −−*accept* statement corresponding to the Ith member
> −−of the entry family D_WRITE
> **accept** D_WRITE(I)(B: **in** BLOCK) **do**
>   −−sequence of statements
> **end** D_WRITE;

As mentioned before, the calling task is blocked (suspended) while information exchange takes place, i.e., until the entry call terminates. Execution of the entry call terminates when the execution of the corresponding *accept* statement has terminated.

4. Delay Statement [9.6]

A task can temporarily suspend its execution by executing a *delay* statement. The statement

    delay T;

causes suspension of the task executing the statement for at least T seconds. T is an arithmetic expression of the predefined fixed point type DURATION. If T is zero or negative, execution of the *delay* statement has no effect.

A more important usage of the *delay* statement occurs in conjunction with the *select* statment. Using it as an alternative in the *select* statement allows a task to time-out, after the specified period, when attempting a rendezvous (see section 5 for more detail).

The *delay* statement is illustrated by a task DISPLAY that is used to control the *time and temperature* display commonly put up by banks for displaying advertisements and performing a public service. The current time and temperature are displayed at regular intervals along with some advertisement.

Task DISPLAY uses a package TIME_AND_TEMPERATURE that provides procedures to clear the display and to display the time, temperature and advertisement. It is assumed that the program unit containing task DISPLAY has been compiled with the package TIME_AND_TEMPERATURE and that the *use* clause

    use TIME_AND_TEMPERATURE;

has been given. The specification and body of task DISPLAY is

    task DISPLAY;

    task body DISPLAY **is**
    begin
      loop
        CLEAR; DISPLAY_TIME; **delay** 15.0;
        CLEAR; DISPLAY_TEMPERATURE; **delay** 15.0;
        CLEAR; DISPLAY_AD("Open a New Account Today" &
              " and Get a Free Toaster"); **delay** 30.0;
      end loop;
    end DISPLAY;

5. Select Statement [9.7]

There are three kinds of *select* statements: the *selective wait*, the *conditional entry* call and the *timed entry* call. The *selective wait* statement allows a task to

- accept entry calls from more than one task in a nondeterministic fashion,

- wait only a specified amount of time for an entry call to be made,

- perform an alternative action if no entry call is pending and

- indicate its readiness to terminate.

The conditional entry call, unlike the normal entry call, is a nonblocking entry call. The calling task does not wait if the called task is not ready, but goes on to do other things. The timed entry call is similar to the conditional entry call except that the calling task waits a specified period for the called task to accept the entry call before it withdraws the entry call.

5.1 Selective Wait [9.7.1]

The *selective wait* statement has the form

```
select
    select_alternative
{or
    select_alternative}
[else
    sequence_of_statements]
end select;
```

where a *select_alternative* is of the form

```
[when condition => ]
        selective_wait_alternative
```

An alternative of the *select* statement is said to be *open* if there is no *when* clause before it or if the condition in the *when* clause is true. Otherwise it is said to be *closed*.

A *selective_wait_alternative* can be one of

```
    accept_statement [sequence_of_statements]
  | delay_statement [sequence_of_statements]
  | terminate;
```

A *selective wait* statement can have at most one *terminate* alternative. If a *terminate* alternative is present, then the *selective wait* statement cannot contain the delay statement as an alternative. An *else* part is not allowed in a *selective wait* statement containing a terminate or a delay alternative.

The use of the *select* statement is illustrated by the following program segment:

```
loop
    select
        when buffer not full =>
                accept WRITE(C: in CHARACTER) do
                    .
                    .
                end WRITE;
                .
                .
    or when buffer not empty =>
                accept READ(C: out CHARACTER) do
                    .
                    .
                end READ;
                .
                .
    or
        terminate;
    end select;
end loop;
```

The *select* statement accepts calls to either of the entries READ or WRITE, depending upon the state of the buffer. Calls to WRITE are accepted when the buffer is not full and calls to READ are accepted when the buffer is not empty. If there are no entry calls pending, the task executing the above segment is also indicating its willingness to terminate.

Execution of a *selective wait* statement is determined according to the following algorithm:

1. Determine all the open alternatives and start counting time for the *delay* statements (if any).

2. If there are open alternatives or if there is an *else* part in the *selective wait* statement, then the steps given below are followed in determining the next course of action:

    a. Select any one of the open alternatives that is an *accept* statement and for which a rendezvous can be established. Perform the rendezvous.

    b. Select an open alternative containing a *delay* statement with the shortest delay period, if no alternative has been selected yet and the specified delay has elapsed. Execute the sequence of statements following the *delay* statement.

    c. A *terminate* alternative may be selected only if its master[9] has completed execution, all other children of the master have terminated or are waiting at a *terminate* alternative, there are no dependent tasks and there are no outstanding entry calls (see section 6 for more details).

A task terminates if the *terminate* alternative is selected.

d. If no open alternative can be selected immediately or all the alternatives are closed, then the *else* part is selected; if there is no *else* part, then execution is suspended until an open alternative can be selected.

3. If all the alternatives are closed and there is no *else* part in the *selective wait* statement, then raise the exception PROGRAM_ERROR.

The body of task CONSUMER, given earlier, is now modified so that it terminates instead of executing forever. The *accept* statement in CONSUMER is made part of a *select* statement that also has a *terminate* alternative:

```
task body CONSUMER is
   X: CHARACTER;
begin
   loop
      select
         accept RECEIVE(C: in CHARACTER) do
            X := C;
         end RECEIVE;
         PUT(UPPER(X));
      or
         terminate;
      end select;
   end loop;
end CONSUMER;
```

CONSUMER will now terminate by the selection of the *terminate* alternative after it has determined that PRODUCER has terminated. (CONSUMER and PRODUCER are the two dependent tasks of their master—procedure CONVERT_TO_UPPER_CASE. Termination of PRODUCER leaves CONSUMER as the only task in a completed master.)

---

9. The *master* of a task is the construct that created the task; see section 6 for more details.

5.2 Conditional Entry Call [9.7.2]

A conditional entry call is used to attempt an immediate rendezvous. If an immediate rendezvous is possible, then the rendezvous takes place and the sequence of statements following the entry call is executed; otherwise the alternative sequence of statements specified in the *else* alternative is executed. A conditional entry call has the form

```
select
    entry_call [sequence_of_statements]
else
    sequence_of_statements
end select;
```

A conditional entry call can be used by a task to poll another task repeatedly to determine if the second task is ready to rendezvous. For example, a task X containing the following loop tries to read a card by calling entry READ of the card reader driver CARD. If CARD is not ready to rendezvous, task X does some local computations instead of wasting time waiting for CARD to be ready. This process is repeated indefinitely until a card can be read. Of course, it might be wiser to restrict the number of rendezvous attempts to a finite number:

```
loop
    select
        CARD.READ(C);
        process the card C
        exit;
    else
        do local computation
    end select;
end loop;
```

5.3 Timed Entry Call [9.7.3]

A timed entry call is an attempt to establish a rendezvous within some specified time period. If a rendezvous can be established within the specified period, then rendezvous takes place and the statements following the entry call are executed. Otherwise the statements following the specified *delay* statement are executed. The timed entry call has the form

```
select
    entry_call [sequence_of_statements]
or
    delay_statement [sequence_of_statements]
end select;
```

The timed entry call can be used to monitor a critical device that must respond within a specified time period. If such a device does not respond within this period, then immediate corrective action must be taken. For example, in a nuclear reactor program a task NEW_TEMP, which measures the temperature of the walls of the vessel containing the fuel rods, must honor a request for a new temperature reading with a delay of at most 0.1 seconds. Otherwise the task requesting the new temperature reading raises an alarm, exception NO_TEMP_READING, so that corrective action can be taken. Monitoring of NEW_TEMP's performance, in the task requesting the new temperature, is implemented as

```
loop
    select
        NEW_TEMP.READ(TEMP);    --get new temperature
        :
        :
        process latest temperature TEMP
        :
        :
    or
        delay 0.1;
                --wait one tenth of a second before raising an alarm
        raise NO_TEMP_READING;
                --alarm is raised; exceptions are discussed in
                --the Appendix
    end select;
end loop;
```

6. Activation, Completion, Dependence and Termination of Tasks [9.3, 9.4]

Tasks declared immediately within a declarative part of a subprogram or a package (i.e., tasks that are not nested within a declaration) become active just prior to the execution of the first statement following the declarative part. (In case a package body does not have any statements, then a *null* statement is assumed.) Tasks are activated in an arbitrary order, e.g., in the most efficient order.

A task, a block or a subprogram is said to have *completed* execution when its body has been executed. In case of a block, execution is also completed upon the execution of an *exit*, a *return* or a *goto* statement that transfers control out of the block. In case of a subprogram, execution of a *return* statement also completes execution of the subprogram. Raising an exception in a task, a block or a subprogram that does not contain an exception handler also causes its completion.

Each task depends upon a *master* which is a construct that created it; the master can be a task, a currently executing block or subprogram, or a library package. A task created using the storage allocator (see Chapter 3 on *Task*

Types) depends upon the master that contains the associated access type definition. Other tasks depend upon the master that created them.

A task terminates if

1. it has completed execution and it has no dependent tasks, or

2. it has completed and all of its dependent tasks have terminated, or

3. it is waiting at a *terminate* alternative (of a *select* statement) and

    - all its dependent tasks have terminated,

    - there are no outstanding entry calls,

    - its master has completed execution, and

    - all dependent tasks of its master have either already terminated or are waiting at a *terminate* alternative.

A block or subprogram is left, i.e., terminated, only if all dependent tasks have terminated.

The termination rules imply that all unterminated tasks depending upon the same master, which has completed execution, can terminate together if each is waiting at a *terminate* alternative of a *select* statement.

As an illustration, consider the PRODUCER and CONSUMER example given earlier. Procedure CONVERT_TO_UPPER_CASE is the master of the two tasks PRODUCER and CONSUMER. Although the body of CONVERT_TO_UPPER_CASE consists of just the *null* statement, it will not terminate until its dependent tasks PRODUCER and CONSUMER terminate. Since CONSUMER does not terminate, procedure CONVERT_TO_UPPER_CASE will not terminate.

7. Mutual Exclusion

The rendezvous mechanism can be used to implement *mutual exclusion* of operations in time. When several tasks update common data, mutual exclusion is needed to ensure consistency of the data [BRI73]. As an example, consider airline Cheap Air's database. There is one seat left on Cheap Air's flight CA211 from New York to New Delhi. Two prospective passengers, X and Y, call to make reservations on flight CA211. These calls are handled by agents A and B, respectively. Each finds one seat available and get ready to update flight CA211's record in the data base.

Updating a record consists of three actions: retrieval of flight record, record update and storage of the updated record. For example, one possible update scenario is

A gets flight CA211's record from the database showing one available seat
B gets flight CA211's record from the database showing one available seat
A updates CA211's record to include X
A stores updated record in the database
B updates CA211's record to include Y
B stores updated record in the database

At the end of these actions, A and B think that they have put X and Y on flight CA211, respectively, whereas in reality, X's information was deleted when B stored the version of the record with Y on flight CA211.

This problem could have been avoided if, during the update operations, each agent had exclusive access to flight CA211's record. Either A should be able to perform the three actions comprising the update before B or after B, but both A and B should not be able update simultaneously. The following scenario could then have occurred:

A gets flight CA211's record from the database showing one available
       seat, updates the record to include X and stores it in the database
B gets flight CA211's record from the database now showing flight
       is full, gives up trying to put Y on CA211 and informs Y
       appropriately

Mutual exclusion is easily achieved in Ada by ensuring that only two tasks are involved in a particular rendezvous (i.e., no nested rendezvous). One task can be assigned to monitor the shared data for which mutual exclusion is desired. Access to the shared data is possible only via the monitoring task. For example, task SHARED_DATA monitors shared data that is updated and read by several tasks:

```
task SHARED_DATA is
    entry UPDATE(formal parameters);
    entry READ(formal parameters);
end SHARED_DATA;

task body SHARED_DATA is
    .
    .
    declarations for the shared data
    .
    .
begin
    loop
        --accept calls, one at a time, to update or read the shared data
        select
            accept UPDATE(formal parameters) do
                Record the formal parameters, i.e., save their values
                    in variables global to the accept statement
            end UPDATE;
            --let the task supplying the update resume execution
            --while the update is done
            Perform the update
        or
            accept READ(formal parameters) do
                Set the formal parameters to appropriate values
            end READ;
        or
            --quit if all tasks interested in the shared data
            --have quit or are ready to quit
            terminate;
        end select;
    end loop;
end SHARED_DATA;
```

The common data is accessed by the entry calls

```
SHARED_DATA.UPDATE(actual parameters);
```

and

```
SHARED_DATA.READ(actual parameters);
```

A task similar to SHARED_DATA can be used to encapsulate the airline database to eliminate the possibility of data inconsistency that could have occurred if the two agents tried to update the database simultaneously. Suppose that agents A and B have determined that one seat is available on flight CA211 (by calling entry READ). Both A and B request allocation of this seat for their customer by calling entry UPDATE. These requests will be successful or unsuccessful depending upon whether or not any seats are available at the time the request is accepted (regardless of the information that was supplied to the agent via the entry READ—this information could have become obsolete by the time the agent's request was accepted).

The UPDATE alternative in task SHARED_DATA must be modified to reflect the fact that an update request may or may not be successful:

```
select
    accept UPDATE(formal parameters) do
        if update can be performed then
            Record the parameters
            Return indication of success
        else
            Return indication of failure
        end if;
    end UPDATE;
    if update was agreed upon then
        Perform the update
    end if;
or
    .
    .
    .
or
    .
    .
    .
end select;
```

It is often desirable to allow more than one task to read the shared data simultaneously, because this results in a smaller average waiting time for the tasks accessing the data. Of course, only one task at a time will be allowed to update the data. Implementation of this scheme requires the design of a task that grants permissions to update or read the shared data, but does not monitor the shared data itself as is done by the task SHARED_DATA. Moreover, the shared data must be global to all the accessing tasks. The accessing tasks inform the permissions task when they are finished with the data so that the permissions task can keep track of the tasks accessing the shared data.

8. Abort Statement [9.10]

A task can be terminated explicitly by means of an *abort* statement. The statement

abort $T_1, T_2, ..., T_n$;

causes all the tasks $T_1, T_2, ..., T_n$ that have not already terminated to become *abnormal*, thus preventing any further rendezvous with these tasks. A task in Ada can abort any task including itself. However, the tasks specified must be visible at the place in the program where they are aborted.

A task that depends upon an abnormal task also becomes abnormal. A task that becomes abnormal terminates immediately if it is waiting at an entry call, an *accept* statement, a *select* statement, or a *delay* statement; otherwise, termination occurs as soon as the task reaches a synchronization point such as the start or the end of a *accept* statement, an exception handler and so on.

If the calling task becomes abnormal during a rendezvous, it is allowed to complete the rendezvous before being terminated (so that data is not left in an inconsistent state); the called task is unaffected. If the task containing the *accept* statement becomes abnormal during a rendezvous, then the exception TASKING_ERROR is raised in the calling task at the point of entry call.

The exception TASKING_ERROR is raised, at the point of entry call, in all tasks waiting for or attempting to rendezvous with an aborted task. The task attribute CALLABLE has the value FALSE if the task has become abnormal (or has completed or terminated).

Although this blanket ability to abort tasks can be misused, it may be needed in applications, such as the control of nuclear reactors and missiles, where misbehaving tasks may have to be terminated in an effort to avoid a catastrophe. The *abort* statement should be used only in well-understood situations with full awareness of its consequences.

9. Task Priorities [9.8]

Each task may be assigned a priority that overrides the default priority assigned to a task by the implementation. Tasks can be assigned a priority by using the PRIORITY pragma (pragmas are discussed in the Appendix), which is of the form

pragma PRIORITY(P);

and is included in the specification of the task. P is a static expression of the implementation defined integer subtype PRIORITY. The higher the value of P, the higher the priority of the task.

By default, all tasks are assigned the same priority.[10] Priorities should be used to indicate the importance and the relative urgencies assigned to tasks. A higher-priority task gets preference in resource allocation.

The priority of a task is static and cannot be changed dynamically, i.e., it cannot be changed at run time. A task with a higher priority is always given preference in the selection of a task for a rendezvous. For example, suppose

_____

10. The default priority is implementation dependent.

that two tasks A and B, A having a higher priority than B, are ready to rendezvous with a third task C. If A and B have called different entries of C, then A will be selected, because of its higher priority. If A and B have called the same entry of C, then the task selected will be the one that called C first; in this case, the priorities do not make any difference. The order of scheduling tasks of equal priority is not specified and is left to the implementation. Priorities should be used to indicate the importance or the urgency of a task. They should not be used to control synchronization. An implementation may completely disregard all priorities.

10. Task and Entry Attributes [9.9]

The following attributes are defined for tasks:

T'CALLABLE	FALSE if task T has completed, terminated or become abnormal, and TRUE otherwise.
T'TERMINATED	TRUE if task T has terminated and FALSE otherwise.
E'COUNT	the number of tasks waiting to rendezvous at entry E (this entry attribute can be used only within the body of a task, say T, that contains the entry; moreover, it cannot be used in a subprogram, package or task nested in T).

These attributes are used in controlling task interaction. For example, attribute CALLABLE can be used to avoid calling a task that has completed or terminated; calling such a task raises the error exception TASKING_ERROR in the calling task. The COUNT attribute can be used to implement a general scheduling scheme—calls to an entry are accepted when no calls to entries designated more important are pending.

In addition to the above attributes, the following representation attributes [13.7.2], which are implementation dependent, are also defined:

T'ADDRESS	the starting address of the machine code associated with task T.
T'SIZE	for a task T, this attribute is the number of bits allocated, and for a task type T (see Chapter 3 on *Task Types*), it yields the minimum number of bits that must be allocated for tasks of type T.
T'STORAGE_SIZE	the number of storage units required for a task T or for each activation of a task type T.

11. The CALENDAR Package [9.6]

Ada programs can determine the current time by using function CLOCK that is provided in the predefined library package CALENDAR. This package also contains subprograms that allow a program to determine the current year and current month, compare two times and so on. Time, which is a value of the private type TIME defined in CALENDAR, is actually a composite value made up of the current year, current month, the current day of the month and the elapsed time for the current day in seconds. The specification of package CALENDAR is

```
package CALENDAR is
  type TIME is private;

  subtype YEAR_NUMBER is INTEGER range 1901..2099;
  subtype MONTH_NUMBER is INTEGER range 1..12;
  subtype DAY_NUMBER is INTEGER range 1..31;
  subtype DAY_DURATION is DURATION range 0.0 .. 86_400.0;

  function CLOCK return TIME;

  function YEAR(DATE: TIME) return YEAR_NUMBER;
  function MONTH(DATE: TIME) return MONTH_NUMBER;
  function DAY(DATE: TIME) return DAY_NUMBER;
  function SECONDS(DATE: TIME) return DAY_DURATION;

  procedure SPLIT(DATE: in TIME;
                  YEAR: out YEAR_NUMBER;
                  MONTH: out MONTH_NUMBER;
                  DAY: out DAY_NUMBER;
                  SECONDS: out DAY_DURATION);

  function TIME_OF(YEAR: YEAR_NUMBER;
                   MONTH: MONTH_NUMBER;
                   DAY: DAY_NUMBER;
                   SECONDS: DAY_DURATION := 0.0) return TIME;

  function "+"(LEFT: TIME; RIGHT: DURATION) return TIME;
  function "+"(LEFT: DURATION; RIGHT: TIME) return TIME;
  function "-"(LEFT: TIME; RIGHT: DURATION) return TIME;
  function "-"(LEFT: TIME; RIGHT: TIME) return DURATION;

  function "<"(LEFT, RIGHT: TIME) return BOOLEAN;
  function "<="(LEFT, RIGHT: TIME) return BOOLEAN;
  function ">"(LEFT, RIGHT: TIME) return BOOLEAN;
  function ">="(LEFT, RIGHT: TIME) return BOOLEAN;

  TIME_ERROR: exception;  --can be raised by TIME_OF, "+" and "-"

private
  --implementation dependent
end CALENDAR;
```

It is not necessary to declare operators, other than those defined in CALENDAR, for values of the predefined fixed point type DURATION, such as

> **function** "+"(LEFT, RIGHT: DURATION) **return** DURATION;
> **function** "−"(LEFT, RIGHT: DURATION) **return** DURATION;

because they are automatically made available with the declaration of DURATION.

11.1 Cumulative Drift in Performing an Action Repeatedly at Regular Intervals

Suppose action P has to be performed repeatedly after every INTERVAL seconds. Consider the use of the following program segment to execute the action P repeatedly:

```
        ⋮
    INTERVAL: DURATION := ...;
    NEXT_TIME: TIME := ...;
               −−next time the action is to be performed
        ⋮
begin
        ⋮
    delay NEXT_TIME − CLOCK;
    loop
        Action P
        delay INTERVAL;
    end loop;
        ⋮
end ...;
        ⋮
```

where function CLOCK is from the predefined package CALENDAR [9.6].

Although this program segment looks fine superficially, it suffers from the problem of *cumulative time drift*, i.e., the actual interval between two successive executions of the desired action P drifts away from the desired gap INTERVAL, because of an error that accumulates. The actual interval between the ith and the $i+1^{th}$ $(i \geqslant 1)$ executions of the action P is not INTERVAL, but is

$$INTERVAL + i*\tau$$

where τ is the time required to perform the action P.

When performing actions where it is undesirable to have such a cumulative drift, a program segment of the form given below should be used [BAR80]:

```
    .
    .
    INTERVAL: DURATION := ...;
    NEXT_TIME: TIME := ...;
    .
    .
begin
    .
    .
    loop
       delay NEXT_TIME − CLOCK;
       Action P
       NEXT_TIME := NEXT_TIME + INTERVAL;
    end loop;
    .
    .
end ...;
    .
    .
```

12. Shared Variables [9.11]

The Ada programming language also allows shared variables, i.e., global variables accessed by several tasks. The use of global variables has been considered detrimental to program understandability and reliability [WUL73]. Their use in concurrent programming aggravates the hard task of writing understandable and reliable programs. However, use of global variables is necessary in Ada so that more than one task can access the same data simultaneously.[11] (Of course, simultaneous updates of shared data are meaningful only if each update is performed on a disjoint portion of the shared data; similarly, simultaneous querying and updating of shared data must involve disjoint portions of the shared data.)

If two tasks access a shared variable, then neither of them can assume anything about the order in which the other task performs its operations, except at the points where they synchronize. Two tasks synchronize at the start and end of their rendezvous. At the start and end of its activation, a task synchronizes with the task causing its activation.

A program containing tasks sharing variables of scalar or access types will produce unpredictable results if it violates either of the following rules:

1.   If a task reads a shared variable between two synchronization points, then no other task must update this shared variable between these synchronization points. However, other tasks are allowed to read the

---

11. The use of global variables also makes it difficult to implement concurrent programs on multi-computers [GEH81b].

shared variable.

2. If a task updates a shared variable between two synchronization points, then no other task is allowed to read or update the shared variable between these two synchronization points.

These rules allow an implementation to maintain local copies of the shared variable, e.g., in a register, with the following properties:

- Reading a local copy is equivalent to reading the shared variable itself, provided the task does not reach a synchronization point and does not update the variable.

- Storing the updated value of the local copy into the shared variable can be deferred until a synchronization point, provided that the local copy is used for every additional read or update (before the synchronization point).

Every read and update of a shared variable whose type is a scalar or an access type can be made into a synchronization point by using the SHARED pragma. For example, the pragma

   pragma SHARED(G);

makes every reading and updating of the variable G a synchronization point. An implementation must restrict the objects for which the pragma SHARED is allowed to those objects for which reading and updating can be implemented as indivisible operations.

13. Examples

The first example illustrates the use of an intervening task to buffer communication between two tasks explicitly. The second example illustrates the use of an entry family to partition requests into several categories. This is followed by an example illustrating various solutions of the classic *readers and writers* problem. The chapter concludes after three more examples: shortest job scheduler, programmer-controlled task scheduling and implementation of path expressions.

13.1 Task Communication Using a Buffer Task

Communication between tasks in Ada is not automatically buffered. If buffering is needed, then it may be explicitly provided by an intervening task.

The tasks PRODUCER and CONSUMER, in the procedure CONVERT_TO_UPPER_CASE given earlier, have to rendezvous once for each character transmitted. Variations in speed of the tasks PRODUCER and CONSUMER are not possible, since there is no buffering of communication between them.

Procedure CONVERT_TO_UPPER_CASE2, which is a modified version of procedure CONVERT_TO_UPPER_CASE, is now presented in which communication between PRODUCER and CONSUMER is buffered to allow variations in speed. Buffering is accomplished by introducing an intervening task called BUFFER (see Figure 2.5) with a maximum buffering capacity of 50 characters.

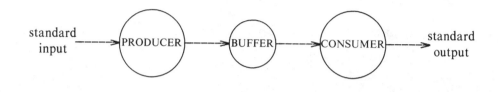

Figure 2.5: Using a task to buffer communication

Both PRODUCER and CONSUMER now call BUFFER to send and receive characters instead of interacting directly with each other. PRODUCER is forced to wait if it is producing characters much faster than CONSUMER can digest them (i.e., when BUFFER contains 50 characters). On the other hand, CONSUMER is forced to wait if it consumes much faster than PRODUCER produces (i.e., when BUFFER is empty).

```
with TEXT_IO; use TEXT_IO;
procedure CONVERT_TO_UPPER_CASE2 is

   task PRODUCER;      --sends characters to the buffer
   task CONSUMER;      --reads characters from the buffer
   task BUFFER is      --buffers up to 50 characters
      entry WRITE(C: in CHARACTER);
      entry READ(C: out CHARACTER);
   end BUFFER;

   function UPPER(C: in CHARACTER) return CHARACTER is
   begin
      :
   end UPPER;

   task body PRODUCER is
      C: CHARACTER;
   begin
      while not END_OF_FILE(STANDARD_INPUT) loop
         GET(C);
         BUFFER.WRITE(C);
      end loop;
   end PRODUCER;

   task body CONSUMER is
      X: CHARACTER;
   begin
      loop
         BUFFER.READ(X);
         PUT(UPPER(X));
      end loop;
   end CONSUMER;

   task body BUFFER is
      N: constant INTEGER := 51;
      Q: array(1..N) of CHARACTER;
             --max number of elements in the buffer will be N-1
      INB, OUTB: INTEGER range 1..N := 1;
             --INB mod N + 1: next free space in Q
             --OUTB mod N + 1: first element in Q, if any
             --INB = OUTB: Q is empty; initially true
             --INB mod N + 1 = OUTB: Q is full; as a
             --consequence the buffer always has one unused
             --element in this implementation scheme
```

```
        begin
          loop
            select
              when INB mod N + 1 /= OUTB =>     --Q not full
                --a character can be accepted
                  accept WRITE(C: in CHARACTER) do
                    Q(INB mod N + 1) := C;
                  end WRITE;
                        --PRODUCER can resume execution
                  INB := INB mod N + 1;
              or when INB /= OUTB =>          --Q not empty
                --a character can be read
                  accept READ(C: out CHARACTER) do
                    C := Q(OUTB mod N + 1);
                  end READ;
                        --CONSUMER can resume execution
                  OUTB := OUTB mod N + 1;
            or
                terminate;
              end select;
            end loop;
          end BUFFER;


      begin
          --PRODUCER, CONSUMER and BUFFER become active
        null;
      end CONVERT_TO_UPPER_CASE2;
```

On reaching the end of standard input, task PRODUCER terminates. However, CONSUMER does not terminate after all the characters supplied by PRODUCER have been processed. BUFFER cannot terminate until both PRODUCER and CONSUMER have terminated or are willing to terminate.

CONSUMER cannot be modified easily, as was possible in case of the procedure CONVERT_TO_UPPER_CASE given earlier; modification is not straightforward, because a *terminate* alternative cannot be used in CONSUMER as it does not accept entry calls (the terminate alternative can be used only in *selective wait* statements). However, this problem can be resolved in one of several ways. For example, we can:

1. Modify PRODUCER to send an *end of transmission* character when it is done; modify CONSUMER to terminate when it gets this character from BUFFER. With this approach one character must be reserved to indicate termination.

2. Add additional entries to BUFFER by which PRODUCER informs BUFFER that it will not be sending any more data and CONSUMER determines that no more data will be available. CONSUMER aborts when it determines that no more data is available.

3. Add an entry to BUFFER by which a task can determine if BUFFER has any characters. CONSUMER completes execution by terminating the loop when it determines that PRODUCER has completed or terminated (using the attribute CALLABLE), and BUFFER has no characters.

4. Restructure the program.

None of these alternatives is very satisfactory. The first one seems to be the best.

Tasks PRODUCER and CONSUMER are suspended by BUFFER as long as it is necessary for BUFFER to communicate with them, i.e., until the end of the *accept* statement corresponding to the entry called by them. It would be inefficient to hold up these tasks longer than necessary. For example, the *accept WRITE* statement in BUFFER could alternatively have been written as

```
accept WRITE(C: in CHARACTER) do
    Q(INB mod N + 1) := C;
    INB := INB mod N + 1;
end WRITE;
```

This would be inefficient, since PRODUCER will be unnecessarily suspended while BUFFER is doing its internal bookkeeping (incrementing INB). The body of an *accept* statement should be kept to a minimum to avoid delaying the calling task unnecessarily.

13.2 Using Entry Families—A Disk Manager

The problem is to implement a disk manager. A package, called DISK, which provides operations to interface with the physical disk is available. The disk consists of several recording *platters* mounted on a spindle (see Figure 2.6). Both surfaces of the platter can be used for recording. Each platter consists of many circular *tracks*. The set of all tracks that are the same distance away from the spindle is called a *cylinder*. A track is identified by its cylinder and surface numbers. Each track contains an equal number of *sectors*.

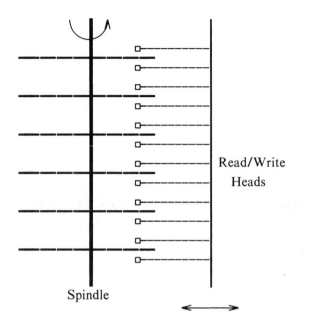

Figure 2.6: Multiplatter disk

Each platter surface has its own read/write head. The read/write heads access tracks on the same cylinder at any given time. These heads can be moved back and forth from one cylinder to another. Disk accesses are slow, because moving the disk heads is a slow process. Consequently, disk algorithms [HOA74, TEO72] try to minimize disk head movement in order to give best performance. In trying to maximize disk performance, care must be taken to ensure that no requests for disk access are made to wait an unreasonable amount of time.

The basic unit of storage that can be transferred to and from the disk is a sector. Let us assume, for this example, that a sector holds 512 characters and that this amount is equal to the main memory unit of storage allocation, called the *block*.

A block of memory is transferred to or from the disk by first moving the disk head to the desired cylinder. Next, the starting location of the block, surface and sector numbers, and the direction of the data transfer are placed in the hardware registers associated with the disk. An interrupt from the disk signals the end of the data transfer.

This detail is encapsulated in the package DISK, which is specified as

```
package DISK is
  procedure READ(SURFACE_NO: SURFACES;
             SECTOR_NO: SECTORS; BLOCK: ADDRESS);
  procedure WRITE(SURFACE_NO: SURFACES;
             SECTOR_NO: SECTORS; BLOCK: ADDRESS);
  procedure MOVE(CYLINDER_NO: CYLINDERS);
end DISK;
```

where the subtypes SURFACES, SECTORS and CYLINDERS are defined as

```
subtype SURFACES is INTEGER range 0..MAX_SURFACES − 1;
subtype SECTORS is INTEGER range 0..MAX_SECTORS − 1;
subtype CYLINDERS is INTEGER range 0..MAX_CYLINDERS − 1;
```

and type ADDRESS is a predefined type provided in the package SYSTEM [13.7]. The address in storage where an object X is allocated is given by the attribute X′ADDRESS [13.7.2].

The algorithm implemented by the disk manager to control the disk head movement is straightforward. Tracks are scanned starting from cylinder 0 up to cylinder MAX_CYLINDERS−1. Upon reaching the last track the scanning direction is reversed.

All requests for accessing tracks on a specific cylinder are serviced when the disk read/write heads are positioned at the cylinder. Disk access requests are therefore segregated by cylinder number. Two entry families—one for disk read requests and one for disk write requests—are used to partition the requests by cylinder number. Cylinder i is associated with the ith member of the entry families. Requests for accessing a specific cylinder are accepted by accepting calls to the corresponding member of the entry family.

The specification of the disk manager task DISK_MANAGER is

```
task DISK_MANAGER is
  entry READ(CYLINDERS) (SURFACE_NO: SURFACES;
             SECTOR_NO: SECTORS; BLOCK: ADDRESS);
  entry WRITE(CYLINDERS) (SURFACE_NO: SURFACES;
             SECTOR_NO: SECTORS; BLOCK: ADDRESS);
end DISK_MANAGER;
```

where READ and WRITE are the entry families.

The body of task DISK_MANAGER can be abstractly described as

```
CYLINDER_NO := −1; STEP := 1;
LIMIT := MAX_CYLINDERS − 1;
loop
   while CYLINDER_NO /= LIMIT loop
      CYLINDER_NO := CYLINDER_NO + STEP;
      Accept all requests to access this cylinder
   end loop;
   STEP := − STEP;
   LIMIT := (MAX_CYLINDERS − 1) − LIMIT;
end loop;
```

The statement *Accept all requests to access this cylinder* is refined as

```
while WRITE(CYLINDER_NO)'COUNT /= 0 loop
   Accept call WRITE(CYLINDER_NO);
end loop;
```

```
while READ(CYLINDER_NO)'COUNT /= 0 loop
   Accept call READ(CYLINDER_NO);
end loop;
```

The body of DISK_MANAGER is obtained by incorporating this refinement into the abstract version of the DISK_MANAGER and by supplying some more detail:

```
task body DISK_MANAGER is
   CYLINDER_NO: INTEGER := -1;
   STEP: INTEGER := 1;
   LIMIT : CYLINDERS := MAX_CYLINDERS - 1;
begin
   loop
      while CYLINDER_NO /= LIMIT loop
         CYLINDER_NO := CYLINDER_NO + STEP;
         DISK.MOVE(CYLINDER_NO);
         while WRITE(CYLINDER_NO)'COUNT /= 0 loop
            accept WRITE(CYLINDER_NO)
                        (SURFACE_NO: SURFACES;
                         SECTOR_NO: SECTORS;
                         BLOCK: ADDRESS) do
               DISK.WRITE(SURFACE_NO, SECTOR_NO, BLOCK);
            end WRITE;
         end loop;

         while READ(CYLINDER_NO)'COUNT /= 0 loop
            accept READ(CYLINDER_NO)
                        (SURFACE_NO: SURFACES;
                         SECTOR_NO: SECTORS;
                         BLOCK: ADDRESS) do
               DISK.READ(SURFACE_NO, SECTOR_NO, BLOCK);
            end READ;
         end loop;
       end loop;
      STEP := - STEP;
      LIMIT := (MAX_CYLINDERS - 1) - LIMIT;
   end loop;
end DISK_MANAGER;
```

The performance of the disk manager can be improved by modifying the algorithm so that[12]

---

12. John Linderman, a colleague at Bell Labs, likens the disk manager algorithm given to an escalator algorithm (instead of an elevator algorithm). In escalators, there is a big delay on each floor (the disk heads stop at each cylinder). Just as there are no escalators in a 100-story building, one would also not see the above algorithm used for real disks.

The modifications suggested make the disk manager algorithm similar to an elevator algorithm.

- The disk heads skip past cylinders for which there is no activity. As a result of the physics of speeding up and slowing the arms on which the disk heads are mounted, it takes only slightly more time in moving to any arbitrary cylinder than moving to the next cylinder.

- The disk heads are moved only when it is determined that there is a request for reading or writing.

13.3 The Concurrent Readers and Writers Example

Suppose several tasks want to access the same shared data. Tasks are of two kinds—*readers* and *writers* [COU71]. A reader task reads the shared data, but does not update it; a writer task updates it. What strategy should be used to allow concurrent access to the shared data? Several readers should be able to access the shared data simultaneously, but a writer should have exclusive access to the shared data.

One example of an application where concurrent readers and writers occur is a database (such as the airline reservation database described earlier). Database transactions are either queries (i.e., readers) or updates (i.e., writers) and these transactions may occur simultaneously.

Several strategies will be examined and implemented:

1. *One Reader or One Writer*: Only one reader task or one writer task is allowed to access the shared data at any time.

2. *Many Readers or One Writer*: The first strategy is unduly restrictive because it prevents multiple readers from accessing the data. There is no harm in allowing multiple readers to read the shared data simultaneously, because they do not change it. Not allowing multiple readers reduces the amount of concurrent computation in the system and increases the average waiting time for the tasks because each reader must wait until it gets exclusive access to the shared data.

3. *Many Readers or One Writer with the Writers Having a Higher Priority*: In the second strategy, it is possible that a steady stream of readers may indefinitely block the writers from accessing the shared data. This problem can be avoided by giving the writers a higher priority than the readers. Once a writer indicates its desire to access the shared data, all additional requests by readers are delayed until no write requests are pending.

4. *Many Readers or One Writer with the Writers Having a Higher Priority, But All Waiting Readers Are Given Access after a Writer Has Finished*: The third strategy is fine as long as the number of writers is small compared to the number of readers. Otherwise, the writers will block the readers indefinitely from getting access to the shared data. This blocking

can be prevented by requiring that all pending requests from readers be accepted after the current writer has finished and before a new writer is allowed access to the shared data.

Readers and writers will access the shared data by calling procedures READ and WRITE of the package RESOURCE; this package will contain the task controlling access to the shared data.

13.3.1 Solution 1a: Task RW_1A will be used to ensure that only one reader or writer accesses the shared data at any time. Its specification is

```
task RW_1A is
   entry READ(X: out SHARED_DATA);
   entry WRITE(X: in SHARED_DATA);
end RW_1A;
```

The body of task RW_1A is

```
task body RW_1A is
   S: SHARED_DATA := ... ;    --the shared data
begin
   loop
      select
         accept READ(X: out SHARED_DATA) do
            X := S;
         end READ;
      or
         accept WRITE(X: in SHARED_DATA) do
            S := X;
         end WRITE;
      end select;
   end loop;
end RW_1A;
```

Only one request to READ or WRITE is accepted at a time. Acceptance of a READ or a WRITE entry call is nondeterministic and will depend upon the implementation.

Package RESOURCE, which will contain task RW_1A, is declared as

```
package RESOURCE is
   type SHARED_DATA is ... ;
   procedure READ(X: out SHARED_DATA);
   procedure WRITE(X: in SHARED_DATA);
end RESOURCE;
```

```
package body RESOURCE is

   --specification and body of task RW_1A come here

   procedure READ(X: out SHARED_DATA) is
   begin
      RW_1A.READ(X);
   end READ;

   procedure WRITE(X: in SHARED_DATA) is
   begin
      RW_1A.WRITE(X);
   end WRITE;


end RESOURCE;
```

13.3.2 Solution 1b: The use of separate entries for the readers and writers does not guarantee that requests by readers and writers are accepted in first-in first-out (FIFO) order. Acceptance of these requests in FIFO order can be ensured by using a task with only one, instead of two, entries and indicating the desired kind of access to the shared data by means of a parameter:

```
task RW_1B is
   entry REQUEST(X: in out SHARED_DATA; WHAT: in SERVICE);
end RW_1B;

task body RW_1B is
   S: SHARED_DATA := ... ;   --the shared data
begin
   loop
      accept REQUEST(X: in out SHARED_DATA;
                                   WHAT: in SERVICE) do
         case WHAT is
            when READ => X := S;
            when WRITE => S := X;
         end case;
      end REQUEST;
   end loop;
end RW_1B;
```

The specification of package RESOURCE is modified to include the definition of the enumeration type SERVICE, which consists of two elements READ and WRITE. The body of the package RESOURCE is modified to include task RW_1B instead of RW_1A. Finally, the procedures READ and WRITE are modified to call entry REQUEST of RW_1B:

```
procedure READ(X: out SHARED_DATA) is
begin
    RW_1B.REQUEST(X, READ);
end READ;

procedure WRITE(X: in SHARED_DATA) is
begin
    RW_1B.REQUEST(X, WRITE);
end WRITE;
```

The above calls to entry REQUEST, in procedures READ and WRITE, are semantically incorrect, because the first formal parameter of REQUEST has mode **in out** while the corresponding actual parameters in these calls have the mode **out** and **in**, respectively. The first formal parameter of REQUEST was declared to be of mode **in out** so that both requests for reading and writing the shared variable could be accepted.

In the case of an **in out** parameter, the actual parameter is copied to the corresponding formal parameter at the start of each call (and the formal parameter copied back at the end of the call). Consequently, an uninitialized variable error occurs at the start of the call to REQUEST in procedure READ, because an attempt is made to copy the value of the formal parameter into the actual parameter, even though this value is not needed. X is a formal parameter of mode **out** in READ and therefore has no initial value transmitted to it by the corresponding actual parameter in the call to READ.

Moreover, an actual parameter corresponding to an **in out** parameter must be a variable, since a value is returned at the end of a subprogram or an entry call. The first actual parameter in WRITE is a constant, since formal parameters of mode **in** are constants. Consequently, a semantic error occurs when calling REQUEST from procedure WRITE, because at the end of the call a value cannot be returned by means of the first actual parameter even though no value is to be returned.

Procedures READ and WRITE are modified to eliminate these semantic problems as follows:

```
procedure READ(X: out SHARED_DATA) is
begin
   X := ...;
      --some initial value to avoid the uninitialized variable problem
   RW_1B.REQUEST(X, READ);
end READ;

procedure WRITE(X: in SHARED_DATA) is
   Y: SHARED_DATA;
begin
   Y := X;
   RW_1B.REQUEST(Y, WRITE);
end WRITE;
```

13.3.3 Solution 2: The above two solutions cannot be extended to allow simultaneous access by multiple readers because the task controlling access can accept requests only from one task at a time. Consequently, an alternative design must be considered. Instead of performing the mutual exclusion itself, the controlling task, called RW_2, will be used for synchronization.

Synchronizing entries of RW_2 will be called by procedures READ and WRITE of the package RESOURCE. The shared data will not be kept inside the controlling task, since that will restrict data access to only one task at a time. Instead, the shared data will be kept in the body of package RESOURCE and will be global to the procedures READ and WRITE. This will make it possible for multiple calls to the procedure to be executed simultaneously, provided the controlling task RW_2 allows this.

Synchronizing entry calls will be used to prevent multiple writers from simultaneously updating the shared data, to prevent a writer from updating data when a reader is in the middle of accessing the data or to prevent a reader from accessing the shared data when a writer is updating it.

The specification of the controlling task RW_2 is

```
task RW_2 is
   entry START_READ;
   entry END_READ;
   entry START_WRITE;
   entry END_WRITE;
end RW_2;
```

Entry START_READ is called from procedure READ to request permission to access the shared data prior to accessing it. Entry END_READ is called after completing access to inform RW_2 that access to the shared data has been completed. Similarly, entries START_WRITE and END_WRITE are called from procedure WRITE.

The body of the controlling task RW_2 is

```
task body RW_2 is
   NO_READERS: NATURAL := 0;
   WRITER_PRESENT: BOOLEAN := FALSE;
begin
   loop
      select
         when not WRITER_PRESENT =>
            accept START_READ;
            NO_READERS := NO_READERS + 1;
      or
            accept END_READ;
            NO_READERS := NO_READERS - 1;
      or
         when not WRITER_PRESENT and NO_READERS = 0 =>
            accept START_WRITE;
            WRITER_PRESENT := TRUE;
      or
            accept END_WRITE;
            WRITER_PRESENT := FALSE;
      end select;
   end loop;
end RW_2;
```

Package RESOURCE has the same specification as shown earlier in solution 1a. However, its body is now changed to

```
package body RESOURCE is

    S: SHARED_DATA := ... ;    --the shared data

    --specification and body of task RW_2 come here

    procedure READ(X: out SHARED_DATA) is
    begin
       RW_2.START_READ;
       X := S;
       RW_2.END_READ;
    end READ;

    procedure WRITE(X: in SHARED_DATA) is
    begin
       RW_2.START_WRITE;
       S := X;
       RW_2.END_WRITE;
    end WRITE;

end RESOURCE;
```

Since only one writer will be allowed to access the shared data at any given time, statements for updating the shared data can be moved inside the controlling task and the two synchronizing entries replaced by one entry WRITE as in the case of RW_1A (in solution 1a). This movement of code to update the shared data will save one rendezvous for every access of the shared data by a writer task.

13.3.4 Solution 3: Writers can be given a higher priority by accepting readers only when no writer is updating the shared data or when no writer is waiting for permission to update the shared data (i.e., at the entry START_WRITE). According writers a higher priority can be accomplished by changing task RW_2 as follows (the modified version is called RW_3):

```
task body RW_3 is
   NO_READERS: NATURAL := 0;
   WRITER_PRESENT: BOOLEAN := FALSE;
begin
   loop
      select
         when not WRITER_PRESENT
                        and START_WRITE'COUNT = 0 =>
            accept START_READ;
            NO_READERS := NO_READERS + 1;
      or
         .
         .
         .
      end select;
   end loop;
end RW_3;
```

Package RESOURCE is the same as in solution 2 except that task RW_3 replaces task RW_2 and calls to RW_2 are replaced by calls to RW_3.

13.3.5 Solution 4: By changing RW_2 into RW_4 as follows, all waiting readers are accepted after a writer has updated the shared data and before another writer is accepted:

```
    task body RW_4 is
      NO_READERS: NATURAL := 0;
      WRITER_PRESENT: BOOLEAN := FALSE;
    begin
      loop
        select
          when not WRITER_PRESENT
                  and START_WRITE'COUNT = 0 =>
            accept START_READ;
            NO_READERS := NO_READERS + 1;
        or
            :
        or
          accept END_WRITE;
            WRITER_PRESENT := FALSE;
            for I in 1..START_READ'COUNT loop
                --readers arriving after the evaluation of the
                --COUNT attribute will not be accepted here
              accept START_READ;
              NO_READERS := NO_READERS + 1;
            end loop;
        end select;
      end loop;
    end RW_4;
```

Package RESOURCE is the same as in solution 2 except that task RW_4 replaces task RW_2 and calls to RW_2 are replaced by calls to RW_4.

13.4 Shortest-Job-Next Scheduler

The problem is to implement a task that schedules jobs in the order of increasing execution time, i.e., shortest-job-next order. The scheduler is given jobs (job identification number, of type ID, and execution time of the job) by several input tasks. Several job dispatching tasks ask for the next job to be executed from the scheduler. The scheduler selects a job with the shortest execution time to give to the next dispatching task requesting a job.

The scheduler uses the package ORDERED_SET declared in the section on packages given in the Appendix. The specification of ORDERED_SET is reproduced:

```
package ORDERED_SET is
    procedure INSERT(JOB: in ID; T: in DURATION);
            --add JOB to the set; JOB is a job that requires
            --T seconds of execution time
    procedure SMALLEST(JOB: out ID);
            --Store in JOB, a job from the ordered set with the
            --smallest execution time; this job is deleted from the
            --set; SMALLEST should be called after ensuring
            --that the set is not empty.
    function EMPTY return BOOLEAN;
end ORDERED_SET;
```

The specification of task SCHEDULER is

```
task SCHEDULER is
    entry ADD(JOB: in ID; T: in DURATION);
    entry NEXT(JOB: out ID);
            --return the next job to be executed and delete
            --it from the list of jobs to be scheduled
end SCHEDULER;
```

SCHEDULER accepts jobs from the input tasks and inserts them into the ordered set. When there are jobs in the ordered set, SCHEDULER accepts requests from the dispatching tasks to which it hands out jobs in increasing execution-time order. Provided that the *use* clause

```
use ORDERED_SET;
```

has been given, the body of SCHEDULER is declared as

```
task body SCHEDULER is
   I: ID;
   PERIOD: DURATION;
begin
   loop
      select
            accept ADD(JOB: in ID; T: in DURATION) do
               I := JOB;
               PERIOD := T;
            end ADD;
            INSERT(I, PERIOD);
      or when not EMPTY =>
            accept NEXT(JOB: out ID) do
               SMALLEST(JOB);
            end NEXT;
      end select;
   end loop;
end SCHEDULER;
```

13.5 Controlling Task Scheduling

Entry calls are accepted in FIFO order. In some situations, a different scheduling discipline is desired. For example, disk access requests may be accepted in an order that minimizes head movement and an operating system may schedule jobs with the smallest execution times first to minimize the average waiting time.

One strategy that can be used to implement a different scheduling scheme is to use a family of entries. Suppose requests for service are classified into three categories declared as

   type REQUEST_LEVEL **is** (URGENT, NORMAL, LOW);

Urgent requests are accepted before any other kind of requests. Normal requests are accepted only if there are no urgent requests pending. Finally, requests in the low category are accepted only if there are no urgent or normal priority requests pending. Within each category, requests are accepted in FIFO order.

This scheme may be implemented by a task SERVICE that contains the declaration of an entry family REQUEST:

   task SERVICE **is**
      entry REQUEST(REQUEST_LEVEL) (D: **in out** DATA);
   end SERVICE;

Each member of REQUEST handles one request category. For example, the entry call

SERVICE.REQUEST(URGENT)(D);   ——D is the data

is a request for urgent service.

The body of task SERVICE is

```
task body SERVICE is
    ——local declarations
begin
    loop
        select
            accept REQUEST(URGENT)(D: in out DATA) do
            .
            .
            process the request
            .
            .
            end REQUEST;
            .
            .
        or when REQUEST(URGENT)'COUNT = 0 =>
                    ——the number of tasks waiting at an entry is
                    ——given by the COUNT attribute
            accept REQUEST(NORMAL)(D: in out DATA) do
            .
            .
            process the request
            .
            .
            end REQUEST;
            .
            .
        or when REQUEST(URGENT)'COUNT = 0
                    and REQUEST(NORMAL)'COUNT = 0 =>
            accept REQUEST(LOW)(D: in out DATA) do
            .
            .
            process the request
            .
            .
            end REQUEST;
            .
            .
        end select;
    end loop;

    end SERVICE;
```

Scheduling algorithms such as those for minimizing disk head movement or average process waiting time cannot be implemented with this scheme. To implement a general scheduling scheme, a two-stage process involving two entry calls is used. First, the task requesting service gets an identification number and issues an entry call indicating that it wants service. This call is accepted immediately and the identification of the calling task is noted by SERVICE—this is the signing-in stage. Next, the caller issues another entry call that is accepted by SERVICE only when it can perform the service—this is the waiting-for-service stage.

The reason for making two entry calls is that SERVICE cannot schedule the calling task, say A, until it establishes a rendezvous with A to get information about the request and the resources required. Task A is then given a unique identification number, which it must use to get service. Tasks waiting to get service are scheduled according to some scheduling algorithm.

Task SERVICE is an implementation of the abstract algorithm

loop
    Accept all jobs waiting to sign in for service
    Provide service to one job (if any)
end loop

It is inconvenient and error prone to let the calling task actually make the two entry calls. Instead, they are encapsulated in a procedure body and the task requesting service issues only one procedure call (which is syntactically similar to an entry call). A subprogram specification cannot be in a task specification. Consequently, task SERVICE is enclosed in a package SERVICE_PACKAGE:

```
package SERVICE_PACKAGE is
    ——definition of type DATA
    procedure GET_SERVICE(D: in out DATA);
end SERVICE_PACKAGE;

package body SERVICE_PACKAGE is

    subtype ID is INTEGER range 1..100;
    ——procedure NEXT_ID, FREE_ID and data to allocate/deallocate
    ——identification for tasks requesting service. These are used
    ——in procedure GET_SERVICE.

    ——other local declarations of SERVICE_PACKAGE

    task SERVICE is
        entry REGISTER_REQUEST(ID)(D: in out DATA); ——sign in
            ——Family of entries with index type ID
            ——A job that is assigned the unique identification
            ——number J of type ID calls entry J for service
        entry SERVE_REQUEST(ID)(D: in out DATA);
    end SERVICE;

    procedure GET_SERVICE(D: in out DATA) is
    begin
```

```
        Get a unique identifier I (by calling a task; a task
          is used instead of a function so that requests are
          sequentialized in order to ensure identifier uniqueness)
        --register service request; member I of the entry
        --family REGISTER_REQUEST is called with data D
          SERVICE.REGISTER_REQUEST(I)(D);
        --wait for service
          SERVICE.SERVE_REQUEST(I)(D);
        Free identifier I (by calling an entry of the above task
          that supplied the identifier)
    end GET_SERVICE;

    task body SERVICE is
    begin
      loop
        for I in ID loop
              --a loop is used to accept calls of an entry family
            select
                  --poll each member of the entry family;
                  --there can be only one call per member, since
                  --jobs requesting service are assigned unique
                  --identification numbers
              accept REGISTER_REQUEST(I)(D: in out DATA) do
                    :
                  --add job I to waiting list
              end REGISTER_REQUEST;
            else
              null;
            end select;
        end loop;

        if any job is waiting for service then
              --Let K be the next job to be provided service; K is
              --determined by using the specified scheduling algorithm
              accept SERVE_REQUEST(K)(D:in out DATA) do
                    :
              end SERVE_REQUEST;
        end if;
      end loop;

    end SERVICE;

end SERVICE_PACKAGE;
```

13.6 Implementation of Path Expressions

Path expressions [CAM74, BRI78, AND79] are a synchronization tool used in specifying meaningful sequences of entry call acceptance. Path expression operators

$$; \quad | \quad *$$

are used to specify simple path expressions:

P; Q   Acceptance of entry call P must be followed only by accepting a call to entry Q.

P | Q   An entry call to either P or Q can be accepted next.

P*   Accept zero or more occurrences of calls to entry P.

Implementation of path expressions in Ada is straightforward. For example, path expression P; Q is implemented by the sequence of *accept* statements

```
accept P;
accept Q;
```

Path expression P | Q is implemented by the *select* statement

```
select
    accept P;
or
    accept Q;
end select;
```

Path expression P* is implemented by the program fragment

```
loop
    select
        accept P;
    else
        exit;
    end select;
end loop;
```

Chapter 3: **Task Types** [9.2]

Ada allows the programmer to define task types in much the same way as other data types, such as integers and reals, are defined. Task types facilitate the declaration of multiple instances of identical tasks and allow for the dynamic creation of task instances. By and large, task types can be used just like other types, but there are some restrictions.

Multiple instances of identical tasks can be created by declaring an array with elements of a task type or by many individual declarations of task type objects. Tasks are created dynamically by first declaring an access type that refers to objects of a task type. Then this access type is used in conjunction with the allocator *new* to allocate storage for the tasks. Newly allocated tasks begin executing immediately after allocation.

The ability to create tasks dynamically gives a programmer flexibility in designing efficient systems. One can instantiate new tasks as needed instead of instantiating the maximum number of tasks that might be needed in the program at the beginning. Creation of tasks prior to their being needed is undesirable, since tasks consume resources, e.g., CPU time (tasks must be scheduled) and storage. In an example illustrating the tracking of airplanes [GEH83a], each airplane is tracked by a dedicated task. A new task is created when a new airplane is to be tracked, and this task is terminated and its storage deallocated when it is no longer necessary to track the airplane. The program is designed to handle up to 512 airplanes. If a facility to create tasks dynamically is not available, then all 512 tasks must be allocated in the beginning of the program, resulting in program inefficiency.

A facility for dynamic task creation complicates the language, its implementation and its run-time support. For example, a dynamic task creation facility was not included in Concurrent Pascal [BRI75] because Brinch Hansen wanted to avoid a complicated storage allocation scheme [BRI81b]. Such a facility is not necessary in programs that perform the same function again and again, e.g., some operating systems and real-time programs [BRI81b]. However, as mentioned above, the lack of a facility for dynamic task creation can lead to inefficient programs.

1. Declaration of Identical Tasks [9.1, 9.2]

The declaration of a task type is syntactically similar to the declaration of a task, the only difference being the presence of the keyword **type** in the task specification. For example, a task type FORK is declared as

```
task type FORK is
    entry PICK_UP;
    entry PUT_DOWN;
end FORK;
```

The declaration

```
F1, F2: FORK;
```

declares two tasks F1 and F2. These tasks become active just prior to execution of the first statement of the subprogram or package in which they are declared.

Arrays with elements of a task type are declared and accessed just like arrays with elements of other types. For example, each element of array F declared as

```
F: array(ID) of FORK;
```

is a task, and $F(I)$ refers to the Ith task.

Task types are limited types; limited type objects cannot be assigned a value or compared. Values of task objects are implicitly defined by their declaration, by parameter association or by the storage allocator (for dynamically instantiated tasks). Constant declarations of task objects, i.e., declarations using the reserved word **constant**, are not allowed, because such declarations require an explicit initialization, which is prohibited. Tasks can be passed as **in** or **in out** parameters; the actual parameter task and the corresponding formal parameter task designate the same task for both parameter modes.

2. Dynamic Task Creation/Exchanging Identities

If an application needs to create tasks dynamically or to store and exchange the identities of the tasks, then access types must be used. For example, consider the access type ANOTHER_FORK declared as

```
type ANOTHER_FORK is access FORK;
```

and variable EXTRA_FORK declared as

```
EXTRA_FORK: ANOTHER_FORK;
```

A task of type FORK, referred to by variable EXTRA_FORK, is created dynamically by calling the allocator **new**:

```
EXTRA_FORK := new FORK;
```

Allocated tasks become active immediately after they are allocated. All allocated tasks must have terminated or be ready to terminate to allow the block, subprogram or task, in which the associated access type has been declared, to terminate.

3. Examples

The use of task types can be illustrated by examples that vary in size and complexity—from small and simple to large and complex. The first example illustrates the use of a task type to declare many instances of semaphores. The second example, the classic dining-philosophers problem first posed by Dijkstra [DIJ71], illustrates the use of a task array. The third and fourth examples both illustrate the dynamic creation of tasks. The third example uses tasks to simulate an alarm clock. The fourth and final example simulates job scheduling in a machine shop.

3.1 Semaphores

The following task type SEMAPHORE is used to implement semaphores:

```
task type SEMAPHORE is
    entry P;
    entry V;
end SEMAPHORE;

task body SEMAPHORE is
begin
    loop
        accept P;
        accept V;
    end loop;
end SEMAPHORE;
```

Semaphores are declared by declaring tasks of type SEMAPHORE:

```
S1, S2, S3: SEMAPHORE;
```

Mutually exclusive access to the shared data can be implemented by requiring that all concurrent processes accessing shared data use code fragments of the form

```
S1.P;
access the shared data
S1.V;
```

to access the shared data.

3.2 The Mortal Dining Philosophers

This problem is an adaptation of the one posed by E. W. Dijkstra. Five philosophers spend their lives eating spaghetti and thinking. They eat at a circular table in a dining room (see Figure 3.1). The table has five chairs around it and chair number I has been assigned to philosopher number I $(1 \leqslant I \leqslant 5)$. Five forks have also been laid out on the table so that there is precisely one fork between every adjacent two chairs. Consequently there is

one fork to the left of each chair and one to its right. Fork number I is to the
left of chair number I.

Figure 3.1: The five philosophers

In order to be able to eat, a philosopher must enter the dining room and sit in
the chair assigned to her. A philosopher must have two forks to eat (the forks
placed to the left and right of every chair). If the philosopher cannot get two
forks immediately, then she must wait until she can get them. The forks are
picked up one at a time with the right fork being picked up first. When a
philosopher is finished eating (after a finite amount of time), she puts the forks
down and leaves the room.

The dining philosophers problem has been studied extensively in the computer science literature. It is used as a benchmark to check the appropriateness of concurrent programming facilities and of proof techniques for concurrent programs. It is interesting because, despite its apparent simplicity, it illustrates many of the problems, such as shared resources and deadlock, encountered in concurrent programming. The forks are the resources shared by the philosophers who represent the concurrent processes.

The five philosophers and the five forks will be implemented as tasks using two arrays of tasks in procedure DINING. On activation, each philosopher is given an identification number[13] (equal to the array index she is associated with). Using this number, a philosopher can determine the identification numbers of the forks on either side of her. Each philosopher is mortal and passes on to the next world soon after having eaten 100,000 times (about three times a day for 90 years).

```
procedure DINING is
    subtype ID is INTEGER range 1..5;

    task type PHILOSOPHER is
        entry GET_ID(J: in ID);
                --get an identification number
    end PHILOSOPHER;

    task type FORK is
        entry PICK_UP;
        entry PUT_DOWN;
    end FORK;

    F: array(ID) of FORK;          --the 5 forks
    P: array(ID) of PHILOSOPHER;   --the 5 philosophers

    task body FORK is
            --A fork can be picked up by one philosopher at a time.
            --It must be put down before it can be picked up again.
            --The forks terminate after the philosophers terminate.
        begin
```

---

13. A task must be explicitly given an identification since Ada tasks cannot identify themselves. The ability of tasks to identify themselves can be convenient, especially in the context of an array of tasks. Moreover, the inelegance and unnecessary sequentialization resulting from the explicit supplying of identifications would be avoided. One strategy for task self-identification would be to introduce a new attribute into Ada especially for this purpose.

```
        loop
            select
                    accept PICK_UP;
                    accept PUT_DOWN;
            or
                    terminate;
            end select;
        end loop;
    end FORK;

    task body PHILOSOPHER is
        I: ID;  --index or number of this philosopher
        LIFE_LIMIT: constant := 100_000;
        TIMES_EATEN: INTEGER := 0;
        LEFT, RIGHT: ID;          --fork numbers
    begin
        accept GET_ID(J: in ID) do
                            --get the identification number
            I := J;
        end GET_ID;

        LEFT := I;      --number of the left fork
        RIGHT := I mod 5 + 1;   --number of the right fork

        while TIMES_EATEN /= LIFE_LIMIT loop
            --think for a while; then enter dining room and sit down
            --pick up forks
                F(RIGHT).PICK_UP;
                F(LEFT).PICK_UP;
            --eat
            --put down forks
                F(LEFT).PUT_DOWN;
                F(RIGHT).PUT_DOWN;

            TIMES_EATEN := TIMES_EATEN + 1;
            --get up and leave dining room
        end loop;
    end PHILOSOPHER;

begin
    for K in ID loop
            --give identification numbers to the philosophers
        P(K).GET_ID(K);
    end loop;
```

end DINING;

Philosophers and forks were both implemented as arrays of tasks. It would have been convenient if Ada had allowed a task that is an element of an array to determine its index in the array so that it could distinguish itself from the other elements of the array. The above program would then become simpler, since there would be no need to supply the identification numbers explicitly to the philosophers.

A variation of the above problem for the reader to try is to allow a philosopher to sit in any chair. This variation will result in a smaller average waiting time for eating for the philosophers. *Hint*: This scheme can be implemented by declaring a new task that is called by every philosopher to request a chair (preferably one with free forks). On leaving the dining room, a philosopher informs this task that the chair is vacant.

In the solution given, no individual philosopher will be blocked indefinitely from eating, i.e., *starve*, because the philosophers pick up the forks in first-in first-out order (the discipline associated with all entry queues). However, there is a possibility of deadlock in the solution given above, e.g., each philosopher picks up one fork and waits to get another fork so that she can start to eat. Assuming that all the philosophers are obstinate and that none of them will give up her fork until she gets another fork and has eaten, everything will be in a state of suspension and all the philosophers will starve (see Figure 3.2).

Figure 3.2: Who eats next?

Deadlock can be avoided in several ways; for example, a philosopher may pick up the two forks needed by her only when both forks are available (*Hint*: by using *when* conditions in the *select* statement). Alternatively, one could add another task called the HOST that makes sure there are at most four philosophers in the dining room at any given time. Each philosopher must request permission to enter the room from the HOST and must inform him on leaving.

Task HOST is declared as

```
task HOST is
   entry ENTER;
   entry LEAVE;
end HOST;

task body HOST is
   I: INTEGER := 0;    ——number of philosophers in the room
begin
   loop
      select
         when I < 4 =>
               ——a philosopher can enter if there are less
               ——than 4 philosophers in the dining room
            accept ENTER;
            I := I + 1;
      or
            accept LEAVE;    ——philosopher is leaving
            I := I − 1;
      or
         terminate;
      end select;
   end loop;
end HOST;
```

There is no possibility of a deadlock with this change, since at least one philosopher in the room will be able to eat. Since they all eat for a finite time, she will leave and some other philosopher will be able to eat.

3.3 An Alarm Clock

Suppose there is a user-command interpreter,[14] written in Ada, with which users interact with a machine. This command interpreter has a body of the form

---

14. A simple command interpreter similar to the *shell* interpreter that is the user-interface in Unix™ operating systems.

Unix is a trademark of Bell Laboratories.

```
with TEXT_IO; use TEXT_IO;
with CALENDAR; use CALENDAR;
procedure COMMAND_INTERPRETER  is
      :
      :
begin
      :
      :
         loop
            Read the next user command
            if command is C₁ then Execute command C₁
            elsif command is C₂ then Execute command C₂
               :
               :
            elsif command is Cₙ then Execute command Cₙ
            else
               :
               :
            end if;
         end loop;
      :
      :
exception
      :
      :
   end COMMAND_INTERPRETER;
```

The problem is to implement an alarm clock as one of the commands that a user can execute. When the user executes the command *alarm*, the command interpreter arranges for the alarm to be sounded at the appropriate time; the interpreter does not wait for *alarm* to complete, but goes on to execute the next user command.

Command *alarm* has the form

ALARM hh mm message

where *hh mm* is the time in hours and minutes (both being integer values) and *message* is the message that is to be displayed on the user's terminal when the alarm goes off. The *bel* character (from the package ASCII), which causes a beeping sound on the user's terminal, is used to attract the user's attention when the alarm goes off.

If *hh mm* is greater than the current time, but less than or equal to 2400 hours (midnight), then the alarm is to be sounded the same day; otherwise, the alarm is intended by the user to be set off the next day.

Some example commands are

ALARM 12 00 Lunch with visitor
ALARM 09 45 Do not forget the meeting at 10 a.m.
ALARM 16 00 Time to play squash

Every request for an alarm setting will be implemented in the COMMAND_INTERPRETER by dynamically allocating a task of type USER_ALARM and supplying it with the appropriate information. It is the responsibility of the allocated task to sound the alarm at the specified time. Task type USER_ALARM will be declared in the body of procedure COMMAND_INTERPRETER. Upon receiving an *alarm* command from the user, the COMMAND_INTERPRETER executes a program fragment of the form

```
:
if command is ALARM then
   GET(HOURS); GET(MINUTES);
   Clear MSG by putting blanks in it; GET_LINE(MSG);
   P := new USER_ALARM;
   P.SET_OFF(HOURS, MINUTES, MSG);
elsif
   :
```

to set the alarm. Variables HOURS and MINUTES are subtypes of type INTEGER with ranges 0..24 and 0..59, respectively. MSG is of the subtype REASON which is declared as

```
subtype REASON is STRING(1..60);
```

TEXT_IO is assumed to be instantiated appropriately for INTEGER input and output in the body of the COMMAND_INTERPRETER.

The specification of task type USER_ALARM is

```
task type USER_ALARM is
   entry SET_OFF(HOURS, MINUTES: INTEGER; MSG: REASON);
end USER_ALARM;
```

Task type USER_ALARM can be abstractly described as

```
record information about the alarm
determine if the alarm is to be sounded today or tomorrow
wait until it is time to sound the alarm
sound the alarm and display message at the user's terminal
```

Based on this abstract description, the body of task type USER_ALARM is

```
    task body USER_ALARM is
       HR, MIN: INTEGER;
       M: REASON := (1..60 => ' ');
       CUR_TIME, ALARM_TIME: TIME;
       INTERVAL: DURATION;
    begin
       --record information about the alarm
          accept SET_OFF(HOURS, MINUTES: INTEGER MSG: REASON) do
             HR := HOURS; MIN := MINUTES;
             M := MSG;
          end SET_OFF;


       --store in ALARM_TIME the time to give alarm
       --Functions CLOCK, TIME_OF, YEAR, MONTH and DAY, and the
       --subtype DAY_DURATION are from the package CALENDAR
          CUR_TIME := CLOCK;
          ALARM_TIME := TIME_OF(YEAR(CUR_TIME),
                                MONTH(CUR_TIME),
                                DAY(CUR_TIME),
                                DAY_DURATION(HR*3600 + MIN*60));
       --determine if the alarm is to be sounded today or tomorrow
          if ALARM_TIME < CUR_TIME then
             ALARM_TIME := ALARM_TIME + DURATION(24.0*3600.00);
          end if;


       delay ALARM_TIME-CUR_TIME;

       --sound the alarm and display message at the user's terminal
          PUT(ASCII.BEL); PUT(ASCII.BEL);
          PUT_LINE(M);


    end USER_ALARM;
```

Every instance of task type USER_ALARM terminates after sounding the alarm.

3.4 Job Shop Scheduling—An Example from Simulation

The problem is to simulate a machine job shop that has several groups of identical machines and processes *orders*—i.e., *jobs*—that involve the use of these machines [KAU76]. This example is known in the simulation literature as the *job shop model*.

Job orders arrive at random intervals. Each order consists of a number of steps, each step involving the use of a machine from one of the different machine groups for a period of time, called the *processing time*, as shown in

Figure 3.3:

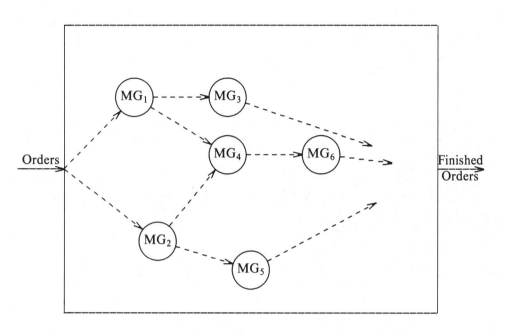

MG$_I$: Machine Group I

Figure 3.3: The machine shop

The maximum number of machine groups to be catered for is 10 and the maximum number of steps allowed for each order is 20. The simulation data is supplied in the following format:

number of machine groups, followed by their sizes
{ arrival time of next order
number of steps in the order
list of the machine groups and corresponding processing times }

where the brackets {} indicate repetition of the items enclosed by them.

The strategy used to simulate the machine shop involves assigning a task (of type MACHINE_GROUP) to manage each one of the machine groups— allocation of the machines in the groups is controlled by these tasks. An array of controlling tasks, MG, is used for this purpose. Allocation of machines in group I will be controlled by task MG(I).

To request allocation of a machine from group I, entry REQUEST of task MG(I) is called. If there are no more free machines in a group, then honoring the request to allocate a machine is delayed until a machine is free. After a machine has been used to perform a step in an order, it is returned to its group, say I, by the entry call MG(I).RELEASE.

Each order is represented by a task of type ORDER in the simulation. Every time a new order comes to the machine shop a new task, of type ORDER, is allocated and given the necessary information about the order. This task manages the execution of the order by requesting machines for the various steps in the order.

Main procedure JOB_SHOP controls the simulation. This procedure contains the tasks controlling the machine groups, creates tasks for the orders and gives them the necessary information about the orders. Procedure JOB_SHOP can be abstractly described as

```
set up the machine groups MG
while there are more orders loop
    wait until it is time for the next order to arrive
    get the next order
    initiate processing of this order by creating
        a task for it
end loop;
```

The tasks controlling each machine group can be abstractly described as

```
loop
    select
        when there are free machines =>
            accept a request for allocating a machine
    or
        take back a freed machine
    or
        terminate;
    end select;
end loop;
```

Specification of task type MACHINE_GROUP is

```
task type MACHINE_GROUP is
   entry SIZE(N: in INTEGER);      --number of machines in the group
   entry REQUEST;
   entry RELEASE;
end MACHINE_GROUP;
```

The body of MACHINE_GROUP is

```
task body MACHINE_GROUP is
   NO_OF_MACHINES: INTEGER;
begin
   accept SIZE(N: in INTEGER) do
      NO_OF_MACHINES := N;
   end SIZE;
   loop
      select
         when NO_OF_MACHINES > 0 =>
            accept REQUEST;
            NO_OF_MACHINES := NO_OF_MACHINES - 1;
      or
            accept RELEASE;
            NO_OF_MACHINES := NO_OF_MACHINES + 1;
      or
            terminate;
      end select;
   end loop;
end MACHINE_GROUP;
```

Tasks of type ORDER can be abstractly described as

```
for each step in the order loop
      request a machine from the appropriate group
      wait until processing is done
      release the machine back to its group
end loop;
```

Upon getting the details of an order, an order task requests the machine needed in each step from the appropriate machine group, holds onto it for the time required to perform the step and then returns the machine to its group. The specification of task type ORDER is

```
task type ORDER is
   entry INFO(I: GROUP_IDS; T: PROCESSING_TIMES);
end ORDER;
```

The body of ORDER is

```
task body ORDER is
   GI: GROUP_IDS(1..MAX_STEPS);
                  --array indicating the machine required in each step
   PT: PROCESSING_TIMES(1..MAX_STEPS);
                  --processing time needed for each step
   NO_OF_STEPS: INTEGER;
begin
   accept INFO(I: GROUP_IDS; T: PROCESSING_TIMES) do
      NO_OF_STEPS := I'LAST;
      for J in 1..NO_OF_STEPS loop
         GI(J) := I(J);
         PT(J) := T(J);
      end loop;
   end INFO;
   for STEP in 1..NO_OF_STEPS loop
      MG(GI(STEP)).REQUEST;
      delay DURATION(PT(STEP));
      MG(GI(STEP)).RELEASE;
   end loop;
end ORDER;
```

The final version of JOB_SHOP is obtained by expanding its abstract description and using the task types MACHINE_GROUP and ORDER:

```ada
with TEXT_IO; use TEXT_IO;
procedure JOB_SHOP is
    package IO_FLOAT is new FLOAT_IO(FLOAT);
    package IO_INTEGER is new INTEGER_IO(INTEGER);
    use IO_FLOAT; use IO_INTEGER;
    MAX_GROUPS: constant := 10;
    MAX_STEPS: constant := 20;

    type GROUP_IDS is array(INTEGER range <>) of INTEGER;
    type PROCESSING_TIMES is array(INTEGER range <>) of FLOAT;

    --specification of task type MACHINE_GROUP
    --specification of task type ORDER

    type NEW_ORDER is access ORDER;

    MG: array(1..MAX_GROUPS) of MACHINE_GROUP;
    GI: GROUP_IDS(1..MAX_STEPS);
    PT: PROCESSING_TIMES(1..MAX_STEPS);
    ARRIVAL_INTERVAL: FLOAT;
    NO_OF_GROUPS, NO_OF_MACHINES: INTEGER;
    NO_OF_STEPS: INTEGER;
    NEXT_ORDER: NEW_ORDER;

    --bodies of task types MACHINE_GROUP and ORDER

begin
    PUT("MAX_GROUPS="); PUT(MAX_GROUPS); NEW_LINE;
    PUT("MAX_STEPS="); PUT(MAX_STEPS); NEW_LINE;
    --set up the machine groups and kill the extra tasks
    GET(NO_OF_GROUPS);
    for I in 1..NO_OF_GROUPS loop
        GET(NO_OF_MACHINES);
        MG(I).SIZE(NO_OF_MACHINES);
    end loop;
    for J in NO_OF_GROUPS+1..MAX_GROUPS loop
        abort MG(J);
    end loop;
    --process the orders
    while not END_OF_FILE(STANDARD_INPUT) loop
        GET(ARRIVAL_INTERVAL);
        delay DURATION(ARRIVAL_INTERVAL);

        GET(NO_OF_STEPS);
```

```
      for I in 1..NO_OF_STEPS loop
         GET(GI(I));     --group ids
         GET(PT(I));     --processing times
      end loop;

      NEXT_ORDER := new ORDER;
      NEXT_ORDER.INFO(GI(1..NO_OF_STEPS),
                      PT(1..NO_OF_STEPS));  --initialize order
   end loop;
end JOB_SHOP;
```

In this solution the maximum number of machine groups and number of processing steps have been hard-wired into the program. Not only is this strategy inefficient (since extra tasks and storage will be allocated), but it will not run if the number of groups or number of processing steps exceeds the predefined limits. How can these predefined limits be eliminated? (*Hint*: Use a *block* statement).

Does this solution suffer from the *cumulative time drift* discussed in Chapter 2? If so, then how can this drift be eliminated?

Each machine group in this program is controlled by a task. As an alternative strategy, instead of allocating one task to control each group of machines in the job shop, one task could have been used to control all the machine groups in the shop. Although this would have required less resources (fewer tasks), centralized allocation of machines by one controlling task unnecessarily makes the simulation more sequential. Requests for machines from different groups would then have to be accepted sequentially.

The main purpose of a simulation program is to collect statistics to analyze the problem being simulated. Instructions to collect statistics were omitted from the above program to emphasize the focus on the dynamic creation of tasks; these instructions can be easily added to appropriate parts of the program.

Chapter 4: **Exceptions and Tasking** [9.3, 11]

Raising and handling exceptions in tasks is similar to raising and handling them in subprograms with one important difference: exceptions cannot be propagated out of a task. Propagation of exceptions out of a task was prohibited because it meant that a task could asynchronously interfere with its parent and, in turn, it could be subject to the same kind of interference from tasks local to it [DOD79b]. In contrast, communication by means of the rendezvous mechanism is synchronous, since both the calling and called tasks must synchronize at the *entry call* and *accept* statements, respectively.

In this chapter, the interaction of exceptions and tasks will be examined in detail. Specifically, the effect of raising an exception in a task depends upon where the exception is raised—in a task declaration, in a task activation, during task execution or during task communication.

1. Exceptions Raised in Task Declarations and During Task Activation [9.3, 11.4.2]

If an exception occurs when processing the declaration of task objects, then this processing is abandoned and the exception raised again immediately after the declaration in the enclosing declarative part.

The activation of a task includes processing declarations in its body. The raising of an exception when processing a declaration in a task body results in the completion of the task and raising of the exception TASKING_ERROR at the point of task activation.

The point of activation for declared tasks is immediately after the reserved word **begin**, but just before the first executable statement. Exception TASKING_ERROR is raised only once even if exceptions are raised in the activation of many tasks. In the case of tasks that are dynamically created using the allocator *new*, exception TASKING_ERROR is raised when the allocator is invoked.

2. Statement in a Task Raising an Exception [11.4.1]

An exception occurring in a statement contained in a task (i.e., the immediately enclosing frame[15] is a task) is handled by the exception handler provided in the task. After execution of the exception handler, the task becomes completed. If an exception handler is not provided, then the task becomes completed immediately.

An exception raised in a task cannot be propagated out of the task—either implicitly by not providing an exception handler, or explicitly by raising or reraising the exception. An exception can be propagated out of a block or a subprogram, but only after all dependent tasks have terminated.

3. Exceptions During Task Communication [11.5]

An exception can be raised in a task during a rendezvous or when attempting a rendezvous. The following situations cause exceptions to be raised in the called task or raised in the calling task:

1. *The called task completes before accepting an entry call or is already completed at the time of the call.* Exception TASKING_ERROR is raised in the calling task at the point of the entry call.

2. *The called task becomes abnormal during rendezvous.* Exception TASKING_ERROR is raised in the calling task at the point of the entry call.

3. *An exception raised in the accept statement is not handled locally within an inner frame.* The exception is raised in the calling task at the point of the entry call and it is also raised in the part of the program containing the *accept* statement, i.e., the called task. Raising an exception during execution of the *accept* statement is the *only* situation which results in an exception being raised in two parts of a program.

Abnormal termination of the calling task does not cause an exception to be raised in the called task. If the rendezvous has not started, then the rendezvous is canceled. Otherwise, the rendezvous is allowed to complete normally and the called task is unaffected.

4. Examples

The examples in this section illustrate the raising and handling of exceptions in several different contexts. The first example, the automatic cruising speed controller found in some automobiles, illustrates both the handling of an exception raised in a task without letting the task terminate and the

---

15. A *frame* is either a *block* statement, or the body of a subprogram, package, task or generic unit.

termination of a task after the exception raised in the task has been handled. The next two examples, asynchronous copying of files and storage allocation, illustrate raising and handling of exceptions during rendezvous.

4.1 Cruising Speed Control

Some automobiles come equipped with a cruise control mechanism that automatically maintains the automobile at a constant speed selected by the driver. The cruise control mechanism is set in action by driving the automobile at the desired cruising speed and then pushing the cruise control button. The cruise control mechanism is disengaged by depressing either the brake or the gas pedal (the accelerator).

The problem is to write a task CRUISE_CONTROL that implements such a mechanism. A package AUTO_CONTROL that contains several subprograms which can be used to control the automobile is available. In particular, AUTO_CONTROL contains the subprograms SPEED, CHANGE_SPEED and ALARM and the exception SPEEDOMETER_MALFUNCTION:

```
package AUTO_CONTROL is
    :
    :
    function SPEED return FLOAT;
    procedure CHANGE_SPEED(S: in FLOAT);
    procedure ALARM(MSG: in STRING); --both audible and visual
    :
    SPEEDOMETER_MALFUNCTION: exception;
    :
    :
end AUTO_CONTROL;
```

Function SPEED returns the speed at which the automobile is currently traveling. Exception SPEEDOMETER_MALFUNCTION is raised by function SPEED if something goes wrong with the speedometer. In this case the cruise control mechanism is disengaged and task CRUISE_CONTROL is terminated. The driver is alerted by the sounding of an alarm using procedure ALARM. An audible version of the argument in the call to ALARM is played, using the speakers in the automobile, to warn the driver.

Calling procedure CHANGE_SPEED with a value x causes the automobile speed to be increased by x mph if x is positive and to be decreased by x mph if x is negative. It takes about half a second for the automobile to respond to the change-of-speed instruction. The speed of the car is changed in a manner that optimizes fuel consumption. If for some reason the speed of the automobile cannot be maintained within 2 mph of the desired cruising speed, the cruise control mechanism is disengaged and task CRUISE_CONTROL terminated. As before, an alarm is to be sounded by calling procedure ALARM with an appropriate message.

The cruise control mechanism is designed to work for speeds between 35 mph and 55 mph. If the driver tries to set the cruise control with the automobile speed outside this limit, the alarm is sounded along with an appropriate message. However, in this case, task CRUISE_CONTROL does not terminate, but allows the driver to set the cruising speed again.

Interrupts are raised by pressing the cruise control initiation button, by depressing the gas pedal and by depressing the brake. Addresses of these interrupts are

> cruise control button interrupt   8#60#
> brake   8#62#
> gas pedal   8#64#

Interrupts can be made to appear like entry calls by associating the interrupt locations with entries. (See Chapter 5 on *Device Drivers* for further details.)

It is assumed that the entities in package AUTO_CONTROL have been made directly visible to task CRUISE_CONTROL by means of the clauses

> **with** AUTO_CONTROL; **use** AUTO_CONTROL;

given at an appropriate place in the procedure containing CRUISE_CONTROL.

Task CRUISE_CONTROL has the specification

```
task CRUISE_CONTROL is
    entry TAKE_OVER;
    entry BRAKE;
    entry GAS_PEDAL;

    for TAKE_OVER use at 8#60#;
            ——associate interrupt at location 8#60#
            ——with entry TAKE_OVER
    for BRAKE use at 8#62#;
    for GAS_PEDAL use at 8#64#;
end CRUISE_CONTROL;
```

Entry TAKE_OVER is associated with the interrupt generated when the cruise control button is pressed to indicate that the cruise control mechanism should take over control of the automobile's speed.

The algorithm implemented by task CRUISE_CONTROL can be abstractly described as

```
loop
    wait until the driver activates the cruise control mechanism
    check whether the cruising speed is within the specified limits;
            if not, warn driver but do not activate the mechanism
    loop
        select
            deactivate mechanism if brake is depressed
        or
            deactivate mechanism if gas pedal is depressed
        or
            Try and maintain automobile speed around the cruising
                speed; otherwise, deactivate mechanism.
            Wait 0.1 seconds for the automobile speed change
        end select;
    end loop;
end loop;
```

The body of CRUISE_CONTROL is

```
task body CRUISE_CONTROL is
    LOW_CRUISING_LIMIT: constant FLOAT := 35.0;
    HIGH_CRUISING_LIMIT: constant FLOAT := 55.0;
    VARIATION: constant FLOAT := 2.0;
    RESPONSE_TIME: constant DURATION := 0.5;
    CURRENT_SPEED, CRUISING_SPEED: FLOAT;
    OUTSIDE_CRUISE_LIMITS: exception;
    CRUISE_CONTROL_MALFUNCTION: exception;
begin
    loop
        begin
            accept TAKE_OVER;
            CRUISING_SPEED := SPEED;
                --SPEED is the function that yields the current
                --automobile speed (from package AUTO_CONTROL)
            if CRUISING_SPEED < LOW_CRUISING_LIMIT
                or CRUISING_SPEED > HIGH_CRUISING_LIMIT then
                raise OUTSIDE_CRUISE_LIMITS;
            end if;
            loop
                select
                    accept GAS_PEDAL; exit;
                or
                    accept BRAKE; exit;
                else
                    CURRENT_SPEED := SPEED;
```

```
                    if abs (CRUISING_SPEED − CURRENT_SPEED)
                                         <= VARIATION then
                       CHANGE_SPEED(CRUISING_SPEED
                                         − CURRENT_SPEED);
                    else
                       raise CRUISE_CONTROL_MALFUNCTION;
                    end if;
                    delay RESPONSE_TIME;
                  end select;
                end loop;
              exception
                when OUTSIDE_CRUISE_LIMITS =>
                   ALARM("Cruising Speed Too High or Too Low");
                   −−this execution of block statement terminates;
                   −−execution of the loop continues
              end;
            end loop;
          exception
            when SPEEDOMETER_MALFUNCTION =>
               ALARM("Speedometer Malfunction−Cruise Control Disabled");
            when CRUISE_CONTROL_MALFUNCTION =>
               ALARM("Cruise Control Problem, Cruise Control Disabled");
          end CRUISE_CONTROL;
```

The statements inside the first loop have been enclosed inside a *block* statement **begin** ... **end**. Why is it necessary to use the *block* statement? The reader should try and answer this question before reading the next paragraph.

If the driver attempts to set the cruising speed outside the specified limits, exception OUTSIDE_CRUISE_LIMITS is raised. However, raising this exception must not terminate the task, since the driver is allowed to set the cruising speed again. Consequently, the *block* statement is used to handle exception OUTSIDE_CRUISE_LIMITS locally.

However, if exception CRUISE_CONTROL_MALFUNCTION is raised, indicating that the cruise control mechanism is not able to keep the car within 2 mph of the desired cruising speed, then task CRUISE_CONTROL terminates after the completion of the exception handler for CRUISE_CONTROL_MALFUNCTION.

4.2 Asynchronous File Copying [DOD79b]

Task SPOOLER, which is described below, provides a facility for the asynchronous copying of text files. Exceptions END_OF_FILE and NAME_ERROR are handled locally; exception NAME_ERROR is also raised in the calling task. Exception NAME_ERROR is raised when the calling task supplies illegal external names for the source or destination files.

Task SPOOLER can be abstractly described as

> **loop**
>   Accept a request to copy one file to another
>   Copy the file
> **end loop**;

Accepting a request to copy file SOURCE to file DESTINATION involves associating the external file names with internal file names by opening the files. The task making the file copy request is suspended while the files are opened, so that an exception raised when opening the files is conveyed to the calling task by means of exception propagation. Such an exception may arise because a file does not exist or because it has the wrong access permission.

It will be assumed that the package or subprogram containing task SPOOLER is compiled in the context

> **with** TEXT_IO; **use** TEXT_IO;

Task SPOOLER will now have access to the file operations OPEN and CLOSE, input operations GET and PUT, type FILE_MODE, enumeration literals IN_FILE and OUT_FILE (of type FILE_MODE), and exceptions NAME_ERROR and END_ERROR. (Of course, other entities in TEXT_IO will also become accessible to task SPOOLER, but they are not needed.)

The specification of task SPOOLER is

> **task** SPOOLER **is**
>   **entry** COPY(SOURCE, DESTINATION: **in** STRING);
> **end** SPOOLER;

The body of SPOOLER is

```
            task body SPOOLER is
              X, Y: FILE_TYPE;
              C: CHARACTER;
          begin
            loop
              begin
                accept COPY(SOURCE, DESTINATION: in STRING) do
                  OPEN(X, IN_FILE, SOURCE);
                       --X is the internal name of file SOURCE
                  begin
                    OPEN(Y, OUT_FILE, DESTINATION);
                         --Y is the internal name of file DESTINATION
                  exception
                    when NAME_ERROR => CLOSE(X); raise;
                  end;
                end COPY;

                loop
                  GET(X, C); PUT(Y, C);
                end loop;
              exception
                when END_ERROR => CLOSE(X); CLOSE(Y);
                when NAME_ERROR => null;  --restart main loop
              end;
            end loop;
          end SPOOLER;
```

If an error results from opening the first file, exception NAME_ERROR is propagated to the calling task, since the exception is raised during the rendezvous and is not handled locally within the *accept* statement. For the second file, NAME_ERROR is handled locally, to allow file X (i.e, SOURCE) to be closed, but this exception is then reraised, which causes it to be propagated to the calling task as well as outside the *block* statement. (As mentioned earlier, an exception is propagated outside a task only if it occurs during a rendezvous and is not handled locally.)

If NAME_ERROR is raised when opening file SOURCE or DESTINATION, it is eventually raised just after the end of the *accept* statement and is handled by the exception handler specified in the enclosing *block* statement. Enclosing the *accept* statement in the *block* statement prevents termination of SPOOLER because of an exception.

Exception NAME_ERROR, when propagated to the calling task, can be handled by an exception handler associated with the calling task or locally in association with the entry call as illustrated by the following program segment:

```
begin
    SPOOLER.COPY("QUICKSORT.ADA", "TEMP");
exception
    when NAME_ERROR => take appropriate action
end;
```

4.3 A Storage Allocation Facility

The occurrence of an exception inside an *accept* statement (but not within any enclosing frame) causes the termination of the *accept* statement and the exception to be raised just after the *accept* statement within the called task; this exception is also propagated to the calling task. Propagation of the exception to the calling task can be prevented by enclosing the potential source of the exception inside an inner frame, such as a *block* statement.

As an example, consider task BLOCK_STORAGE that allocates storage for objects of type BLOCK. If there is no storage available, execution of the storage allocator *new*, within BLOCK_STORAGE, causes exception STORAGE_ERROR to be raised. Propagation of the first occurrence of the exception STORAGE_ERROR is hidden from the calling task, because first an attempt is made to reclaim any unused storage by calling the garbage collection procedure, GARBAGE_COLLECTOR; then storage allocation is attempted a second time. If it is not possible to allocate storage even after calling GARBAGE_COLLECTOR, STORAGE_ERROR is propagated to the calling task.

Task BLOCK_STORAGE uses types BLOCK and PTR_TO_BLOCK, which are declared as

```
type BLOCK is array(1..512) of CHARACTER;
type PTR_TO_BLOCK is access BLOCK;
```

The specification of task BLOCK_STORAGE is

```
task BLOCK_STORAGE is
    entry ALLOCATE(P: out PTR_TO_BLOCK);
end BLOCK_STORAGE;
```

The body of task BLOCK_STORAGE is

```
task body BLOCK_STORAGE is
begin
   loop
      begin
         accept ALLOCATE(P: out PTR_TO_BLOCK) do
            begin
               P := new BLOCK;
            exception
               when STORAGE_ERROR =>
                     GARBAGE_COLLECTOR;
                     P := new BLOCK;
            end;
         end ALLOCATE;
      exception
         when STORAGE_ERROR => null;
      end;
   end loop;
end BLOCK_STORAGE;
```

The *block* statement inside the *accept* statement prevents the first occurrence of the exception STORAGE_ERROR from being propagated to the calling task. This exception is handled locally—the garbage collector is called in an attempt to reclaim unused storage so that the storage allocation request can be honored.

If storage allocation is not possible after calling GARBAGE_COLLECTOR, exception STORAGE_ERROR is then propagated to the calling task and is also raised within BLOCK_STORAGE just after the *accept* statement. As in task SPOOLER in the earlier example, a *block* statement is used to prevent termination of the task BLOCK_STORAGE. An exception handler must be provided, even it is one with a *null* statement, since in the absence of an exception handler, the exception will propagate outside the loop and cause termination of the task.

Chapter 5: **Device Drivers** [9, 13.5.1]

A *device driver* is a task dedicated to controlling a hardware device, such as a disk, a CRT display or a line printer. The device driver shields the rest of the program from such peculiarities of the device as the location of its hardware registers and the details of its interrupts. It is good programming practice to design programs so that they do not interact directly with hardware devices, but instead interact using their drivers. Programs can be unaffected by changes to a device, because device drivers shield them from the changes. Only device drivers, which constitute a small fraction of a system and which are isolated from the application programs, need to be modified when the device is changed.

Device drivers must be able to access device registers, such as buffers and status words, that are assigned absolute locations in memory, handle interrupts generated by the device and execute privileged instructions. Access to the status word of a device allows a driver to determine the status of a device, e.g., whether or not the device is ready to perform the next action and to control its behavior, such as turning off interrupts generated by it.

Traditionally, device drivers were written in assembly or machine language even if a high-level language, such as Concurrent Pascal [BRI75], was being used to implement the rest of the system, because the high-level languages did not provide facilities to access the hardware. Modula [WIR77a, WIR77b, WIR77c] was the first programming language to provide high-level facilities for writing device drivers. Ada's facilities are similar, but more elaborate.

The Ada facilities that allow high-level access to device registers and interrupt handling are the *representation* clauses (see section on Representation Clauses in the Appendix). With the *address* clause, program variables can be associated with device registers and interrupts can be associated with entries. One can access specific bits of a device register by using *length* and *record representation* clauses together with *address* clauses.

1. Device Registers [13.5.1]

To access a device register, one instructs the compiler, by means of an *address* clause, to allocate a program variable of an appropriate type at the hardware address corresponding to the device register. References to this variable translate into references to the device register. For example, the declarations

PRINTER_BUFFER: CHARACTER;
for PRINTER_BUFFER **use at** 8#177566#;

allow the memory location 8#177566#, representing the printer buffer, to be accessed using variable PRINTER_BUFFER, which is of type CHARACTER.

Specific bits of a location in computer memory can be accessed by mapping a boolean array onto the word or by specifying the layout of a record that is allocated at the memory location. For example, the boolean array STATUS, declared as

STATUS: **array**(0..15) **of** BOOLEAN;

is mapped to the location 8#177564# and the compiler is told to use only 16 bits for it by means of the *representation* and *length* clauses

for STATUS **use at** 8#177564#;
for STATUS'SIZE **use** 16;

Bit i of memory location 8#177564# is accessed using STATUS(i). (For additional details and examples of accessing bits in specific memory locations see the *Chain Line Printer Driver* example, given later in this chapter, and the *Typing Speed* example in Chapter 6 on *Real-Time Programming*.)

2. Interrupts [13.5.1]

A hardware interrupt is treated like an entry call—the task making the call in this case being the hardware device. An interrupt is associated with an entry by means of the *address* clause; such a clause specifies that the entry is to be called whenever an interrupt associated with the given address occurs. An entry associated with an interrupt is called an *interrupt entry*. As an example, consider the association of entry DONE with an interrupt that is associated with the address 16#40# [DOD83]:

task INTERRUPT_HANDLER **is**
entry DONE;
for DONE **use at** 16#40#;
end INTERRUPT_HANDLER;

The occurrence of an interrupt acts as an entry call whose priority is greater than that of any user-defined task [13.5.1]. The occurrence of an interrupt entry call effectively raises the priority of the task containing that entry to the priority associated with the hardware device, because the rendezvous takes place with the higher priority. Consequently, a device driver gets preference in being scheduled for execution whenever it can accept an entry call issued by an interrupt.[17] The motivation for having a rendezvous occur at the higher priority is to allow device interrupts to be handled quickly; this maximizes peripheral-device use by minimizing the time required to handle their interrupts.

A queued interrupt corresponds to an ordinary entry call, an interrupt that is lost if not processed immediately corresponds to a conditional entry call and an interrupt that is lost if not processed before the occurrence of the next interrupt (an unbuffered interrupt) corresponds, approximately, to a timed entry call. The exact nature of an interrupt entry call depends upon the nature of the device and the Ada implementation.

Control information supplied by an interrupt can be passed to the associated interrupt entry by means of parameters (this facility is implementation-dependent). Only formal parameters of mode **in** are allowed in interrupt entries.

If a *select* statement contains both a *terminate* alternative and an *accept* alternative for an interrupt entry, then an implementation may impose additional requirements on the selection of the *terminate* alternative.

3. Low-Level Input/Output Package [14.6]

Device drivers can also be written using a low-level input/output standard package called LOW_LEVEL_IO. Devices are controlled by means of memory references (as discussed in detail above) or by means of privileged instructions. The use of package LOW_LEVEL_IO is necessary when devices are controlled by means of privileged instructions [PER82]. Package LOW_LEVEL_IO contains the procedures SEND_CONTROL and RECEIVE_CONTROL that are used for writing device drivers. Each procedure has two parameters that specify the type of the device and the type of data sent to and received from the device. The overloaded procedure SEND_CONTROL is used to send control information to the device. The overloaded procedure RECEIVE_CONTROL is used to monitor the execution of the device by requesting information from the device.

Package LOW_LEVEL_IO, which is implementation dependent, has the specification

---

17. An interrupt entry can also be called by another task.

```
package LOW_LEVEL_IO is
    --declarations of the possible types for DEVICE and DATA
    --declarations of overloaded procedures for these types

    procedure SEND_CONTROL (DEVICE: device_type;
                                    DATA in out data_type);
    procedure RECEIVE_CONTROL (DEVICE: device_type;
                                    DATA in out data_type);
end LOW_LEVEL_IO;
```

4. Examples

The examples in this section illustrate the control of two diverse kinds of
devices—the chain line printer (a vanishing breed with the arrival of laser
printers) and the familiar typewriter terminal.

4.1 A Chain Line Printer Driver

The problem is to write a device driver for a chain line printer. Wear and tear
of the printer chain is to be minimized by stopping the chain when the printer
is not being used. If the printer driver does not receive a request to print a line
for 10 seconds, the driver stops the chain. Once the chain is stopped, further
requests for printing will cause the chain to be restarted; however, a 1-second
delay occurs before printing recommences. (This example is a modified and
expanded version of the example in DOD79b.)

Some characteristics of the chain printer that are relevant to this problem are

Printer status register (2 bytes)	8#777500#
Printer buffer register (1 byte)	8#777502#
Address of interrupt indicating	
printer is ready to accept the next character	8#200#

Bits in the status register are used to control the behavior of the printer.
Setting bit 5 to 1 (0) enables (disables) interrupts. Setting bit 7 to 1 causes
the printer chain to start moving, while setting it to 0 causes the chain to stop.

Bits 5 and 7 of the printer status register will be accessed using boolean
variables INTERRUPT_ENABLED and CHAIN_RUNNING that will be
mapped to these bits. Instead of a boolean array to access the bits, as
illustrated earlier (in section 1 of this chapter), components of a record object
will be used. First, a record type containing two components is declared:

```
type STATUS_REGISTER is
  record
    INTERRUPT_ENABLED: BOOLEAN;
    CHAIN_RUNNING: BOOLEAN;
  end record;
```

Next the layout in storage of objects of type STATUS_REGISTER is declared using the representation clause:[18]

```
for STATUS_REGISTER use
  record
    INTERRUPT_ENABLED at 0*WORD range 5..5;
          --map INTERRUPT_ENABLED to bit 5 of the first
          --word of the storage allocated to variables
          --of type STATUS_REGISTER
    CHAIN_RUNNING at 0*WORD range 7..7;
                --map CHAIN_RUNNING to bit 7
    --other bits are not used
  end record;
```

WORD is a constant representing the number of bytes per word:

```
WORD: constant := 2;
```

After this, the amount of storage that is to be allocated for objects of this type is specified:

```
for STATUS_REGISTER'SIZE use WORD;
          --allocate exactly one word (two bytes per word)
```

Finally, a variable PRINTER_REGISTER is declared to be of type STATUS_REGISTER and the compiler is instructed, by means of an *address* clause, to allocate this variable at 8#777500#, the printer status register address:

```
PRINTER_REGISTER: STATUS_REGISTER;
for PRINTER_REGISTER use at 8#777500#;
```

Bits 5 and 7 can now be accessed as components INTERRUPT_ENABLED and CHAIN_RUNNING, respectively, of the record PRINTER_REGISTER.

---

18. Assume that FALSE is mapped to 0 and TRUE is mapped to 1. An Ada implementation may choose a different mapping. An Ada implementation can be specifically instructed to use the above mapping by means of the *enumeration representation* clause [13.3], e.g.,

```
for BOOLEAN use (FALSE => 0, TRUE => 1);
```

Requests for printing a line are passed on by the device driver to the printer, one character at a time, via the buffer register of the printer. These characters are automatically transferred from the buffer register to an internal buffer (size 132 characters) in the printer. The contents of the internal buffer are printed when the buffer is full or when the last character sent to be printed is the line feed character (ASCII.LF) or the form feed character (ASCII.FF). A carriage return is automatically performed when the internal buffer is printed.

The printer device driver, task PRINTER_DRIVER, uses the following declarations:

```
LINE_LENGTH: constant := 132;
subtype LINE is STRING(1..LINE_LENGTH);
```

The specification of task PRINTER_DRIVER is

```
task PRINTER_DRIVER is
    entry PRINT(L: LINE);
    entry READY;    --printer ready for next character
    for READY use at 8#200#;
end PRINTER_DRIVER;
```

Task PRINTER_DRIVER implements the abstract algorithm

```
Enable interrupt
Ensure chain is stopped
loop
    select
        Accept a request to print a line and put line in BUFFER
        If chain is stopped, then start the chain and wait one second
        Give the line BUFFER to the printer for printing
    or
        If chain has been in motion for 10 seconds without
        any printing, then stop it
    end select;
end loop;
```

The abstract instruction *Give the line BUFFER to the printer for printing* is refined as

```
for I in 1..LINE_LENGTH loop
    Put BUFFER(I) in printer buffer; wait for character to print
    exit when BUFFER(I) is the line feed or form feed character;
    end if;
end loop;
```

The body of task PRINTER_DRIVER is

```
task body PRINTER_DRIVER is
    --all the declarations and representation clauses for
    --the type STATUS_REGISTER are included here

    PRINTER_REGISTER: STATUS_REGISTER;
    for PRINTER_REGISTER use at 8#777500#;
    BUFFER: LINE;
    PRINTER_BUFFER: CHARACTER;
    for PRINTER_BUFFER use at 8#777502#;
begin
    PRINTER_REGISTER.INTERRUPT_ENABLED := TRUE;
    PRINTER_REGISTER.CHAIN_RUNNING := FALSE;
    loop
        select
            accept PRINT(L: LINE) do
                BUFFER := L;
            end PRINT;

            if not PRINTER_REGISTER.CHAIN_RUNNING then
                --start the chain and wait one second
                    PRINTER_REGISTER.CHAIN_RUNNING := TRUE;
                    delay 1.0;
            end if;
            --Give the line BUFFER to the printer for printing
                for I in 1..LINE_LENGTH loop
                    PRINTER_BUFFER := BUFFER(I);
                    accept READY;
                    exit when BUFFER(I) = ASCII.LF or
                                    BUFFER(I) = ASCII.FF;
                end loop;
        or
            when PRINTER_REGISTER.CHAIN_RUNNING =>
                delay 10.0;  --stop the chain
                PRINTER_REGISTER.CHAIN_RUNNING := FALSE;
        end select;
    end loop;
end PRINTER_DRIVER;
```

4.2 Typewriter Input and Output

The problem is to write a package TYPEWRITER for a PDP-11 computer that provides the user (most likely a systems programmer) with procedures to read a character from the keyboard and to write a character via the typewriter printer.[19] These procedures will call upon the keyboard and printer device drivers to read a character and write a character, respectively. The relevant hardware specifications of the typewriter are

Keyboard hardware buffer address	8#177562#
Keyboard interrupt address	8#60#
Printer hardware buffer address	8#177566#
Printer interrupt address	8#64#
Interrupt priority	4

The keyboard interrupt occurs after the hardware buffer has been filled with a new character.[20] The printer interrupt occurs after the character put into the hardware buffer has been printed.

One driver task will be defined for the typewriter keyboard and one for the printer. The keyboard driver will have an internal buffer of 64 characters and will be willing to accept characters from the keyboard as long as the buffer is not full. It is from this buffer that the user can read characters using the procedure READ_CHAR. The printer driver has a similar structure.

The specification of the package TYPEWRITER is

```
package TYPEWRITER is
   procedure READ_CHAR(C: out CHARACTER);
   procedure WRITE_CHAR(C: in CHARACTER);
end TYPEWRITER;
```

and its body is

---

19. This problem is an adaptation of an example in WIR77a.

20. The character in the hardware buffer should be retrieved before the next character arrives, since otherwise the first one will be lost. We will assume that the task reading characters from the hardware buffer will be able to respond with the required speed to avoid the loss of any characters. The priority rules imply that an accept statement executed in response to an interrupt has precedence over those executed in response to normal entry calls.

```
package body TYPEWRITER is

  task KEYBOARD is
    pragma PRIORITY(4);
          --must have at least the priority of the interrupt
    entry GET(C: out CHARACTER);
    entry PUT;
    for PUT use at 8#60#;
  end KEYBOARD;

  task PRINTER is
    pragma PRIORITY(4);
          --must have at least the priority of the interrupt
    entry GET;
    entry PUT(C: in CHARACTER);
    for GET use at 8#64#;
  end PRINTER;

  procedure READ_CHAR(C: out CHARACTER) is
  begin
    KEYBOARD.GET(C);
  end READ_CHAR;

  procedure WRITE_CHAR(C: in CHARACTER) is
  begin
    PRINTER.PUT(C);
  end WRITE_CHAR;

  --body of task KEYBOARD, described below, is to be included here
  --body of task PRINTER, described below, is to be included here


end TYPEWRITER;
```

Entries KEYBOARD.PUT and PRINTER.GET have been associated with interrupts; as mentioned earlier, interrupt entry calls are issued by the hardware.

The bodies of the two tasks KEYBOARD and PRINTER are

```
task body KEYBOARD is
   MAX: constant := 64;    --internal buffer size
   A: array(1..MAX) of CHARACTER;    --internal buffer
   INB, OUTB: INTEGER := 1;    --internal buffer pointers
   N: INTEGER := 0;    --buffer count

   HARDWARE_BUFFER: CHARACTER;
   for HARDWARE_BUFFER use at 8#177562#;
begin
   loop
      select
         when N > 0 =>
            accept GET(C: out CHARACTER) do
               C := A(OUTB);
            end GET;
            OUTB := OUTB mod MAX + 1;
            N := N - 1;
      or
         when N < MAX =>
            accept PUT do
               A(INB) := HARDWARE_BUFFER;
            end PUT;
            INB := INB mod MAX + 1;
            N := N + 1;
      end select;
   end loop;
end KEYBOARD;


and
```

```
task body PRINTER is
   MAX: constant := 64;    --internal buffer size
   A: array(1..MAX) of CHARACTER;    --internal buffer
   INB, OUTB: INTEGER := 1;    --buffer pointers
   N: INTEGER := 0;    --buffer count

   HARDWARE_BUFFER: CHARACTER;
   for HARDWARE_BUFFER use at 8#177566#;
   HARDWARE_BUFFER_EMPTY: BOOLEAN := TRUE;
begin
   loop
      select
         accept GET;    --character printed
         if N > 0 then
            HARDWARE_BUFFER := A(OUTB);
            OUTB := OUTB mod MAX + 1;
            N := N - 1;
         else
            HARDWARE_BUFFER_EMPTY := TRUE;
         end if;
      or
         when N < MAX =>
            accept PUT(C: in CHARACTER) do
               A(INB) := C;
            end PUT;
            INB := INB mod MAX + 1;
            N := N + 1;
            if HARDWARE_BUFFER_EMPTY then
               HARDWARE_BUFFER := A(OUTB);
               OUTB := OUTB mod MAX + 1;
               N := N - 1;
               HARDWARE_BUFFER_EMPTY := FALSE;
            end if;
      end select;
   end loop;
end PRINTER;
```

Chapter 6: **Real-Time Programming** [9.6, 13.5.3]

Real-time programs can be informally described as programs that have concurrent components and operate under time constraints. As a consequence of these characteristics, they do not possess two important properties possessed by sequential programs [BRI73b]:

1. *The effect of a sequential program is independent of its execution speed.* Consequently, a programmer need not worry about details such as the speed of the CPU or of the peripheral devices and the scheduling policy used by the implementation.

2. *A sequential program exhibits reproducible behavior*, i.e., repeated execution of a sequential program with the same initial data results in the same output. This property is heavily relied upon during program debugging and testing.

Certain programs, however, have to be designed with their execution speeds as part of their specifications, because otherwise the data being produced for these programs will be lost. For example, programs gathering telemetry data from satellites must be able to gather the data with at least the speed at which it arrives, programs monitoring unbuffered interrupts must be able to process one interrupt before the arrival of the next one, and keyboard drivers must provide quick response.

It is not easy to give exact definitions of real-time programs, since the term real-time means different things to different people. However, the essence of real-time programs is captured by the following two definitions:

First Definition of **Real-Time Programs** [WIR77d]: If the validity of a program depends upon its execution speed, then it is termed a *real-time* (or processing-time-dependent) program.

Second Definition of **Real-Time Programs** [MEL83]: Real-time programs are programs that interact with digital/analog peripheral devices. Data acquisition by the program must be keyed to the time scale of the physical phenomena. The program must be able to respond within the time constraints of the real-world phenomena.

Real-time programs interact with an environment in which events may happen simultaneously and nondeterministically at high speed. Real-time programs may be designed to execute forever (i.e., in practice until they are aborted or there is system failure). Since real-time programs are usually concurrent and time-dependent, it is hard to reproduce the sequence of events that resulted in a particular output. This difficulty in reproducing results makes it hard to determine the sequence of events that resulted in erroneous output—debugging is a serious problem! Consequently, extra care should be taken in designing real-time programs. This warning should not be taken lightly—real-time programs are used in critical applications such as those for controlling spacecraft, missiles and nuclear reactors. Software failure may result in a catastrophe.

1. Requirements for Real-Time Programming Languages

A programming language for real-time programming should provide facilities for [STO82, YOU82]

1. *Explicit Programmer Control of Task Scheduling*: A programmer should be able to supply an alternative scheduling algorithm to be used instead of the one provided by the implementation of the programming language. Alternatively or in conjunction with programmer-defined scheduling, a programmer should be able to specify task priorities. Specification of task priorities provides a limited degree of control over scheduling. Programmer control of scheduling may be necessary for meeting critical timing constraints.

2. *Timeout in Task Communication*: A task should be able to abandon its attempt to interact with another task if a rendezvous cannot be established within some specified time period. Timeout is illustrated in an example illustrating *Home Fire/Energy/Security Monitoring* [GEH83a]. In this example, a task ALARM times out after 4.5 seconds, abandoning its attempt to rendezvous with the fire and burglar alarms, to report that all is well to task STATUS. If such a report is not made within 5.0 seconds, STATUS assumes that ALARM is inoperative (possibly because of tampering) and initiates emergency procedures (e.g., informing the police).

3. *Direct Communication with Hardware Devices*: It should be possible to confine interrupt handling to well-defined language constructs.

4. *Error Handling*: Whenever possible, a real-time program should be able to recover from errors and, in severe cases, it should be able to terminate errant tasks.

It is important to note that none of these facilities for real-time programming will be of any help if the hardware, consisting of the underlying computer and peripheral devices, is not fast enough to perform the required task within the specified time constraints.

Ada provides facilities that meet these requirements:

1. Scheduling can be done explicitly or implicitly:

   a. *Explicit Scheduling*: Although entry calls are handled by default in first-in first-out order, a programmer can implement any desired scheduling scheme by using entry families. The one-stage process of calling the entry of a server task and getting service upon acceptance of the entry call can be replaced by a two-stage process. The task requesting service first registers its request by calling an entry of the server task which gives it an index of some member of an entry family. The requesting task then calls this member of the entry family. The server accepts calls to the entry family using the desired scheduling policy. This two-stage process can be made secure, i.e., a user can be prevented from calling the entry family directly by using forged or old indices of the entry family, by encapsulating the two-stage sign-in process in a procedure. Tasks requesting service call this procedure.

   However, it is not possible to deschedule a task explicitly in Ada [ROB81]. Such a facility would be very desirable to ensure the immediate scheduling of some critical task.

   b. *Implicit Scheduling*: Ada tasks can be assigned priorities by means of the **PRIORITY** pragma [9.8], which is implementation dependent, i.e., the implementation defines the valid range of priorities. An implementation may define a null range of priorities, thus disallowing user specification of task priorities.

   One must take care when using priorities in Ada. For example, calls to an entry are accepted in FIFO order regardless of the priority of the waiting tasks.

2. Ada's time-out facilities are the *timed entry* calls for the task calling an entry and the *delay* alternative in the *selective wait* statement for the acceptor of an entry call.

3. As mentioned in Chapter 5 on *Device Drivers*, Ada provides high-level facilities for interfacing with hardware devices. With *representation* clauses, program variables can be mapped to device buffer and status registers—the variables can even be mapped to specific register bits. Associating an entry with the address of the interrupt makes the interrupt behave exactly like an entry call.

   Interrupt entry calls are accorded a higher priority than that of any user-defined tasks (and therefore entry calls of user-defined tasks). Different devices (and therefore their interrupts) may be assigned different priorities by an Ada implementation. In addition to communication with a device by means of its device registers, information can be received from the device by means of parameters of interrupt entries associated with the interrupts.

4. The exception mechanism in Ada is the basis of its elaborate error-handling facilities. Tasks in Ada may be unconditionally terminated using the *abort* statement.

2. Designing Real-Time Systems

The *Ada Reference Manual* [DOD83] says nothing about scheduling details, leaving them up to the implementation. An Ada implementation may use any scheduling strategy as long as the above scheduling rules are honored. Consequently, the correct design of a real-time system requires that the system designer understand the details of the task scheduling policy used by the Ada implementation so that critical timing constraints can be met.

As an example, suppose task A is executing and task B receives an entry call from a critical device that has the highest priority. Will the execution of task A be suspended so that task B can be scheduled to handle the critical device? Or will task B be forced to wait until task A reaches a point where its execution can be suspended, e.g., a *delay* statement or an *accept* statement with no pending entry calls? The system designer will have to learn about these details for critical applications.

3. Scheduling

Every Ada run-time system will maintain a list of tasks that are *eligible for execution*. If two tasks with different priorities are both eligible for execution, using the same physical processors and same resources, then the task with the higher priority must be executed. In cases of tasks with the same priority, the order of scheduling is not defined and is left to the implementation.

For tasks with no explicitly specified priority, the scheduling rules are not defined except when these tasks engage in a rendezvous with a task whose priority has been specified explicitly. Since tasks with different priorities may interact with each other, Ada gives rules to determine the priority of task interaction. The priority of a rendezvous is

1. the higher of the priorities of the two tasks if their priorities are specified,

2. the priority of the task with a specified priority if one task has no specified priority and

3. unspecified if both tasks have no explicitly specified priority.

Whether or not the timing constraints can be met depends upon system design, hardware characteristics and scheduling policies of the Ada implementation.

The moment when the next task is selected for execution depends upon when the scheduler is invoked. Invocation of the scheduler depends upon the scheduling policy. Consequently, when designing real-time systems, it is important to know when the scheduler will be invoked to determine whether or not timing constraints will be satisfied.

4. Timing Constraints and Scheduling Policies

Different scheduling policies may have an impact on system characteristics, such as response time, leading to different system designs. How does one design a system taking the timing constraints into account? Timing information obtained from the static program text is not enough, since the processor may be shared among many tasks.

A scheduler may not be invoked (by the Ada run-time system) at any arbitrary place; it may be invoked (causing the descheduling of a task) only at the following points [DOD79b]:

- Task initiation.

- Task completion and termination.

- Entry call (including an interrupt entry call).

- Reaching an *accept* statement for which no call has been issued.

- Reaching a *select* statement with no open alternatives.

- Completion of a rendezvous.

- Execution of a *delay* statement.

- Termination of a *delay* statement.

Two scheduling policies are examined in detail.

4.1 Nonpreemptive Scheduling

In nonpreemptive scheduling, a device driver is allowed to execute as long as it can. The next device driver is scheduled only after the currently executing one can no longer continue. The drivers are scheduled in the order in which their interrupt entries are called. The priority of the device drivers is effectively raised above that of any user task when accepting an interrupt entry call.

Consider, as an example, a real-time program interacting with several hardware devices, all having the same priority. Each device is controlled by one dedicated driver. Assume that the drivers accept entry calls but do not make any calls themselves. (As examples, see the drivers KEYBOARD and DISPLAY of the *Typewriter Input and Output* example of Chapter 5 on *Device Drivers*.) What is the maximum delay that can occur in accepting an interrupt entry call?

The maximum delay that can occur before a driver j can accept an interrupt entry call is

$$\sum_{i, i \neq j} t(S_i)$$

where $t(S_i)$ is the time to execute the longest possible sequence of statements before a driver i cannot continue, and i ranges over all the other device drivers (i.e., $i \neq j$).

4.2 Preemptive Priority Scheduling

In practice, it may be desirable to assign different priorities to different devices, especially if the real-time system controls many devices and a few of them need a fast response [WIR77d]. A running task is immediately suspended when a higher priority task becomes eligible for execution; the latter is then scheduled for execution. Analysis of such a scheme is very complicated unless a programming discipline is followed. Wirth [WIR77d] advocates the use of the following programming strategy for the design of real-time systems:

1. A task should be devoted to each device.

2. Each device task should be cyclic—the cycle consists of some statement sequence S_i and the *accept* statement corresponding to the interrupt entry.

Then the cycle time t_i of device task i is

$$t_i = t(S_i) + t(\mathbf{accept}_i)$$

where $\mathbf{accept}_i$ is the *accept* statement corresponding to interrupt entry in the ith device task. The time $t(\mathbf{accept}_i)$ depends upon the device itself and represents the time spent waiting for the corresponding interrupt to occur. The cycle time of a process at a priority level P must be considerably larger than that of all processes at priority level $P-1$. This condition ensures that at most one interrupt from a higher priority input occurs while processing of an input.

Out of every second of execution time, r_i, defined as

$$r_i = \frac{t(S_i)}{t(S_i) + t(\mathbf{accept}_i)} \ll 1.0$$

is the fraction of time needed to serve the ith device task.

The *effective execution* time is the real time required for execution. The effective execution time will be different from the actual execution time if the processor is being shared with other tasks. Under the above conditions the effective execution time $t(S)$ of any statement S in a device task at priority level P is

$$t(S) = \frac{t'(S)}{1.0 - \Sigma r_j}$$

where $t'(S)$ is the execution time of statement S using a dedicated processor and where j ranges over all the tasks with priority greater than P.

5. Examples

The first example is a simple application of the preemptive scheduling analysis. The second example illustrates the use of polling, instead of interrupts, to control a device. This problem involves measuring the typing speed of a user. The final example is a backyard irrigation system where the backyard must be watered for specific time periods. The two kinds of devices available for measuring the ground moisture content have different characteristics, leading to different solutions.

5.1 Example of Real-Time Constraint Analysis

As an example of real-time analysis, consider the task KEYBOARD taken from the typewriter example in Chapter 5 on *Device Drivers*:

```
task KEYBOARD is
    pragma PRIORITY(4);
    entry GET(C: out CHARACTER);
    entry PUT; for PUT use at 8#60#;
end KEYBOARD;
```

```
task body KEYBOARD is
  :
  :
  HARDWARE_BUFFER: CHARACTER;
  for HARDWARE_BUFFER use at 8#177562#;
begin
  loop
    select
      when N > 0 =>
        accept GET(C: out CHARACTER) do
          C := A(OUTB);
        end GET;
        OUTB := OUTB mod MAX + 1;
        N := N - 1;
    or
      when N < MAX =>
        accept PUT do
          A(INB) := HARDWARE_BUFFER;
        end PUT;
        INB := INB mod MAX + 1;
        N := N + 1;
    end select;
  end loop;
end KEYBOARD;
```

Characters are typed in by the user every θ milliseconds. KEYBOARD shares the processor with several other tasks; KEYBOARD must be able to accept characters from the terminal without losing them. The keyboard interrupts are not queued and the input characters are not buffered by the hardware.

Task KEYBOARD will be able to accept characters from the keyboard without losing any one of them only if the *total effective execution time* of all the statements in both *select* alternatives is less than θ. Statements in both the select alternatives need to be considered to take care of the worst-case situation. This situation occurs if a call to the interrupt entry PUT is issued just after KEYBOARD has accepted a call to entry GET.

Suppose several calls to entry PUT are pending, having been issued before the first GET entry call. The worst-case situation, described above, does not include the processing time for more than one GET entry call, since calls to entry PUT are given preference over calls to entry GET, because of the higher priority accorded to a rendezvous associated with interrupt entry.

Note that characters will be lost if the internal buffer gets full, because other tasks are not requesting characters fast enough from KEYBOARD using entry GET. Task KEYBOARD does not accept characters from the keyboard if its internal buffer is full.

5.2 Typing Speed

The problem is to write a program to measure the typing speed of a person [BRI81c]. Characters typed at the keyboard are displayed on the screen. When the user types the character #, the typing speed (in words/minute) is displayed and the program terminates. (A word is considered to be a sequence of upper-case and lower-case letters.)

Most examples given in this book have illustrated the control of devices using the interrupt mechanism. The solution to the typing-speed problem, on the other hand, uses *polling*, i.e., repeated checking to determine if some event has occurred or if some condition has become true. The keyboard is polled to determine whether or not another character has been input; the display is polled to determine whether or not it is ready to accept another character to be output.

Although polling solutions are generally wasteful of system resources, they may be necessary or even preferable in some cases. For example, polling may be necessary if a microprocessor does not have an interrupt mechanism or a programming language does not have interrupt-handling constructs. In dedicated applications, determination of event occurrence by polling can be more efficient than the use of interrupts, since polling avoids the overhead associated with the context switches required for handling interrupts. This overhead becomes significant if the frequency of event occurrence is high.

Input from the keyboard and output to the display will be done after examining the status registers associated with these devices. The registers will have to be examined repeatedly to determine the state of the devices.

The typewriter display and keyboard interface with the computer using the following status and buffer registers:

device	register	address
Keyboard	status	8#177560#
	buffer	8#177562#
Display	status	8#177564#
	buffer	8#177566#

Each word and register of the microcomputer[21] being used in this example is

---

21. It is assumed that the microcomputer being used for this problem has an architecture similar to that of an LSI-11. The device interface information given in this example is extracted from that given for an asynchronous serial I/O device for an LSI-11 [DIG80].

16 bits long (bits are numbered from 0 to 15):

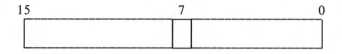

Bit 7 of the keyboard status register is set when the next character typed at the keyboard has been received in the keyboard buffer. This bit is automatically cleared when the keyboard buffer is accessed. Bit 7 of the display status register is set when the display buffer is empty and ready to accept another character for transmission. This bit is automatically cleared when a character is put into the display buffer.

Bit 7 of the keyboard status register will be accessed as the 7th element of a 16-element boolean array STATUS which will be mapped onto the keyboard status register. STATUS is declared as

    type STATUS_ARRAY **is array**(0..15) **of** BOOLEAN;
    STATUS: STATUS_ARRAY;

Through an *address* clause [13.5], the Ada compiler is first instructed to allocate STATUS starting at the keyboard status register's address:

    for STATUS **use at** 8#177560#;

Next a *length* clause [13.2] is used to specify that exactly 16 bits of storage should be allocated for objects of type STATUS_ARRAY:

    for STATUS_ARRAY'SIZE **use** 16;

ensuring that each element of the array is allocated exactly one bit of the keyboard device register.[22]

The use of representation clauses, which are implementation dependent, has some ramifications on the semantics of a program. For example, STATUS(7) will not be initialized or assigned a value in the program. Bit 7, of the keyboard (display) status register, which corresponds to this element cannot be changed by the programmer; it can only be read. As mentioned earlier, this bit is automatically set and reset by the device keyboard. It is assumed that the

---

22. *Representation* clauses [13], i.e., the *address* and *length* clauses, can be implementation dependent. For example, I have assumed that the combination of the *address* and *length* clauses given leads to the mapping of STATUS(0) to bit 0 of the status register, STATUS(1) to bit 1 and so on. It is possible that an Ada implementation may use the reverse mapping, i.e., STATUS(0) to bit 15, STATUS(1) to bit 14 and so on.

Ada compiler will not flag usage of STATUS(7) without initialization as an error, realizing that STATUS is mapped onto a device register.[23]

Similarly, variable BUFFER, which will be mapped to the keyboard buffer, will not be initialized or assigned a value in the program. BUFFER will be automatically set to the character input at the keyboard.

The typing speed will be computed by procedure TYPING_SPEED, which can be described abstractly as

```
NO_WORDS := 0;
Read a character; START_TIME := current time;
while character is not # loop
    if character is a letter then
        Read the rest of the word
        NO_WORDS := NO_WORDS + 1;
    else
        Read a character
    end if;
end loop;
FINISH_TIME := current time;
Compute and print the speed in words per minute
```

The statement *Read the rest of the word* is refined as

```
Read a character
while character is a letter loop
    Read a character
end loop;
```

The condition *character is a letter* is refined as

character **in** ′A′..′Z′ **or** character **in** ′a′..′z′

The statement *Compute and print the speed in words per minute* is refined as

Display INTEGER(DURATION(60*NO_WORDS) /
(FINISH_TIME−START_TIME))

START_TIME and FINISH_TIME will be declared to be of type TIME (declared in the library package CALENDAR). The difference between the two values of type TIME results in a value of type DURATION. Appropriate conversions, as shown, are necessary to compute the speed in words per minute

---

23. Presumably all memory locations associated with hardware devices will be known to the Ada compiler.

as an integer value.

Characters are displayed by calling entry WRITE of the display driver DISPLAY. The specification of task DISPLAY is

```
task DISPLAY is
   entry WRITE(C: in CHARACTER);
end DISPLAY;
```

The body of DISPLAY is

```
task body DISPLAY is
   type STATUS_ARRAY is array(0..15) of BOOLEAN;
   STATUS: STATUS_ARRAY;
   STATUS: array(0..15) of BOOLEAN;
   for STATUS use at 8#177564#;
   for STATUS_ARRAY'SIZE use 16;
   READY: BOOLEAN renames STATUS(7);
            --shorthand and mnemonic way of accessing bit 7
   BUFFER: CHARACTER;
   for BUFFER use at 8#177566#;
   TEMP: CHARACTER;
begin
   loop
      accept WRITE(C: in CHARACTER) do
         TEMP := C;
      end WRITE;
      while not READY loop null; end loop;
                        --note the polling
      BUFFER := TEMP;
   end loop;
end DISPLAY;
```

Characters typed at the keyboard are read by calling entry READ of the keyboard driver KEYBOARD. The specification of task KEYBOARD is

```
task KEYBOARD is
   entry READ(C: out CHARACTER);
end KEYBOARD;
```

All characters typed are immediately echoed on the display. A line feed character is inserted in the sequence of characters displayed whenever the user types the carriage return character. The body of KEYBOARD is

```
task body KEYBOARD is
    type STATUS_ARRAY is array(0..15) of BOOLEAN;
    STATUS: STATUS_ARRAY;
    for STATUS use at 8#177560#;
    for STATUS_ARRAY'SIZE use 16;
    READY: BOOLEAN renames STATUS(7);

    BUFFER: CHARACTER;
    for BUFFER use at 8#177562#;

    TEMP: CHARACTER;
begin
    loop
        while not READY loop null; end loop;
        TEMP := BUFFER;
        accept READ(C: out CHARACTER) do
            C := TEMP;
        end READ;
        DISPLAY.WRITE(TEMP);
        if TEMP = ASCII.CR then  --carriage return character
            DISPLAY.WRITE(ASCII.LF);  --line feed character
        end if;
    end loop;
end KEYBOARD;
```

Procedures WRITE_TEXT and WRITE_INTEGER are used to display strings and integers using task DISPLAY. The body of WRITE_TEXT is

```
procedure WRITE_TEXT(S: in STRING) is
begin
    for J in S'RANGE loop
        DISPLAY.WRITE(S(J));
    end loop;
end WRITE_TEXT;
```

Procedure WRITE_INTEGER first converts its integer parameter to a string by using the procedure PUT from an appropriate instantiation of the INTEGER_IO package provided by package TEXT_IO. This string is then displayed by calling WRITE_TEXT:

```
procedure WRITE_INTEGER(I: in INTEGER) is
    S: STRING(1..4);    ——typing speed as a sequence of characters
    package IO_INTEGER is new INTEGER_IO(INTEGER);
begin
    IO_INTEGER.PUT(S, I);   ——convert I to a character sequence S
    WRITE_TEXT(S);
end WRITE_INTEGER;
```

The final version of procedure TYPING_SPEED is obtained by incorporating the refinements into its abstract description and including the tasks and procedures defined for interacting with the keyboard and display:

```
with TEXT_IO, CALENDAR; use TEXT_IO, CALENDAR;
procedure TYPING_SPEED is
   NO_WORDS: INTEGER := 0;
   START_TIME, FINISH_TIME: TIME;
                     --TIME is defined in CALENDAR
   C: CHARACTER;

   --include specification of task DISPLAY
   --include specification of task KEYBOARD
   --include body of task DISPLAY
   --include body of task KEYBOARD
   --include procedure WRITE_TEXT
   --include procedure WRITE_INTEGER
begin
   KEYBOARD.READ(C);
   START_TIME := CLOCK;
          --CLOCK (from CALENDAR) returns the current time
   while C /= '#' loop
     if C in 'A'..'Z' or C in 'a'..'z' then
        KEYBOARD.READ(C);
        while C in 'A'..'Z' or C in 'a'..'z' loop
           KEYBOARD.READ(C);
        end loop;
        NO_WORDS := NO_WORDS + 1;
     else
        KEYBOARD.READ(C);
     end if;
   end loop;
   FINISH_TIME := CLOCK;

   DISPLAY.WRITE(ASCII.CR); DISPLAY.WRITE(ASCII.LF);
                     --move to a new line
   WRITE_TEXT("Your typing speed is ");
   WRITE_INTEGER(INTEGER(DURATION(60*NO_WORDS) /
                     (FINISH_TIME-START_TIME)));
   WRITE_TEXT(" words/min");

   abort KEYBOARD, DISPLAY;
end TYPING_SPEED;
```

The two terminal driver tasks KEYBOARD and DISPLAY must be aborted
because TYPING_SPEED will not terminate until all its dependent tasks have
terminated.

Note that if a user types in characters too fast for the microcomputer, then these characters will be lost. Such an event is unlikely because of the mechanical characteristics (i.e., slow speed compared to the microcomputer) of the keyboard.

5.3 Backyard Irrigation System

A backyard irrigation system is to be implemented with the aid of a microcomputer.[24] A set of solenoid operated valves is available to turn on and off the eight watering lines individually—one for each of the eight plots constituting the backyard. The amount of moisture in the soil can be determined by using sensing elements. Two kinds of sensing elements are available in the market:

1. A binary output device that switches on when the ground moisture content drops below the factory set value of 10%.

2. A continuous measuring device that gives an output between 0 and 4095 ($2^{12}-1$) in a linear relationship to the ground moisture content as it varies from 0% to 100%.

Once the plot is determined to be dry, the water is turned on. If the time is between 9:00 a.m. and 5:00 p.m., then the water is turned on for 10 minutes; otherwise, it is turned on for 8 minutes. The longer watering period during the day is to compensate for the substantial water evaporation from higher daytime temperatures. The watering times are sufficient to raise the moisture content of a plot above 10%.

The water lines can be turned on for some specified time period and explicitly turned off by using package WATER_LINES with procedures WATER_ON and WATER_OFF:[25]

```
package WATER_LINES is
    procedure WATER_ON(LINE_NO: INTEGER; T: DURATION);
    procedure WATER_OFF(LINE_NO: INTEGER);
end WATER_LINES;
```

Appropriate interfaces are available to connect the sensors with the hardware. With these interfaces, the following interrupt locations and registers are associated with the sensors for the measuring devices:

---

24. This problem is an adapted version of the one posed by D. A. Mellichamp [MEL83a, MEL83b].

25. Procedure WATER_OFF is not used in this example.

Interrupt address   8#60#

Control register address   8#2000# (continuous measuring device only)
Buffer address   8#2002# (continuous measuring device only)

For the binary device an interrupt occurs when the ground becomes too dry, i.e., when the ground moisture content goes below 10%.[26] For the continuous buffering device, putting value I into the control register initiates a reading of sensor I. The value read is put into the associated buffer. Completion of this operation is indicated by an interrupt.

Two versions of a task WATER_CONTROL, one for each kind of sensor device will be developed. The task WATER_CONTROL must be encapsulated in a procedure, since tasks cannot exist on their own in Ada. WATER_CONTROL could not have been written as a procedure, because only tasks can handle interrupts. Procedure IRRIGATION (a main program) that encapsulates the tasks has the form

```
with WATER_LINES, CALENDAR;
use WATER_LINES, CALENDAR;
procedure IRRIGATION is
    ——specification & body of WATER_CONTROL
begin
    null;   ——required by Ada syntax
end IRRIGATION;
```

5.3.1 Binary-Output-Device Solution: The specification of the task WATER_CONTROL is

```
task WATER_CONTROL is
    entry TOO_DRY(PLOT_NO: in INTEGER);
    for TOO_DRY use at 8#60#;
end WATER_CONTROL;
```

The body of the task WATER_CONTROL is

---

26. The interrupt occurs only when the moisture content goes from above 10% to below 10%; the interrupt does not occur when the moisture content goes from below 10% to above 10%.

```
task body WATER_CONTROL is
  T1: constant DAY_DURATION := DAY_DURATION(9.0*3600.0);
                                              --9:00 a.m.
  T2: constant DAY_DURATION := DAY_DURATION(17.0*3600.0);
                                              --5:00 p.m.
  T: DAY_DURATION;
  WATERING_TIME: DURATION;
  TEN_MIN: constant DURATION := DURATION(10.0*60.0);
  EIGHT_MIN: constant DURATION := DURATION(8.0*60.0);
begin
  loop
    accept TOO_DRY(PLOT_NO: in INTEGER) do
      T := SECONDS(CLOCK);
      if T >= T1 and T <= T2 then
        WATERING_TIME := TEN_MIN;
      else
        WATERING_TIME := EIGHT_MIN;
      end if;
      WATER_ON(PLOT_NO, WATERING_TIME);
    end TOO_DRY;
  end loop;
end WATER_CONTROL;
```

5.3.2 Continuous-Measuring-Device Solution: In contrast to the binary device, a sensor reading of the continuous measuring device must be explicitly initiated by task WATER_CONTROL. Unless a plot has been watered recently, its moisture content must be checked regularly to determine whether or not the plot should be watered. Assume that a plot has been found too dry. Watering of the plot is started, but the consequent increase in moisture content will not be immediately reflected by the sensor. It takes about 30 minutes for the water to soak into the ground and the sensors to report the correct readings. Consequently, once watering has been stopped, sensor readings should not be taken for 30 minutes.

The specification of the task WATER_CONTROL is

```
task WATER_CONTROL is
  entry MEASURING_DONE;
  for MEASURING_DONE use at 8#60#;
end WATER_CONTROL;
```

The algorithm implemented by WATER_CONTROL can be abstractly described as

```
loop
   for I in 1..8 loop
      if plot I has not been watered in the last 30 minutes then
         Read sensor I
         if plot I is dry then
            Determine WATERING_TIME
            WATER_ON(I, WATERING_TIME);
            Update last watering time
         end if;
      end if;
   end loop;
end loop;
```

The body of task WATER_CONTROL is

```
task body WATER_CONTROL is
    T1: constant DAY_DURATION := DAY_DURATION(9.0*3600.0);
                                        --9:00 a.m.
    T2: constant DAY_DURATION := DAY_DURATION(17.0*3600.0);
                                        --5:00 p.m.
    T: DAY_DURATION; WATERING_TIME: DURATION;

    SCALE_FACTOR: constant := 4095.0;    --for the measuring device

    TEN_MIN: constant DURATION := DURATION(10.0*60.0);
    EIGHT_MIN: constant DURATION := DURATION(8.0*60.0);
    DRYING_TIME: constant DURATION := DURATION(30.0*60.0);
    LAST_WATERED: array(1..8) of TIME := (1..8 => CLOCK);

    CONTROL, READING: INTEGER;
    for CONTROL use at 8#2000#;
    for READING use at 8#2002#;
begin
    loop
        for I in 1..8 loop
            if CLOCK - LAST_WATERED(I) >= DRYING_TIME then
                CONTROL := I; accept MEASURING_DONE;
                if FLOAT(READING)/SCALE_FACTOR < 0.10 then
                                        --<10%
                T := SECONDS(CLOCK);
                if T >= T1 and T <= T2 then
                    WATERING_TIME := TEN_MIN;
                else
                    WATERING_TIME := EIGHT_MIN;
                end if;
                WATER_ON(I, WATERING_TIME);
                LAST_WATERED(I) := CLOCK + WATERING_TIME;
            end if;
        end if;
      end loop;
    end loop;
end WATER_CONTROL;
```

What is the impact of initializing array LAST_WATERED to (1..8 =>
CLOCK)? What other initial values could be assigned to it? How can this be
made more flexible? These questions are left as quick exercises for the reader.

5.3.3 An Exercise: The binary output devices are considerably cheaper than
the analog versions, because the analog devices require an analog to digital
converter. When would a continuous measuring device be preferable?

Chapter 7: **Some Issues in Concurrent Programming** [9.3, 11]

Deadlock, unnecessary sequentialization and unnecessary polling are concurrent programming problems that are usually not of interest in, or even relevant to, sequential programming. These problems occur in concurrent programming regardless of the concurrent programming facilities provided in the programming language. However, the exact specifics of the concurrent facilities in a programming language do have an impact on the severity and frequency of such problems.

Three concurrent programming issues are discussed in this chapter: deadlock, maximization of concurrency in a program and the polling bias in Ada.

1. Deadlock

Deadlock occurs when one or more tasks in a program are blocked forever, because of requirements that can never be satisfied [DIJ68a, HOL72a, BRI73, HOL78]. Deadlock can cause in an indefinite circular wait among some tasks. The requirements of each task can be satisfied only by the actions of the other tasks. However, because each task expects the other tasks to resolve the situation, all the tasks stay blocked forever [BRI73].

Deadlock was first recognized and analyzed in 1965 by E. W. Dijkstra [DIJ68a], who termed it as the *problem of the deadly embrace*. (The problem of deadlock had occurred often in earlier operating systems [BRI73].) Deadlock caused by tasks competing for shared resources[27] will occur if the following four conditions hold [COF71, CAL82]:

1. *Mutual Exclusion*: The tasks require exclusive access to the resources.

2. *Partial Resource Allocation*: A task can acquire its resources incrementally.

3. *Nonpreemptive Scheduling*: Resources allocated to a task cannot be taken back from it until after the task has released them.

---

27. The term *resource*, in the context of deadlocks, applies not only to devices such as tape and disk drives, to CPUs and to storage media such as core store and disks, but also to programs, subprograms, data [COF71] and rendezvous.

4. *Circular Waiting*: There exists a circular wait among the competing tasks for the resources held by the other tasks.

Deadlocks occur because of poor program design and the occurrence of unanticipated events. Deadlock can be avoided by ensuring that the four conditions necessary for deadlock are not satisfied at the same time [COF71, BRI73, CAL82]. Satisfaction of the first condition necessary for deadlock, that of *mutual exclusion*, may be unavoidable in the case of some resources [COF71]. However, it is possible to ensure that all three remaining conditions are not satisfied simultaneously by using one of the following approaches [HAV68, COF71]:

1. *Avoid Partial Resource Allocation, i.e., Require Total Resource Allocation*: Each task must request all the resources it needs at once and its execution is delayed until it has acquired all the resources.

2. *Avoid Nonpreemptive Scheduling, i.e., Use Preemptive Scheduling*: If a task holding some resources requests additional resources, then the task must release all the resources held by it and, if necessary, request them again together with the additional resources needed by it.

3. *Avoid Circular Waiting*: A linear ordering is imposed on the different resources. If a task has been allocated resource i, then it can subsequently request only resources that follow resource i in the ordering.

Avoiding circular waiting appears to be the best approach to avoiding deadlock [COF71]. Complete resource allocation by allocating all the resources to the requesting task at once can be costly, since several resources may not be used for a long time. Preemptive scheduling is convenient only for preemptible resources whose state can be easily saved and restored later, e.g., a CPU.

Deadlock is often detected after the system has been inactive for a long time. The deadlocked tasks will remain blocked until some special action is taken to remedy the situation (e.g., aborting one of the deadlocked tasks to let the other ones continue).

1.1 Example: Deadlock Caused by Resources Competition

Consider a program with two tasks X and Y executing on a system with two disk drives. Each of X and Y needs both disk drives together, say for copying a file from one disk to the other, to accomplish its objectives. Deadlock will occur if each task has been granted permission to use one disk drive and is waiting for permission to use the other drive and neither task is willing to give up the permission granted to it, even temporarily, until they accomplish their objectives.

Potential for deadlock can be avoided by granting permission for using both disks simultaneously, instead of one at a time, by requiring a task to give up its resources temporarily or by ordering the resources, e.g., each task must get permission for disk A first and then for disk B, to avoid the circular-wait problem.

1.2 Example—Deadlock from Circularity in Rendezvous

Deadlock may occur if two tasks A and B each want to call the other task before accepting an entry call from the other. This situation is illustrated by the following skeletons of the bodies of tasks A and B:

```
task body A is
   :
begin
   loop
      :
      B.SEND(...);
      accept SEND ... end SEND;
      :
   end loop;
end A;
```

and

```
task body B is
   :
begin
   loop
      :
      A.SEND(...);
      accept SEND ... end SEND;
      :
   end loop;
end B;
```

Tasks A and B deadlock at the entry calls B.SEND and A.SEND, respectively. The four conditions for deadlock listed in the previous section are satisfied here (the rendezvous between A and B can be thought of as the resource). The possibility of deadlock must be eliminated by modifying the program.

1.3 Effective Deadlock

A task is said to be in *effective deadlock* if for all practical purposes the task is blocked, even though there is a small probability that its requirements could be met and it could then continue execution.

As an example of effective deadlock, consider the task SERVICE that was given earlier to illustrate programmer control of scheduling:

```
task body SERVICE is
  --local declarations
begin
  loop
    select
      accept REQUEST(URGENT)(D: in out DATA) do
        .
        .
        process the request
        .
        .
      end REQUEST;
        .
        .
    or when REQUEST(URGENT)'COUNT = 0 =>
      accept REQUEST(NORMAL)(D: in out DATA) do
        .
        .
        process the request
        .
        .
      end REQUEST;
        .
        .
    end select;
  end loop;

  end SERVICE;
```

A task calling SERVICE with priority NORMAL can be effectively deadlocked if there is an unending stream of tasks with the higher priority requesting service and there is always at least one such task waiting for service. How can effective deadlock be avoided in this case? This problem is left for the reader.

Consider, as another example, a task A that repeatedly attempts to rendezvous with another task B, at its entry QUERY, to receive some information:

```
task body A is
    ⋮
begin
    ⋮
    loop
        select
            B.QUERY(...);
            exit;
        else
            Perform some secondary activity
        end select;
        ⋮
    end loop;
end A;
```

If task A is unable to rendezvous immediately with task B, it performs some secondary activity, so that it does not waste time being blocked for a rendezvous, and then tries to rendezvous again. This process is repeated until A is successful in calling B.QUERY. Effective deadlock will occur if every time A attempts to rendezvous with B, B is not ready for a rendezvous, e.g., other tasks may be waiting at entry QUERY or B may be momentarily busy doing something else.

The potential for effective deadlock can be resolved in this example by modifying A so that it blocks when calling entry B.QUERY (the *conditional* entry call is replaced by a simple entry call). Moreover, the code *Perform some secondary activity* can be moved to another task, where it can be executed in parallel with A.

2. Maximizing Concurrency in Ada

A task, like a package, is a data encapsulation mechanism. The data encapsulated by a task is accessed by means of entry calls, whereas the data encapsulated in a package is accessed by means of the objects provided in the package specification such as constants and subprograms. A package has no flow of control of its own; execution of a package subprogram uses the flow of control of the caller. Unlike a package, a task has its own flow of control, i.e., it executes in parallel with the other tasks.[28]

---

28. Data encapsulated in a task cannot be accessed concurrently, i.e., by more than one task interested in using the data. Exclusive access to the data is automatically provided by the encapsulating task, since entry calls are accepted one at a time. Concurrent access of data encapsulated in a package, on the other hand, may produce unpredictable results when several concurrent procedures operate on the same data.

Because tasks have their own flow of control, they can be used to increase concurrency in a program. Tasks should not be used whenever it is possible to use them. If the overhead time required to create and schedule a task is more than the execution time of its body, then creating this new task for the sole sake of concurrency will not pay off.

Concurrency can be maximized by designing the program to reflect the concurrency inherent in the algorithm being implemented and by ensuring that tasks are not suspended unnecessarily. For example, during task interaction the calling task should be suspended by the called task only as long as is necessary to exchange information; internal bookkeeping in the called task can and should be done in parallel with the calling task.

2.1 Implementing Sets as Tasks—An Example

Suppose the concept of a set of integers is to be implemented. Operations to insert, delete and check set membership are to be provided. Addition of duplicate elements to the set is not an error; however, only one copy of an element is kept in the set. Deletion of an element not in the set has no effect on the set and does not result in an error.

Should the set be implemented as a package or a task (either of which can be used to provide data abstraction)? If more than one task is going to use the set, then it would be advantageous to implement it as a task, since mutual exclusion is automatically provided by the task. If only one task is going to use the set, then a task implementation may lead to a greater degree of concurrency, because the internal bookkeeping associated with the set operations can be done in parallel with the tasks manipulating the set. The task implementation of a set will be more desirable if the underlying hardware offers genuine concurrency. However, a task implementation will probably impose a higher execution overhead than a package implementation (e.g., the task implementing the set must be scheduled).

The set will be implemented by a task named SET which uses a linked list to keep track of the set elements (see Figure 7.1):

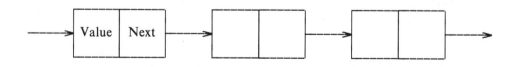

Figure 7.1: The list of set elements

The specification of the task SET

```
task SET is
    entry INSERT(X: INTEGER);
    entry DELETE(X: INTEGER);
    entry IN_SET(X: INTEGER; PRESENT: out BOOLEAN);
end SET;
```

The body of SET may be abstractly described as

```
loop
    select
        Accept a call to INSERT and record element to be inserted
        Insert the element in the list

    or
        Accept a call to DELETE and record element to be deleted
        Delete the element in the list

    or
        Accept a call to IN_SET and store TRUE or FALSE in
         PRESENT depending upon whether or not the element
         is present in the set.

    or
        terminate;
    end select;
end loop;
```

Note that the abstract instructions *Insert the element in the list* and *Delete the element in the list* are executed by SET concurrently with the tasks interacting with SET.

The body of task SET is obtained by using the abstract description of SET and supplying more details:

```
task body SET is
   type NODE;
   type PTR_TO_NODE is access NODE;
   type NODE is
        record
           VALUE: INTEGER;
           NEXT: PTR_TO_NODE;    --automatically initialized to null
        end record;

   HEAD, T: PTR_TO_NODE;    --automatically initialized to null
   E: INTEGER;

begin
   loop
      select
         accept INSERT(X: INTEGER) do
            E := X;
         end INSERT;
         T := HEAD;
         while T /= null and then T.VALUE /= E loop
            T := T.NEXT;
         end loop;
         if T = null then
            T := new NODE;
            T.VALUE := E; T.NEXT := HEAD; HEAD := T;
         end if;
      or
         accept DELETE(X: INTEGER) do
            E := X;
         end DELETE;
         if HEAD = null then    --empty list
            null;
         else --many elements in list
            if HEAD.VALUE = E then    --first element contains E
               HEAD := HEAD.NEXT;
            else    --list not empty, first element not E
               T := HEAD;
               while T.NEXT /= null and then T.NEXT.VALUE /= E loop
                  T := T.NEXT;
               end loop;
               if T.NEXT /= null then
                  T.NEXT := T.NEXT.NEXT;
               end if;
            end if;
```

```
            end if;
    or
        accept IN_SET(X: INTEGER; PRESENT: out BOOLEAN) do
            T := HEAD;
            while T /= null and then T.VALUE /= X loop
                T := T.NEXT;
            end loop;
            PRESENT := T /= null;
        end IN_SET;
    or
        terminate;
    end select;
    end loop;
end SET;
```

Note that the tasks calling entries of SET are delayed only long enough to record the necessary information and that this information is processed by SET concurrently with the calling task.

3. The Polling Bias in Ada [GEH83b]

Concurrent programming facilities similar to those in Ada have never been tried out in a programming language. Consequently, only experience in using these facilities will indicate their appropriateness. Early experience [GEH83b] with Ada's concurrent programming points to inadequacies in its task interaction facilities; they encourage the design of programs that poll.[29] *Polling* is characterized by a task actively and repeatedly checking for the occurrence of an event that originates outside the task. Polling is generally, but not always, undesirable, because it is wasteful of system resources—it burns up CPU cycles. Even if a task is assigned a dedicated CPU in a computer network, polling can be undesirable, because it may generate unnecessary traffic on the network.

Polling in Ada can be classified into two categories—*rendezvous* and *information.*

Definition of **Rendezvous Polling**: Task A *rendezvous polls* task B with respect to entry E if the rendezvous can be preceded by an unbounded number of attempts by A to rendezvous. An attempt may be an unsuccessful entry call or

---

29. This section was adapted and extracted, with the permission of John Wiley & Sons, Ltd., from *Concurrent Programming in Ada: The Polling Bias in the Rendezvous Mechanism* by Narain Gehani and Tom Cargill [GEH83b].

a failure to select the *accept* alternative in a *select* statement.

Definition of **Information Polling**: Task A *information polls* task B with respect to entry E if A and B can rendezvous an unbounded number of times before the desired information is transferred.

Consider the program segment of a task A that wants to access some resource managed by a resource manager task RM:

```
   :
   :
FREE := FALSE;
while not FREE loop
   RM.REQUEST(FREE);
end loop;
   :
   :
```

Task A calls entry REQUEST of task RM, repeatedly rendezvousing with RM until FREE is set to TRUE to indicate that A can go ahead and use the resource. The polling performed by task A is of the second kind, i.e., information polling.

Of course, polling in a program may be a combination of rendezvous and information polling. Between polling, a task may or may not do useful work—leading to the notion of *busy waiting*.

Definition of **Busy Waiting**: A polling task *busy waits* if between (attempted) rendezvous no useful action is performed, i.e., there is no computational progress.

In Ada, both the calling task and the called task can poll—using *the conditional entry call* and *selective wait statement* with the *else* part, respectively. This can lead to a dangerous situation when two tasks try to rendezvous with each other by polling—the rendezvous may never happen.

3.1 Example of a Desirable Polling Program

Polling programs may be desirable in cases where nonpolling programs have additional overhead, such as extra statements or a rendezvous, which may result in real-time constraints being violated. In case of device drivers, polling programs may be necessary when the hardware interface does not provide interrupts or the device is one that must be polled to get readings continuously (see the *Typing Speed* and *Backyard Irrigation System* examples in Chapter 6 on *Real-Time Programming*).

The following example [adapted from KIE79] illustrates a polling program that is more desirable than a nonpolling program simply because it is more efficient. The problem is to display the position of a moving point on a screen (e.g., an airplane on a radar screen) based on the supplied coordinates or from computations based on the most recent coordinates and velocity available. The point position is to be displayed *as fast as possible* so that it is tracked accurately. If an updated position of the point is not available, then a new position should be computed before displaying the point position:

```
loop
    select
        accept UPDATE(coordinates and velocity of point) do
            record X, Y, VX, VY;
        end UPDATE;
    else
        compute new position using old coordinates and velocity;
    end select;
    display point position on screen;
end loop;
```

The critical thing is to display, as fast as possible, the latest position of a point—regardless of whether the position of the point is new or computed. The time required to compute a new position is much less than the average interval between updates of point position.

Rendezvous polling in the task represented by the above program segment can be avoided by rewriting it alternatively as two or more tasks. However, the resulting nonpolling program will not be as efficient because resources will be expended in scheduling the multiple tasks and in task communication.

3.2 Bias Toward Rendezvous Polling

Discussion in this section focuses on examining the specific causes of the undesirable and often needless polling that results from Ada's rendezvous mechanism. The tendency toward rendezvous polling results from a lack of some facilities, from some restrictions and from the presence of some facilities.

3.3 Conditional Entry Call

The *conditional entry call* should be used with care, since it can easily lead to unnecessary polling. For example, the *Ada Reference Manual* [DOD83] contains the following example illustrating the use of a *conditional entry call*:

```
procedure SPIN(R: RESOURCE) is
begin
  loop
    select
        R.SEIZE;
        return;
    else
        null;    -- busy waiting
    end select;
  end loop;
end;
```

This is a poor example of a *conditional entry call*, because the above subprogram involves rendezvous polling, which can be easily avoided by just rewriting it as

```
procedure SPIN(R: RESOURCE) is
begin
    R.SEIZE;
end;
```

Better examples of the use of a *conditional entry call* are the polling solution to the problem of displaying the position of a moving point or the following program segment [BAR82]:

```
loop
    accept FIRE_LOCATION(X: LOCATION);
    select
        OPERATOR.CALL("Put Out Fire at Location", X);
    else
        FIRE_STATION.CALL(X);
    end select;
end loop;
```

which calls the fire station if the operator cannot accept the call immediately. Note that this example does not represent a polling program.

3.4 Handling an Entry Family and Subsets of an Entry Family

The general strategy of handling calls to an entry family (or a subset of an entry family) involves polling [WEL81]. For example, consider the entry family UP declared as

entry UP(FLOORS);

where FLOORS is a discrete range declared as

subtype FLOORS **is** INTEGER **range** 1..N;

The skeleton of a program segment accepting calls to all members of the entry family UP is

```
loop
   for I in FLOORS loop
      select
         accept UP(I) do ... end;
      else
         null;
      end select;
   end loop;
end loop;
```

Polling can be avoided by explicitly writing *accept* statements for each member of the entry family UP:

```
loop
   select
      accept UP(1) do ... end;
   or
      accept UP(2) do ... end;
   or
      accept UP(3) do ... end;
   or
         .
         .
         .
   or
      accept UP(N) do ... end;
   end select;
end loop;
```

This alternative way of handling an entry family is feasible only if N is known at the time the program is written and is convenient only if N is small.

Alternatively, if possible, the entry family may be replaced by a single entry with an additional parameter. However, this replacement is not always a viable alternative. The use of entry families is sometimes essential, e.g., for implementing a general scheduling strategy [DOD79].

3.5 Restrictions on the Selective Wait Statement

Some bias toward polling can be directly attributed to restrictions on the *selective wait* statement. Alternatives in the *selective wait* statement can be only an *accept*, a *delay* or a *terminate* alternative.

An alternative cannot be the optional *when* condition followed by an sequence of nontasking statements, e.g., a sequence of assignment statements. In the light of this restriction consider the following abstract version of a priority scheduler [WEL81]:

```
loop
   select
      accept REQUEST(request details) do
         add request to waiting set;
      end REQUEST;
      next_user := unknown;
   or
      when current_user = no_one and next_user /= unknown =>
         accept ACQUIRE(next_user);
         current_user := next_user; next_user := unknown;
         delete current_user from the waiting set;
   or
      when current_user /= no_one =>
         accept RELEASE(current_user);
         current_user := no_one;
   or
      when next_user = unknown and waiting set is not empty =>
         next_user := highest priority user in waiting set;
   end select;
end loop;
```

This program segment is illegal in Ada, because the last alternative is not a *delay*, a *terminate* or an *accept* alternative. Welsh and Lister [WEL81] suggest that the above program might be written correctly using the *else* clause as

```
loop
   select
      .
      .
      .
   else
      if next_user = unknown and waiting set is not empty then
         next_user := highest priority user in waiting set;
      end if;
   end select;
end loop;
```

However, this program formulation results in busy waiting, since in the absence of any feasible user interaction, the *else* clause is executed to no effect. In many practical applications, busy waiting within a scheduler task is unacceptable. Busy waiting can be avoided by rewriting the program segment to eliminate the *else* clause [WEL81]. The code in the *else* clause is moved to some other place.

A very simple strategy that avoids polling and does not require rewriting of the program segment would be to use a *delay* statement with a null time period:

```
loop
  select
    .
    .
  or
      when next_user = unknown and waiting set is not empty =>
        delay 0.0;
        next_user := highest priority user in waiting set;
  end select;
end loop;
```

Another restriction that can lead to polling is that an *entry call* statement is not allowed as a *selective wait* alternative. As an example, consider the situation when a task X is prepared to accept entry calls E_i from other tasks when the associated conditions B_i are satisfied and would also like to call entry F of Y if the associated condition C is satisfied:

```
loop
  select
      when B₁ => accept call to entry E₁
  or
    .
    .
  or
      when Bₙ => accept call to entry Eₙ
  or
      when C => call entry Y.F
  end select;
end loop;
```

The *select* statement in the above program statement is illegal in Ada, because an entry call is not allowed as a *selective wait* alternative. This program segment can be written using rendezvous polling with the aid of a *conditional* entry call:

```
loop
  select
     when B₁ => accept call to entry E₁
  or
     .
     .
     .
  or
     when Bₙ => accept call to entry Eₙ
  else
     if C then
        select
           call entry Y.F
        else
           null;
        end select;
     end if;
  end select;
end loop;
```

If X and Y are symmetrical tasks, then this design can lead to a situation when both X and Y are polling each other simultaneously—a potentially disastrous situation, since the tasks may never establish a rendezvous.

Alternatively, if the entry call Y.F involves information flow from X to Y only, then this polling can be avoided by using an intervening buffer task B with the following form:

```
loop
     call entry X.G to get information for Y
     call entry Y.F to pass on the information
end loop;
```

where G is now an entry in task X, which is modified so that it now looks like

```
loop
  select
     when B₁ => accept call to entry E₁
  or
     .
     .
     .
  or
     when Bₙ => accept call to entry Eₙ
  or
     when C => accept call to entry G
  end select;
end loop;
```

Such a situation arose in the problem illustrating communication between two computer terminals (see Chapter 8 on *More Examples*). Consider two terminals T_1 and T_2 being used for communication with each other. Every character typed at T_1 is echoed on T_1's display and when the line is completed, it is sent to T_2, where it is displayed between lines typed by the user there. The body of T_1 can be described abstractly as

loop
   select
      Accept a line from T_2 and display it
   or
      when internal buffer is empty $=>$
         Accept a character from the keyboard
         while character not carriage return **loop**
            Accept a character from the keyboard, display and
                  store in internal buffer
         end loop;
         Display and store the carriage return and line feed characters
   or
      when internal buffer has a complete line $=>$
         Send line to T_2 by calling an entry of T_2
   end select;
  end loop;

The characters typed in by the user are collected in the internal buffer and echoed back at the same time. When the internal buffer has a complete line, it is sent to T_2 for display.

Since an entry call cannot be a select alternative, a polling solution was considered. In this case, a polling solution would not be viable, since T_2 would be symmetrical to T_1. The problem was solved by means of intervening buffer tasks. (A more elegant solution than this can be had by devoting one task each to the keyboard and the display. A terminal is really two devices!)

3.6 *else* Clause in the *selective wait* Statement

The use of the *else* clause in the *selective wait* statement is a clear temptation to write polling programs. The *else* clause allows an alternative action to be performed if no alternative of the *selective wait* statement is open. The *else* clause seems to make it natural to do "something else" when a rendezvous is not possible, i.e., poll. An example is the use of the *else* clause in the first attempt to write the scheduling program shown earlier.

The programmer should consider carefully whether this alternative action is part of the task or whether it should be encapsulated in another task, thereby eliminating the polling. Alternatively, rearrangement of the code should be considered.

3.7 Lack of a Selective Call Statement

Ada does not have a *selective call* statement corresponding to the *selective wait* statement. Consequently a program segment of the form

```
loop
    select
        call entry X.E
    or
        call entry Y.F
    end select;
end loop;
```

must be expressed alternatively as the polling program segment

```
loop
    select
        call entry X.E
    else
        select
            call entry Y.F
        else
            null;
        end select;
    end select;
end loop;
```

The above polling alternative is not quite equivalent to its nonpolling counterpart, because it gives preference to calling entry X.E. In discussing the lack of a *selective call* alternative, an article in *Ada Letters* [BOO82] suggested a polling alternative similar to the one given above.

3.8 Careful Program Design

Consider the following abstract version of the body of a task that controls the motion of an elevator [GEH83a]:

```
loop
    Accept calls for elevator service

    if no requests then move car toward home floor
    elsif car at home floor or arriving at destination then
        Compute new destination, etc.
    else
        select
            Accept signal to keep elevator moving
        else
            null;
        end select;
    end if;
end loop;
```

This task represents a first attempt in the design of a program to control an elevator. This design is not a very good one, since the task performs three functions: handles calls for elevator service, computes the destination and controls the elevator motion. Because the task must accept calls for elevator service, it does not wait to receive a signal from the elevator to keep it moving. Instead it polls; if the signal has not come then it goes on to accept requests for service.

A better design, which is also nonpolling, would be to replace this task by three tasks—one for each function. The first task accepts the calls, the second is a database task, and the third is the elevator control task. The first task supplies information to the database task; the third task gets information, such as pending requests and the new destination, from the database task.

A good design principle is to dedicate a task to each function or job to be done instead of letting a task perform several functions (the same design strategy is recommended for designing procedures in sequential programs).

3.9 Summary

Two kinds of polling can occur in Ada programs: rendezvous and information. Rendezvous polling often arises because of Ada's design, whereas information polling comes only from program design.

The bias toward rendezvous polling results from many decisions made in the design of Ada: the lack of *when* conditions followed by an arbitrary statement list in the *select* statements, the lack of a direct facility to handle calls for an entry family or a subset of it, the lack of a *selective call* statement, the disallowing of an *entry call* alternative in the *selective wait* statement, and the presence of the *else* clause in the *selective wait* statement and the *conditional entry call* statement.

It is important that a programmer recognize the bias toward polling in Ada. Care should be taken when designing programs to avoid unnecessary polling, since poor program design can lead to polling programs. As mentioned earlier, a good design principle is to dedicate a task to each function or job to be done instead of letting a task perform several functions.

Chapter 8: **More Examples**

Three concurrent programming examples are presented in this chapter to illustrate the versatility of Ada's concurrent programming facilities. The first and second examples are parallel versions of the quicksort and alpha-beta search algorithms. The third example illustrates the design of a system that allows users to communicate with each other using two terminals connected to a computer. Two solutions of the final example problem are given for comparison. In the first solution there are two device drivers, each controlling two devices, while in the second solution there are four device drivers, one for each device.

The reader is urged to attempt solving the example problems before reading their solutions.

1. Quicksort

Using the quicksort technique [HOA62], write a procedure to sort nonnull arrays of type VECTOR into nondecreasing order. Sorting an array A, with lower bound L and upper bound U $(L \leqslant U)$, results in $A_L \leqslant A_{L+1} \leqslant \cdots \leqslant A_{U-1} \leqslant A_U$—the set of new values of the array A is a permutation of its old values.

Type VECTOR is declared as the unconstrained array type

> **type** VECTOR **is array**(INTEGER **range** <>) **of** FLOAT;

Consider the following sequential QUICKSORT procedure [adapted from GEH83a]:

```
procedure QUICKSORT(A: in out VECTOR) is
    --not to be used with null arrays
L: constant INTEGER := A'FIRST;
U: constant INTEGER := A'LAST;
I, J: INTEGER;
begin
  if U-L <= 1 then --one or two elements
    if A(U) < A(L) then
      SWAP(A(L), A(U));
    end if;
  else        --more than two elements
    PARTITION(A, I, J);
    QUICKSORT(A(L..J));
    QUICKSORT(A(I..U));
  end if;
end QUICKSORT;
```

Procedures SWAP and PARTITION are not defined here. SWAP exchanges the values of its actual parameters while PARTITION partitions its actual parameter array A into slices such that all elements in the slice $A(L..J) \leqslant X$, in the slice $A(I..U) \geqslant X$ and in the slice $A(J+1..I-1) = X$, where X is some arbitrary value. Each partition contains at least one element and therefore each partition is smaller than A.[30]

The two recursive calls to QUICKSORT can be executed in parallel because they operate on disjoint slices of A. It would be nice to be able to specify that the two recursive calls to QUICKSORT are to be executed in parallel. For example, in Concurrent Pascal this parallelism can be specified as

cobegin QUICKSORT(A(L..J)); QUICKSORT(A(I..U)); **coend**;

The *cobegin* statement specifies that the statements inside it are to be executed in parallel.

In Ada, however, execution of the two recursive calls to QUICKSORT in parallel requires more effort from the programmer. Tasks must be declared and used to specify the parallelism. Instances of task type SORT will be used in the body of QUICKSORT to call QUICKSORT in parallel. The specification of task type SORT is

---

30. A complete version of PARTITION is given in *Ada: An Advanced Introduction* by Narain Gehani [GEH83a].

```
task type SORT is
    entry INITIAL_ARRAY(S: in VECTOR);
    entry FINAL_ARRAY(S: out VECTOR);
end SORT;
```

SORT has two entries. The first entry INITIAL_ARRAY is called to supply an instantiation of SORT with the array slice to be sorted. This slice is sorted inside the body of the SORT instantiation by recursively calling QUICKSORT_PARALLEL. The recursive calls are executed in parallel because each call is made from a separate task. The sorted slice is retrieved from the task instance by a call on entry FINAL_ARRAY.

The body of task type SORT is

```
task body SORT is
    type PTR_TO_VECTOR is access VECTOR;
    P: PTR_TO_VECTOR;
begin
    accept INITIAL_ARRAY(S: in VECTOR) do
        P := new VECTOR(S'FIRST..S'LAST);
        P.all := S;
    end INITIAL_ARRAY;

    QUICKSORT_PARALLEL(P.all);

    accept FINAL_ARRAY(S: out VECTOR) do
        S := P.all;
    end FINAL_ARRAY;
end SORT;
```

Procedure QUICKSORT_PARALLEL, which is a modified version of QUICKSORT, sorts the two slices in parallel:

```
procedure QUICKSORT_PARALLEL(A: in out VECTOR) is
    --not to be used with null arrays

type PTR_TO_SORT is access SORT;
P, Q: PTR_TO_SORT;

L: constant INTEGER := A'FIRST;
U: constant INTEGER := A'LAST;
I, J: INTEGER;

begin

    if U-L <= 1 then --one or two elements
        if A(U) < A(L) then
            SWAP(A(L), A(U));
        end if;
    else          --more than two elements

        PARTITION(A, I, J);
        P := new SORT; P.INITIAL_ARRAY(A(L..J));
        Q := new SORT; Q.INITIAL_ARRAY(A(I..U));
        P.FINAL_ARRAY(A(L..J));
        Q.FINAL_ARRAY(A(I..U));

    end if;
end QUICKSORT_PARALLEL;
```

Access type PTR_TO_VECTOR is used inside SORT so that an array of the same size as the actual parameter array slice can be allocated dynamically.

Ada provides only *unit-level* concurrency (i.e., tasks) and no *statement-level* concurrency as provided by the *cobegin* statement of Concurrent Pascal. Consequently, a simple problem requiring that two calls to QUICKSORT be executed in parallel has led to major modifications to QUICKSORT. The tasking facilities in Ada are thus not entirely appropriate for this and some other kinds of concurrent programming problems.

The solution presented here is straightforward and relatively easy to understand, but it is not optimal for many reasons. There is too much copying of the slices and many tasks are created. The number of instantiations of SORT can be reduced by making one recursive call with an instantiation of SORT and letting QUICKSORT_PARALLEL make the second call itself. Cohen [COH82] discusses several ways of optimizing a parallel version of quicksort and points out other inadequacies of the concurrent programming facilities in Ada.

2. The Alpha-Beta Search Algorithm—An Example from Artificial Intelligence

Computer game programs, like those for chess, select the best move by examining the continuations (sequences of moves) of the game that can result from each possible move. One algorithm used to determine the best move is the *minimax* algorithm, which "minimizes losses and maximizes gains". Minimax assumes that the players will always select the best move. Such an algorithm guarantees that a winning position will lead to a win and that a drawing position will lead to at least a draw. Unfortunately, this algorithm is not appropriate for games such as chess where the number of possible continuations can be as high as 2^{38} [MAR82].

The *alpha-beta* algorithm [KNU75, MAR82] improves upon the minimax algorithm by examining only those continuations that are relevant to determining the best move. Alpha-beta always produces the same result as the minimax algorithm.

The alpha-beta algorithm, as described here, returns the ranking of a position (in practice it must also return information about the move that will lead to this ranking). Position rankings are assumed to be positive for the first player and negative for the second player. Computation of a position's ranking depends upon whether or not the position is a terminal position. If the position is a terminal position, i.e., it does not have any successors (next moves), then the value or ranking of this position is the result. If the position has successors, then the result-value is the maximum of the rankings of the successor positions.

The pair (ALPHA, BETA) is called the *search window* [FIN82]. If the position is determined to have a rank of at least BETA, by examining only a subset of its successor positions, then further examination is abandoned and this rank is the result. Similarly, if the position rank is at most ALPHA, then the result is ALPHA.

The problem is to write a parallel version of the alpha-beta algorithm.

The sequential alpha-beta algorithm can be described abstractly by the

```
function ALPHA_BETA(P: POSITION; ALPHA, BETA: INTEGER)
    If P is a terminal position, then the result is the rank of P
    Otherwise, the alpha-beta algorithm is called recursively to compute
      the rank of P based on the rank of its successors of P;
      if the rank of P is ≤ ALPHA, then ALPHA is the result;
      computation of P's rank is stopped when it is determined
      to be at least BETA—this rank is then the result
end ALPHA_BETA;
```

The above abstract algorithm is further refined as[31]

```
function ALPHA_BETA(P: POSITION; ALPHA, BETA: INTEGER)
                              return INTEGER is
   D: NATURAL;
   SUCC: array (1..MAX_MOVES) of POSITION;
   NEW_ALPHA: INTEGER;
begin
   NEW_ALPHA := ALPHA;
   Determine D, the number of possible successor positions of P;
   Determine the successor positions SUCC(1), ..., SUCC(D);
   if D = 0 then return STATIC_VALUE(P); end if;
   for I in 1..D loop
      NEW_ALPHA := MAX(NEW_ALPHA,
            -ALPHA_BETA(SUCC(I), -BETA, -NEW_ALPHA));
      if NEW_ALPHA >= BETA then
         return NEW_ALPHA;      --cut off, i.e., terminate
      end if;
   end loop;
   return NEW_ALPHA;
end ALPHA_BETA;
```

where POSITION is a type indicating the state of the game, STATIC_VALUE is a function that yields the rank of a terminal position, MAX is a function that yields the maximum of two values, and MAX_MOVES is the maximum number of alternative moves possible at any given position. STATIC_VALUE yields positive values for the first player and negative values for the second player.

For a given amount of computing time, a faster search will allow the alpha-beta search algorithm to "see" further into the future [FIN82, MAR82]. A parallel version of the alpha-beta algorithm running in a multiprocessor environment may offer a further look into the future than the sequential alpha-beta algorithm.

In the parallel version of the alpha-beta algorithm, the ranking of a position is computed by first computing in parallel the rankings of the successor nodes using the sequential alpha-beta algorithm; then the ranking of a position is taken to be the maximum of the rank of its successors. The alpha-beta search is done in parallel only on the immediate successors of the position whose rank has to be determined.

---

31. A detailed explanation of the working of the alpha-beta algorithm is not given here, since it is not relevant to the concurrent programming aspects of the problem. Readers can find additional details about the alpha-beta algorithm in MAR82, KNU75, and FIN82.

There is one difference between the sequential alpha-beta algorithm and the parallel alpha-beta algorithm presented here. In the sequential alpha-beta algorithm, the search window used to compute the ranking of the immediate successors is (−BETA, −NEW_ALPHA), where NEW_ALPHA is an improvement over ALPHA; NEW_ALPHA is computed using the rankings of the immediate successors examined so far. NEW_ALPHA is used instead of ALPHA to avoid examining some irrelevant positions; however, using values of the other immediate successors in computing NEW_ALPHA prevents the algorithm from being made parallel. Consequently, in the parallel alpha-beta algorithm given here, the search window used is (−BETA, −ALPHA).

One task, of type POSITION_VALUE, is instantiated for each successor of the position whose ranking is to be computed. Each of these tasks is first initialized with the position of one of the successor nodes in the game continuation tree, and the *alpha* and *beta* cutoff values. The tasks execute in parallel, calling the sequential alpha-beta algorithm recursively and reporting their results to the task EVALUATOR.

The parallel alpha-beta algorithm is

```
function PARALLEL_ALPHA_BETA(P: POSITION;
                    ALPHA, BETA: INTEGER) return INTEGER is
D: NATURAL;
SUCC: array (1..MAX_MOVES) of POSITION;
NEW_ALPHA: INTEGER;

--specification of EVALUATOR comes here
--specification of POSITION_VALUE comes here

type PTR_POSITION_VALUE is access POSITION_VALUE;
T: array(1..MAX_MOVES) of PTR_POSITION_VALUE;

--bodies of task EVALUATOR and POSITION_VALUE

begin
    NEW_ALPHA := ALPHA;
    Determine D, the number of possible successor positions of P;
    Determine the successor positions SUCC(1), ..., SUCC(D);
    if D = 0 then return STATIC_VALUE(P); end if;

    --the tasks for evaluating the nodes will be allocated in a block
    --to ensure that the value of NEW_ALPHA is one computed
    --using the result of all the tasks that post their results.
    --The block statement cannot be left until all the tasks
    --dependent on it have terminated, which happens when all the
    --POSITION_VALUE tasks have reported position rankings to
    --task EVALUATOR.
    --Variable NEW_ALPHA is updated by task EVALUATOR to
    --the maximum of the rankings of the successors of P

    begin
        for I in 1..D loop
            T(I) := new POSITION_VALUE;
            T(I).LOCATION(SUCC(I), -BETA, -ALPHA);
        end loop;
    end;
                    --cannot go ahead until all tasks created in the block
                    --have finished execution

    return NEW_ALPHA;

end PARALLEL_ALPHA_BETA;
```

The specification and body of POSITION_VALUE is

```
task type POSITION_VALUE is
  entry LOCATION(SUCC: POSITION;
                            ALPHA, BETA: INTEGER);
end POSITION_VALUE;

task body POSITION_VALUE is
  VALUE: INTEGER;
  P: POSITION; A, B: INTEGER;
begin
  accept LOCATION(SUCC: POSITION;
                            ALPHA, BETA: INTEGER) do
    P := SUCC; A := ALPHA; B := BETA;
  end LOCATION;
  VALUE := ALPHA_BETA(P, A, B);
  EVALUATOR.RESULT(VALUE);
end POSITION_VALUE;
```

Task EVALUATOR computes the new *alpha* value every time a successor node task returns an evaluation. It is declared as

```
task EVALUATOR is
  entry RESULT(VALUE: INTEGER);
end EVALUATOR;

task body EVALUATOR is
begin
  for I in 1..D loop
    accept RESULT(VALUE: INTEGER) do
      NEW_ALPHA := MAX(NEW_ALPHA, −VALUE);
        −−note that NEW_ALPHA is a global variable
    end RESULT;
  end loop;
end EVALUATOR;
```

D is the number of successor nodes and $T(j)$ is the task evaluating the jth alternative move.

3. Communication Using Computer Terminals

Two persons P1 and P2 communicate with each other using two terminals T1 and T2. When P1 wants to send a message to P2, that person types the message at terminal T1. Each character typed at terminal T1 is also displayed at T1. After a complete line is typed at T1, it is sent to T2 for display. This line is displayed at T2 only when P2 is not in the middle of typing a line, i.e., when P2 is not typing a message or when P2 has typed a complete line but has not started typing the next line. Messages sent by P2 to P1 are treated similarly.

The problem is to design terminal handlers (device drivers) that will allow P1 and P2 to *talk* with each other as described.[32] The terminal handlers always automatically display a *line feed* character LF after every *carriage return* character CR typed by the user. Characters LF and CR are defined in the package ASCII contained in the predefined package STANDARD. To avoid prefixing references to these characters by the package name ASCII, it is assumed that the *use* clause

    use ASCII;

has been given in the environment containing the declarations of the terminal handlers that are developed below.

Each terminal consists of two devices: a display and a keyboard. The buffer and interrupt addresses associated with the displays D1 and D2, and keyboards K1 and K2 are

D1 hardware buffer address	8#177560#
D1 interrupt address	8#60#
K1 hardware buffer address	8#177570#
K1 interrupt address	8#70#
D2 hardware buffer address	8#177564#
D2 interrupt address	8#62#
K2 hardware buffer address	8#177574#
K2 interrupt address	8#72#

The keyboard interrupt occurs after the character typed at the keyboard has been received in the keyboard buffer. On the other hand, the display interrupt occurs after the character put into the display buffer has been displayed.

Two solutions will be presented for comparison. In the first solution each terminal is treated as one device, i.e., one device driver for both the keyboard and the display, while in the second solution each terminal is treated as two separate devices, i.e., one device driver for each keyboard and each display.

---

32. This problem was suggested to the author by Tom Cargill.

3.1 Solution 1—One Device Driver Per Terminal

Tasks T1 and T2 will be declared for managing the two terminals. Communication between T1 and T2 will be indirect, occurring via the buffer tasks B1 and B2. Buffer task B1 takes lines from T1 and delivers them to T2. Buffer task B2 takes lines from T2 and delivers them to T1 (see Figure 8.1).

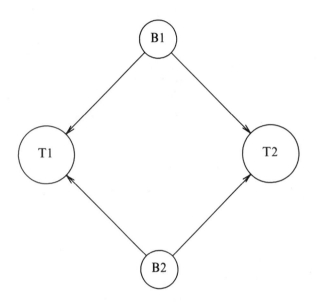

(arrows indicate entry calls and not flow of messages)

Figure 8.1: One task per terminal

Task B1 can be described abstractly as

> **loop**
>> Call T1 to get a line
>> Call T2 to deliver the line
> **end loop**;

Task B2 can be described abstractly as

loop
>   Call T2 to get a line
>   Call T1 to deliver the line

end loop;

Indirect communication is used between T1 and T2 to avoid deadlock, which might otherwise occur. For example, T1 and T2 might block with each attempting to deliver a line to the other. The intervening buffer tasks prevent blocking by giving each task two options: to send a line to the other task or to accept a line from the other task.

Tasks T1 and T2 are similar and, therefore, only one of them, T1, will be developed here. Characters typed in at terminal T1 are accumulated in an internal buffer and at the same time they are also displayed at the terminal. Transmission to T2, via B1, occurs only after a complete line has been accumulated by T1. Task T1 can be abstractly described as

loop
>   **select**
>>   Accept a line from T2, via B2, and display it

>   **or**
>>   **when** internal buffer is empty =>
>>>   ——accept a line from the keyboard
>>>   Accept a character from the keyboard
>>>   **while** character $\neq$ CR **loop**
>>>>   Display the character and store it in the internal buffer
>>>>   Accept a character from the keyboard
>>>   **end loop**;
>>>   Display and store the CR and LF characters

>   **or**
>>   **when** internal buffer has a complete line =>
>>>   Send the line to the other terminal, T2, via B1
>>>   Set buffer to empty
>   **end select**;
end loop;

Type LINE, declared as

subtype LINE **is** STRING;

is used in the final version of T1. It is assumed that the maximum line size will be 200 characters.

The specification of task T1 is

```
task T1 is
   entry GET;
   entry PUT;
   entry FROM_2(X: in LINE);        ——get line from T2 via B2
   entry TO_2(X: out LINE);         ——send line to T2 via B1

   for GET use at 8#60#;    ——keyboard interrupt
   for PUT use at 8#70#;    ——display interrupt
end T1;
```

The statement *Accept a line from T2, via B2, and display it*, given in the abstract description of T1, is refined as

```
accept FROM_2(X: in LINE) do L := X; end FROM_2;
——display the line
   I := 1;
   while L(I) /= LF loop   ——LF was appended by T2
      Display character L(I)
      I := I + 1;
   end loop;
   Display character LF
```

Statements of the form *Display character C* will be refined as

```
DISPLAY_BUFFER := C; accept PUT;
```

where DISPLAY_BUFFER is the hardware buffer associated with the display. An interrupt call to entry PUT, which is issued by the display hardware, indicates that the character put into the display buffer has been displayed.

Variable NUM_BUF reflects the number of characters in the internal buffer LINE_BUFFER. The expression *internal buffer is empty* is therefore refined as

```
NUM_BUF = 0
```

Once the second alternative of the *select* statement in the abstract version of T1 is selected, a complete line will be accepted from the keyboard. Consequently, a nonzero value for NUM_BUF, when the alternatives of the *select* statement are evaluated, indicates that the internal buffer has a complete line. Consequently, the expression *internal buffer has a complete line* can be refined as

```
NUM_BUF /= 0
```

The statement *Accept a character from keyboard* is refined as

```
accept GET do C := KEYBOARD_BUFFER; end GET;
```

The two statements in the abstract version of T1

> **while** *character* $\neq$ CR **loop** ... **end loop**;
> *Display and store ...*

are refined as

> **while** C /= CR **loop**
>   Display character C;
>   NUM_BUF := NUM_BUF + 1;
>   LINE_BUFFER(NUM_BUF) := C;
>   Accept a character from the keyboard
> **end loop**;
>
> Display character CR;
> LINE_BUFFER(NUM_BUF+1) := CR;
> Display character LF;
> LINE_BUFFER(NUM_BUF+2) := LF;

The body of T1, obtained by collecting all the refinements together, is

```
task body T1 is
   LINE_BUFFER: LINE(1..200); NUM_BUF: INTEGER := 0;
   L: LINE(1..200); I: INTEGER;
   C: CHARACTER;

   DISPLAY_BUFFER, KEYBOARD_BUFFER: CHARACTER;
   for DISPLAY_BUFFER use at 8#177560#;
   for KEYBOARD_BUFFER use at 8#177570#;
begin
   loop
      select
         accept FROM_2(X: in LINE) do L := X; end FROM_2;
         I := 1;
         while L(I) /= LF loop
            DISPLAY_BUFFER := L(I); accept PUT;
            I := I + 1;
         end loop;
         DISPLAY_BUFFER := LF; accept PUT;
      or
         when NUM_BUF = 0 =>
            accept GET do C := KEYBOARD_BUFFER; end GET;
            while C /= CR loop
               DISPLAY_BUFFER := C; accept PUT;
               NUM_BUF := NUM_BUF + 1;
               LINE_BUFFER(NUM_BUF) := C;
               accept GET do C := KEYBOARD_BUFFER; end GET;
            end loop;

            DISPLAY_BUFFER := CR; accept PUT;
            LINE_BUFFER(NUM_BUF+1) := CR;
            DISPLAY_BUFFER := LF; accept PUT;
            LINE_BUFFER(NUM_BUF+2) := LF;
      or
         when NUM_BUF /= 0 =>
            accept TO_2(X: out LINE) do
               X := LINE_BUFFER;
            end TO_2;
            NUM_BUF := 0;
      end select;
   end loop;
end T1;
```

The final version of B1 is

```
task B1;

task body B1 is
   L: LINE(1..200);
begin
   loop
       T1.TO_2(L);        --get line for T2 from T1
       T2.FROM_1(L);      --deliver line from T1 to T2
   end loop;
end B1;
```

Task B2 is similar to task B1 and is not given.

The code given in the body of task T1 can be improved by rewriting it to eliminate some duplicate code. For example, the program segment

```
I := 1;
while L(I) /= LF loop
   DISPLAY_BUFFER := L(I); accept PUT;
   I := I + 1;
end loop;
DISPLAY_BUFFER := LF; accept PUT;
```

can be rewritten as

```
I := 1;
loop
   DISPLAY_BUFFER := L(I); accept PUT;
   exit when L(I) = LF;
   I := I + 1;
end loop;
```

Modifications to the refinements leading to such code improvements are left for the reader.

3.2 Solution 2—One Device Driver for Each Keyboard and Display

The first solution does not really reflect the structure of the problem—only two device drivers have been used to control four devices. A terminal really consists of two devices: a *keyboard* and a *display*.

The second solution will be based on the principle that *each device should be controlled by a dedicated device driver* (see Figure 8.2)[33]

---

33. This solution strategy was suggested to the author by Tom Cargill.

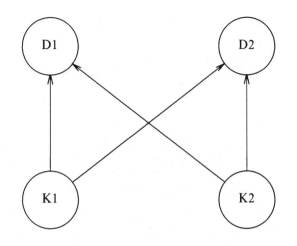

(arrows indicate entry calls and information flow)

Figure 8.2: One task per device

Displays D1 and D2, of terminals T1 and T2, respectively, will be controlled by tasks DISPLAY_1 and DISPLAY_2; their keyboards K1 and K2 will be controlled by tasks KEYBOARD_1 and KEYBOARD_2. Only tasks KEYBOARD_1 and DISPLAY_1 will be developed here; tasks KEYBOARD_2 and DISPLAY_2 are similar.

Task KEYBOARD_1 can be abstractly described as

> **loop**
> ——accept a line from the keyboard
> Accept a character from the keyboard
> **while** character ≠ CR **loop**
> Display the character and store it in the internal buffer
> Accept a character from the keyboard
> **end loop**;
> Display and store the CR and LF characters
> Send line to display D2
> Set buffer to empty
> **end loop**;

Displaying a character in this context means sending it to the task DISPLAY_1 for display at D1.

The specification of task KEYBOARD_1 is

```
task KEYBOARD_1 is
    entry GET; for GET use at 8#70#;
end KEYBOARD_1;
```

The body of task KEYBOARD_1 is

```
task body KEYBOARD_1 is
    LINE_BUFFER: LINE(1..200);
    NUM_BUF: INTEGER := 0;
    KEYBOARD_BUFFER, C: CHARACTER;
    for KEYBOARD_BUFFER use at 8#177570#;
begin
    loop
        --accept a line from the keyboard
        accept GET do C := KEYBOARD_BUFFER; end GET;
        while C /= CR loop
            DISPLAY_1.PUT_CHAR(C);
            NUM_BUF := NUM_BUF + 1;
            LINE_BUFFER(NUM_BUF) := C;
            accept GET do C := KEYBOARD_BUFFER; end GET;
        end loop;
        DISPLAY_1.PUT_CHAR(CR);
        LINE_BUFFER(NUM_BUF+1) := CR;

        DISPLAY_1.PUT_CHAR(LF);
        LINE_BUFFER(NUM_BUF+2) := LF;

        DISPLAY_2.PRINT_LINE(LINE_BUFFER);
        NUM_BUF := 0;
    end loop;
end KEYBOARD_1;
```

Task DISPLAY_1 can be abstractly described as

```
    loop
      select
        Accept a line from the other terminal and display the line
      or
          --accept a line from KEYBOARD_1
          Accept a character from the KEYBOARD_1
          while character ≠ LF loop
            Display the character
            Accept a character from the KEYBOARD_1
          end loop;
        Display the LF character
      end select;
    end loop;
```

The specification of task DISPLAY_1 is

```
    task DISPLAY_1 is
      entry PRINT_LINE(X: in LINE);
      entry PUT_CHAR(A: in CHARACTER);
              --used by KEYBOARD_1 to send characters for display
      entry PUT;

      for PUT use at 8#60#;
    end DISPLAY_1;
```

The body of task DISPLAY_1 is

```
task body DISPLAY_1 is
  L: LINE(1..200);
  I: INTEGER;
  DISPLAY_BUFFER, C: CHARACTER;
  for DISPLAY_BUFFER use at 8#177560#;
begin
  loop
    select
      accept PRINT_LINE(X: in LINE) do
        L := X;
      end PRINT_LINE;
      --display the line
        I := 1;
        while L(I) /= LF loop   --LF is the line feed character
          DISPLAY_BUFFER := L(I); accept PUT;
          I := I + 1;
        end loop;
        DISPLAY_BUFFER := LF; accept PUT;
    or
      accept PUT_CHAR(A: in CHARACTER) do
        C := A;
      end PUT_CHAR;
      while C /= LF loop
        DISPLAY_BUFFER := C; accept PUT;
        accept PUT_CHAR(A: in CHARACTER) do
          C := A;
        end PUT_CHAR;
      end loop;
      DISPLAY_BUFFER := LF; accept PUT;
    end select;
  end loop;
end DISPLAY_1;
```

This solution is simpler and easier to understand than the first solution, since it reflects the underlying hardware organization. Each device is controlled by one task; there are no connecting buffer tasks. Each task reflects the characteristics of the device, thus representing an appropriate logical partitioning of the problem. Information flows from the entry caller to the acceptor of the call; in the first solution, information flowed both ways.

Chapter 9: **Some Concluding Remarks**

Ada is the first major general-purpose programming language to offer high-level concurrent programming facilities. As mentioned earlier, these facilities are essentially untried, and only experience with them will uncover their strengths and limitations—from the points of view of both the user and implementor. Initial experience with the concurrent programming facilities in the preliminary version of Ada [DOD79a] caused these facilities to be modified substantially [DOD83].

Two aspects of the concurrent programming facilities in Ada will be discussed in this chapter:

- Concurrency in Ada and multicomputers.

- Some of the limitations of the concurrent programming facilities in Ada.

This discussion about Ada is based on my study and analysis of the concurrency in Ada, and on my experience in writing a variety of concurrent programs[34] in an effort to understand the concurrent programming facilities.[35]

1. Concurrency in Ada and Multicomputers

Entries are the primary means of communication between tasks. Tasks can also communicate by using common global variables. The *Ada Reference Manual* [DOD83] states that tasks can be implemented on multicomputers, multiprocessors or with interleaved execution on a single processor. An interesting point to examine is the implementation of tasks on a multicomputer.[36] As the cost of computers-on-a-chip keeps going down,

---

34. Including the examples for this book.

35. I must warn the reader that my experience is based on writing relatively small Ada programs. Although the programs were realistic insofar as possible, they were not "real" in the sense that they were not intended for extended use by me nor were they designed for use by others. Exhaustive testing of the programs was not possible because of the enormous resources—both memory and execution time—required by the prototype NYU Ada Compiler. Moreover, programs for controlling devices were tested only in a simulated environment. Consequently, any extrapolation of my evaluation of the facilities in the Ada language to "real" and large programs should be done with some caution.

36. A *multicomputer* is a computer architecture consisting of several different computers, without shared memory, that communicate by sending messages to each other.

multicomputers are being viewed as a means of providing vast amounts of computing power reliably and at low cost. Implementation of Ada's parallel tasks on a multicomputer will require much additional communication overhead and a larger pointer size (name overhead) when tasks share data by using global variables or by using pointers. While this communication overhead is restricted to tasks that share data, the name overhead is imposed even on tasks that do not share data.

Consider two tasks A and B operating on the same global variable G. Tasks operating on global variables imply a hardware architecture that has shared memory as in a multiprocessor environment. Now let us look at a multicomputer architecture. Assume that A and B are implemented to run on different computers. G may reside in the memory of the same computer as one of A or B or possibly in another computer. Assume that G does not reside on the same computer as B. Then every access to G from B will require communication with the memory of the computer on which G resides. This communication overhead may not be obvious to the programmer. Moreover, the programmer may not have control over how the tasks are distributed on the multicomputer. Such extra-language communication will cause additional complexity in the compiler.

A similar problem arises when two tasks share data by means of pointers. The object pointed to will not reside on the same computer as at least one of the tasks. Again, extra-language communications will be required. Also pointer values will now have to indicate which computer's memory is being referenced. Pointer value management will become more complex and the storage allocated for pointers will have to be increased to include the identification of the computer whose memory is being pointed to.

Another problem that arises with Ada's concurrency, not specific to its implementation on multicomputers, is that of synchronization and update when pointers are used to share data between tasks. The Ada designers have recognized the synchronization problem in the context of global variables. The *Ada Reference Manual* [DOD83] states that if global variables are being operated upon by two or more tasks, then it is the responsibility of the programmer to ensure that these tasks do not simultaneously modify the global variables or that a task does not read a shared variable when it is being modified by another task. However the same problem arises when pointers are used to share data between tasks. Additionally, if the tasks are implemented on different computers, then synchronization calls will also require intercomputer communication.

By allowing the use of pointers and global variables to share data across different computers, the designers of Ada, in addition to introducing communication overheads, have also introduced extra complexity from the viewpoints of both the implementors and the users. The use of pointers and global variables is considered to be detrimental to the understanding of sequential programs. Meshing their use with concurrency complicates the issue and seems to be a step in the wrong direction.

Neither the Ada reference manual nor the rationale for its design [DOD79b, DOD83] discusses the above problem or gives any rationale for allowing tasks to share data by means of global variables and pointers. The reasons for the latter were probably "efficiency" and to allow solutions of problems that may not be possible with just the rendezvous mechanism, e.g., the parallel buffer problem. An Ada implementor can simplify an Ada implementation on a multicomputer by ensuring that tasks that share data by means of globals or pointers will reside on the same computer.

2. Some Limitations of the Concurrent Programming Facilities in Ada [GEH83c]

Ada is the first language to base its concurrent programming facilities on the rendezvous concept. Consequently, it is natural to expect problems and limitations of these facilities, such as those enumerated below, to be discovered with use and experience:

- *Level of Concurrency*: The *task-level* concurrent programming facility in Ada is not appropriate for writing some kinds of concurrent programs, e.g., concurrent versions of *divide and conquer* algorithms. Such programs may have several recursive calls that have to be executed in parallel, and there is no easy way to express that in Ada. For example, there is no easy way of saying that the two recursive calls in a quicksort program, e.g.,

  ```
  procedure QUICKSORT(...) is
  .
  .
  begin
  .
  .
      QUICKSORT(...); QUICKSORT(...);
  .
  .
  end QUICKSORT;
  ```

are to be executed in parallel.

- *Parallel Numerical Computations*: The design of concurrent programming facilities in Ada has been motivated by the kind of concurrency that appears in operating systems problems—e.g., the producer-consumer problem—rather than that found in numerical applications. Consequently, it is hard and circuitous to write parallel numerical computations, e.g., parallel vector operations [BLU82].

- *Polling Bias*: As discussed in detail in Chapter 7 on *Some Issues in Concurrent Programming*, the facilities supporting the rendezvous lead to and encourage the design of programs that poll—the *polling bias*. Ada programmers, especially novice programmers, must be aware of this bias.

- *Determination of Self-Identity by a Task*: Tasks cannot determine their identity—an inconvenience in many applications. Suppose, for example, that an array of tasks has been declared. An element task cannot determine its index in the array. The lack of a facility to allow tasks to determine their identity means that some sort of identification, e.g., the index in the array, must be supplied explicitly to the tasks. As a specific example, consider the dining-philosophers problem discussed earlier. If an array of tasks is used to implement the philosophers, each task must first be supplied with its identity, i, so that it knows that it should use only forks i and i **mod** $5 + 1$.

  Preliminary Ada [DOD79a, DOD79b] had a facility that allowed tasks to determine their identity. Instead of the task types, Preliminary Ada had task families. The attribute INDEX when used in the body of a member of the task family yielded its index in the family.[37]

- *Array of Device Drivers*: Task types cannot be parameterized; this limits their usability. For example, an array of device drivers, say for a set of identical terminals, cannot be declared, because the buffer, register and interrupt addresses of the devices cannot be supplied as parameters.

- *Interrupts and Entry Families*: It is not possible to associate entry families with a set of interrupts. Consequently, an entry family cannot be used to handle a number of functionally similar interrupts such as those corresponding to elevator buttons in a computer-controlled elevator mechanism.

2.1 Programmer Control of Ada's Scheduling

Ada does not provide the programmer with sufficient control over the scheduling discipline used in allowing tasks to be executed [ROB81]. For example, when implementing a time-sharing system in Ada it would be natural to implement user processes as tasks. For fairness, time-sharing systems usually allow each process to run for some prespecified time limit. If this limit is exceeded, the executing process is descheduled, scheduled for later execution and another process is allowed to execute. In Ada, there is no way to specify a run-time limit for a task and it is not possible to deschedule a task explicitly.

---

37. Task families in Preliminary Ada were replaced by task types in ANSI Ada to solve some problems with the tasking facilities, e.g., tasks could not be passed as parameters and tasks could not be created dynamically. Using task types, tasks can be created dynamically using access types with objects of a task type in conjunction with the storage allocator *new*.

3. Conclusion

Although the discussion in this chapter focused on weaknesses of the concurrent programming facilities in Ada (as perceived by me), I have enjoyed using these facilities, finding them to be elegant, easy to understand and easy to use. My understanding of concurrent programming has benefited a great deal from using facilities in Ada. Within a short time I was able to write a variety of concurrent programs with ease—even device drivers such as those for controlling a keyboard, a display and a traffic light were easy to write, because interrupts are treated like entry calls.

Appendix: **Sequential Programming in Ada—A Synopsis** [1-6, 8]

Ada is a modern programming language that incorporates many of the advances resulting from programming language research in the 1970s. Programming facilities in the Ada language can be partitioned into two parts: sequential and concurrent. A concurrent Ada program consists of two or more sequential components executing in parallel and cooperating to accomplish a common objective. Consequently, before writing concurrent programs in Ada, we need to understand the sequential programming facilities in the Ada language.

The sequential part of Ada[38] can be partitioned into two parts—the conventional part, which represents the Pascal-like facilities in Ada, and the unconventional part, which represents facilities for modularization, information hiding, separate compilation and generic programming.

The flavor of sequential Ada programs is illustrated by a small program, CALCULATOR, which simulates a simple calculator that can add, subtract, multiply and divide. The data appears as a list of operations in the format

$$A \text{ operator } B$$

where *operator* is one of the symbols $+$, $-$, $*$ or $/$, and the operands A and B are real values.

Program CALCULATOR is defined as

---

38. A more elaborate description of the sequential part of the Ada language can be found in *Ada: An Advanced Introduction* by Narain Gehani [GEH83a].

```
--comments begin with two dashes and continue until the end of the line
with TEXT_IO; use TEXT_IO; --make input/output available
procedure CALCULATOR is
    type REAL is digits 10;
            --precision of real values is specified to be at least 10 digits
    package IO_REAL is new FLOAT_IO(REAL); use IO_REAL;
                    --input/output for REAL values is now available

    A, B: REAL;   --A and B are declared to be real variables
    OPR: CHARACTER;
    RESULT: REAL;
begin
    while not END_OF_FILE(STANDARD_INPUT) loop
            --function STANDARD_INPUT returns the default
            --input file
        GET(A); GET(OPR); GET(B);   --read the input
        case OPR is   --case statement
            when '+' => RESULT := A+B;
            when '-' => RESULT := A-B;
            when '*' => RESULT := A*B;
            when '/' => RESULT := A/B;
            when others => PUT("ERROR***BAD OPERATOR");
                        exit; --exit from the loop on bad input
        end case;
        PUT(RESULT); NEW_LINE;
    end loop;
end CALCULATOR;
```

CALCULATOR is an Ada main program. Any Ada subprogram can be executed as a main program provided all the *contextual information* needed by the subprogram has been specified. The contextual information

with TEXT_IO; **use** TEXT_IO;

makes CALCULATOR complete, i.e., CALCULATOR can be compiled and executed. The *with* clause specifies that CALCULATOR needs to use the predefined package TEXT_IO containing the text input and output facilities. The *use* clause allows subprograms, packages and other facilities (e.g., exceptions) in TEXT_IO to be referenced in CALCULATOR without explicitly stating that they belong to TEXT_IO. Package TEXT_IO provides subprograms to do input and output for some predefined types (e.g., CHARACTER), while for other types it provides templates of subprograms. Using the template FLOAT_IO for floating-point input and output, given in TEXT_IO, the declaration

> **package** IO_REAL **is new** FLOAT_IO(REAL);

creates a package containing input and output subprograms for values of floating-point type REAL.

1. Basics [2]

The *basic character set* of Ada consists of the upper case letters, the digits, the special characters

$$" \# \& ' () * +, - . / :; < = > \_ \ |$$

and the space character. The *expanded character set*, which may not be supported by all the Ada implementations, consists of the 95-character ASCII graphics character set. In addition to the basic character set, the expanded character set includes the lower-case letters and some additional special characters. Any lower-case letter is equivalent to the corresponding upper-case letter except within string and character literals.

Identifiers start with a letter and may be followed by any number of letters, digits and isolated underscore characters. Identifiers differing only in the upper- and lower-case letters, in corresponding positions, are considered identical.

Numeric literals are of two kinds—integers and reals. Some examples are

> 12   12.0   1.2E1 (or 1.2e1)

Isolated underscores may be inserted between adjacent digits to facilitate ease of reading, as in

> 12_000_000

Numeric literals can be written in a base other than decimal. For example, 61.0 decimal can be written in base 8 as

> 8#75.0#   or   8#7.5#E1

where 1 is the exponent in the second example. Both the base and exponent are written in decimal notation. For bases above 10, the letters A through F are used for the extended digits.

A *character literal* is formed by enclosing a character within single quotes. A *string literal* is formed by enclosing a sequence of zero or more printable characters within double quotes. The double-quote character " must be written twice to be included once in a string. Catenation, denoted by &, is used to represent strings longer than one line and strings containing control characters. Control characters such as the carriage return and line feed control characters are denoted as ASCII.CR and ASCII.LF, respectively. There is no direct denotation for them in Ada. They are *imported* from the ASCII *package* by qualification with the identifier that represents them, as will be explained later.

Comments start with two adjacent hyphens anywhere on a line and are terminated by the end of the line.

Ada has some identifiers, designated as *reserved words* [2.9], which have a special meaning in the language. Reserved words may not be used as names of program entities.

2. Types, Constants and Variables [3]

An *object* is an entity with which a type is associated; a value of this type can also be associated with the object. An object is created and its type specified by means of a *declaration*. All objects must be explicitly declared in Ada. (There are some exceptions to this rule, e.g., loop variables are declared implicitly by their presence in the loop heading.) An initial value may be given to an object in its declaration. There are two kind of objects—*constants* and *variables*. The value given to a constant cannot be changed, while that given to a variable can be changed.

2.1 Object Declarations

Object declarations have the form

> identifier_list: [**constant**] T [:= expression];
> identifier_list: **constant** := N;

where T is a type or a *subtype* name, *expression* is the initial value being given to the objects, and N is a *static* expression (i.e., an expression that can be evaluated at compile time). All variables must be given a value before they are used in an expression; otherwise, an error occurs.

2.2 Type Declarations [3.3]

A *type declaration* associates a *name* with a *type definition*. Type declarations have the form

> **type** name **is** type_definition;

where *name* is an identifier.

Types that can be defined are enumeration, integer, real, array, record and access types. A type definition always defines a *distinct* (different from any other) type even if two type definitions are textually identical.

2.3 Scalar Types [3.5]

Scalar types, viz., the *discrete* and *real* types, are types with simple values (the values have no components). *Enumeration* types and *integers* are the discrete scalar types. Integer and real types are called the *numeric* types. Each scalar type T has the attributes T'FIRST and T'LAST which denote the smallest and largest values of type T.

2.3.1 Enumeration Types [3.5.1]: The set of values of an enumeration type is defined by explicitly listing the values. Enumeration type declarations have the form

> **type** ENUM **is** $(a_1, a_2, ..., a_n)$;

where the enumeration literals a_i can be identifiers or character literals. The position of the values a_i determines their ordering, that is, $a_1 < a_2 < a_3$ and so on. Some examples of enumeration type definitions are

> **type** DAY **is** (MON, TUE, WED, THU, FRI, SAT, SUN);
> **type** COLOR **is** (YELLOW, BLUE, RED);

2.3.2 Character and Boolean Types [3.5.2, 3.5.3]: Ada provides two predefined enumeration types—CHARACTER and BOOLEAN. They are declared as

> **type** CHARACTER **is** (*the ASCII character set*);
> **type** BOOLEAN **is** (FALSE, TRUE);

2.3.3 Integers [3.5.4]: Ada provides the predefined type INTEGER. An Ada implementation may also provide other predefined types such as SHORT_INTEGER and LONG_INTEGER. The smallest and largest integers supported by an implementation are given by the constants SYSTEM.MIN_INT and SYSTEM.MAX_INT. The predefined subtypes NATURAL and POSITIVE represent subsets of INTEGER values greater than or equal to zero ($\geqslant 0$) and greater than zero (> 0), respectively.

2.3.4 Reals [3.5.6-3.5.10]: Ada provides elaborate facilities for reals [WIC81]. Values of type real are approximations to the mathematical reals. Reals come in two flavors: floating point and fixed point.

Ada provides the user with the predefined floating-point-real type FLOAT. Additionally, an implementation may provide other predefined reals, such as SHORT_FLOAT and LONG_FLOAT. A user can also define additional floating-point types with different ranges of values and accuracy of representations.

Fixed-point real types are declared as

> **type** NEW_FIXED **is** *fixed_point_constraint*;

where *fixed_point_constraint*, the accuracy constraint for fixed-point types, has the form

> **delta** DEL **range** L..R;

DEL, L and R are static expressions of some real type. The delta value DEL, which must be positive, specifies the maximum absolute error allowed in

representing values of the fixed-point type being specified. Elements of this
fixed-point type are consecutive multiples of DEL.

Two examples of fixed-point types are

> **type** VOLTS **is delta** 0.1 **range** 0.0 .. 1_000_000.0;
> **type** FINE_PRECISION **is delta** 0.00001 **range** 0.0 .. 700.0;

2.4 Arrays [3.6, 4.3, 4.7]

Array types come in two varieties—constrained and unconstrained. In the case
of a *constrained* array type, the bounds of the array are specified when an
array type is defined or when an array object is declared; constrained arrays
are similar to Pascal arrays. In the case of an *unconstrained* array type, the
array bounds are not specified in its declaration. These bounds are supplied
later, in type definitions using the unconstrained array type, in object
declarations or during parameter passage. The unconstrained array type can
be used only in type definitions and parameter declarations. It can be used for
object declarations only if the array bounds are supplied. It is the
unconstrained array type that allows procedures and functions to accept actual
parameter arrays of different sizes.

2.4.1 Constrained Arrays: The constrained array type has the form

> **array** index_constraint **of** C

where subtype C is the type of the array components. C can be any type
including an array (or a task) type. The *index_constraint* specifies the type of
the array indices and is of the form

> (discrete_range {, discrete_range})

where *discrete_range* is a range of the form *L..U*, or is a type or subtype name
followed, possibly, by a range constraint of the form **range** *L..U*. The
expressions L and U defining the bounds of the discrete ranges can be dynamic,
that is, they can depend upon computed results. An array whose bounds are
not static is called a *dynamic array*. Some examples illustrating constrained
array types are

> **type** SALES **is array**(DAY) **of** FLOAT;
> **type** CHESS_BOARD **is array**(1..8, 1..8) **of** CHESS_PIECES;

2.4.2 Unconstrained Arrays: Unconstrained array type definitions have the
form

> **array**(index {, index}) **of** C

where subtype C is the array component type and *index* is of the form

> T **range** < >

T is a type or subtype name. $<>$ is called the *box* and stands for an undefined range whose bounds are to be supplied later.

When declaring unconstrained array type objects, the *index_constraint* must be supplied. Different objects of the same unconstrained array type can have different bounds. An example of an unconstrained array type declaration is

type VECTOR **is array**(INTEGER **range** $<>$) **of** FLOAT;

Two examples of arrays declared using type VECTOR are

X: VECTOR(1..10);   −−1..10 is the index constraint
Y: VECTOR(−200..0);

The use of an unconstrained type in parameter declarations is illustrated by the definition of procedure SORT:

procedure SORT(V: **in out** VECTOR);

Procedure SORT can be called with any array of type VECTOR, such as X, regardless of the size of the array. The bounds of the formal parameter array V are obtained from the corresponding actual parameter and are given by the attributes V'FIRST and V'LAST.

2.4.3 Strings [3.6.3]: Ada provides the predefined string type STRING which is defined as

type STRING **is array**(POSITIVE **range** $<>$) **of** CHARACTER;

The relational operators $=$, $/=$, $<$, $<=$, $>=$ and $>$, and the catenation operator & are predefined for strings.

2.4.4 Array Elements, Slices and Aggregates [4.1.1, 4.1.2, 4.3, 4.3.2]: An element of an n-dimensional array A with subscripts i_1, i_2, ..., i_n is referenced using the notation

A$(i_1, i_2, ..., i_n)$

Portions of one-dimensional arrays, called *slices*, can be referenced by using the notation

A(discrete_range)

Array values, called *array aggregates*, can be constructed directly from component values. Array aggregates can be used for assignment to array objects or in expressions. Array aggregates can be formed using a *positional* notation, a *named* notation or a combination of these two notations. An aggregate must be *complete*; that is, a value must be given for every component of the composite value. The type of an array aggregate is determined from the context unless its type is explicitly stated.

Some examples of array aggregates and slices are given below:

(0, 1, 2, 3, 4)

(1..12 => 25.7)   is a one-dimensional array value with 12 elements, each having the value 25.7; named notation has been used to construct the aggregate.

CARD'(1 | 80 => '*', **others** => '_')

The type of this aggregate is explicitly stated to be CARD. Components 1 and 80 of this aggregate have the value '*'. All other elements have the value '_'.

('T', 'e', 's', 't')

The bounds of a positional aggregate or any aggregate containing the choice **others** are determined from the context [4.3.2]. An N-dimensional array aggregate is written as a one-dimensional array aggregate consisting of (N−1)-dimensional array values.

2.4.5 Array Attributes [3.6.2]: The following attributes are defined for each array object or constrained array subtype A:

A'FIRST(N)   Lower bound of the Nth index

A'LAST(N)   Upper bound of the Nth index

A'LENGTH(N)   Size of the Nth index

A'RANGE(N)   The subtype A'FIRST(N)..A'LAST(N) corresponding to the legal values for the Nth index.

If the index is not specified, then, by default, the index is assumed to be the first one, e.g., A'LENGTH is equivalent to A'LENGTH(1).

2.5 Records [3.7]

A record is a composite object consisting of named components that may be of different types (record components may be *heterogeneous*, whereas the array components are *homogeneous*). Record types are defined as

record
    component_declarations | **null**;
end record

A component declaration declares one or more components to be of a specified type using a type or subtype name followed, optionally, by a constraint. If there are no components in a record, then the record type definition must contain the reserved word **null**; such a record is called a *null record*.

A component C of a record object R is referenced using the *selected component* notation:

> R.C

An example of a record type is

> **type** POSITION **is**
>   **record**
>   X, Y: FLOAT := 0.0;
>   **end record**;

2.5.1 Record Aggregates [4.3.1]: Record values, called *record aggregates*, can be constructed directly from component values. A value must be provided for each component regardless of whether or not a default initial value exists for the component. Like array aggregates, record aggregates can be specified using either the positional or the named notation.

Some record aggregate examples are

> (5.0, 6.0)
> POSITION′(5.0, 6.0) −−aggregate type specified explicitly
> POSITION′(X => 5.0, Y => 6.0)

2.5.2 Record Types with Discriminants [3.7.1]: Discriminants are used to parameterize record type definitions. They allow values of a record type to have alternative forms. Discriminants must be of a discrete type and are specified in the declaration of a record type.

An example of a record type with a discriminant is

> **type** BUFFER(SIZE: BUFFER_SIZE := 128) **is**
>   **record**
>   POS: BUFFER_SIZE;
>   VALUE: STRING(1..SIZE);
>   **end record**;

Objects of type BUFFER may be declared as

> B1: BUFFER := (SIZE=>64, POS=>0, VALUE=> (1..64=>′ ′));
> B2: BUFFER := (64, 0, (1..64 => ′ ′));
>   −−this declaration uses positional notation;
>   −−the discriminant comes before the other components.

2.5.3 Variant Records [3.7.3]: *Variant records* are a special case of records with discriminants. A record may have a variant part that specifies alternative lists of components. A component list can be empty in which case it must be specified as **null**. Each list is prefixed by a set of *choices*. The component list selected is one that has a choice equal to the value of the discriminant. Only components of the selected list can be referenced; referencing components of the other lists in the variant will result in an error.

The general form of a record definition is

record
     component_declarations [variant_part] | **null**;
end record

The variant part of a record has the form

case discriminant_name **is**
    when choice {| choice} => component_list
    {**when** choice {| choice} => component_list}
  end case;

where a choice can be a static expression, a static discrete range or the keyword **others**. The particular list of components selected corresponds to a choice that has a value equal to the discriminant value. A choice that is a discrete range is an abbreviation for a list of choices representing all values of the range. The keyword **others** can appear only as the choice for the last alternative. It appears by itself and stands for all possible values the discriminant can assume that have not been covered by the choices prefixing the preceding alternatives.

2.6 Access Types [3.8, 4.1.3]

Static objects are created by specifying them in a declaration. *Dynamic* objects, on the other hand, are created dynamically and explicitly during program execution. The storage *allocator*, which is called **new**, is used to create dynamic objects. The number of dynamic objects, unlike the number of static objects, is not fixed by the program text—they can be created or destroyed as desired during program execution. Dynamic objects, unlike static objects, do not have an explicit name and must be referred to using *access type* objects that point to them.

The allocator **new** returns a value of an access type when a dynamic object is created. This value is used to refer to the dynamic object. This access type value may be assigned to more than one object of the same access type. Thus, a dynamic object may be referred to using one or more objects of an access type; an object that can be referred to by using two or more access type objects is said to have *aliases*.

Access types are defined by

    access T [constraint]

where T is a type or subtype name and the *constraint* is a discriminant or index constraint. Objects of this access type are used to refer to objects of type T.

The access value **null** is associated with all access types. All objects of an access type are given the **null** value as the default initial value. The value **null** indicates that no object is being referred to by the access type object. Using this value to refer to a dynamic object is an error and raises an exception.

Some examples of access type declarations are

    type TITLE **is access** STRING(1..40);
    type LOCATION **is access** POSITION;

Dynamic objects are created during program execution by a call to the allocator, which is of the form

    new T ['(expression) | 'aggregate | discriminant or index constraint]

where T is a type or subtype name. An initial value for the dynamic object may be explicitly supplied at creation time. If T is an unconstrained type, then a constraint or an initial value must be supplied when creating dynamic objects of type T.

Using access type objects declared as

    T1, T2: TITLE;
    A, B: LOCATION;

some examples of dynamic objects created using the allocator are

    T1 := **new** STRING(1..40);   —index constraint supplied
    T2 := **new** STRING'(1..40 => ' ');   —initial value supplied
    A := **new** POSITION'(Y => 5.0, X => 10.0);
    B := **new** POSITION;

The access value represented by an access type object P is referred to simply as P. The notation for referring to dynamic objects is P.**all**, where P is an access type object or a function call returning a value of an access type. If P refers to an object of a record type, then component C of that record object is referred to as P.C. For example, using variables A and B as declared above, the assignment

    B.**all** := A.**all**;

copies the value of the object referred to by A into the object referred to by B. This assignment is equivalent to the assignments of the components of A to the components of B

    B.X := A.X;
    B.Y := A.Y;

On the other hand, the assignment

    B := A;

just copies the value of A into B, with the result that B also refers to the object pointed to by A. The object, if any, referred to by B prior to the assignment becomes inaccessible unless another access type object refers to it.

2.6.1 Lifetime of a Dynamic Object: A dynamic object remains in existence as long as it can be accessed. Conceptually, dynamic objects can be accessed only as long as the declaration of the corresponding access type is available. The storage allocated for the dynamic objects may be reclaimed when they are no longer accessible or have been deallocated. Inaccessible objects will be automatically deallocated if the implementation provides a *garbage collector.* Otherwise, these objects must be deallocated explicitly if the space occupied by them has to be used for other purposes. Explicit deallocation is done using *instantiations* of the generic procedure UNCHECKED_DEALLOCATION.

3. Expressions and Operator Precedence [4.4, 4.5]

Expressions are formed using operators and operands. In evaluating an expression, operators with a higher precedence are applied first. Operators having the same precedence are applied in textual order from left to right. Parentheses may be used to change the order of evaluation imposed by the precedence of the operators.

A *static expression* [4.9] is an expression whose operands have values that can be determined without program execution. Static expressions can therefore be evaluated at compile time (without executing the program).

Operator precedence is given by the following table, the operators being listed vertically in order of increasing precedence:

Logical	**and** | **or** | **xor** | **and then** | **or else**
Relational/Membership	= | /= | < | <= | > | >= | **in** | **not in**
Adding (binary)	+ | − | &
Adding (unary)	+ | −
Multiplying	* | / | **mod** | **rem**
Highest precedence	** | **abs** | **not**

The operators have their usual meanings.

4. Statements [5]

In this section, Ada statements pertaining to sequential programs are discussed.

4.1 Null Statement [5.1]

Ada has a statement that does nothing. This statement is

null;

The *null* statement is used in situations where no action is to be performed, but where the Ada syntax requires the presence of at least one statement.

4.2 Assignment [5.2]

Assignment statements have the form

V := E;

where V is a variable name and E is an expression. Executing the assignment statement causes the value of E to be assigned to the variable represented by V. The type of both V and E must be the same. Assignment is defined for all types. For example, whole arrays, slices or records can be assigned values directly.

4.3 If Statement [5.3]

The *if* statement has the form

if boolean_expression **then**
    sequence_of_statements
{**elsif** boolean_expression **then**
    sequence_of_statements}
[**else**
    sequence_of_statements]
end if;

The sequence of statements corresponding to the first boolean expression that is true is executed. Otherwise, the sequence of statements corresponding to the *else* part, if any, is executed.

4.4 Case Statement [5.4]

The *case* statement is used to select one alternative sequence of statements out of many. It has the form

case expression **is**
    when choice {| choice} => sequence_of_statements
    {**when** choice {| choice} => sequence_of_statements}
end case;

The expression in the *case* statement must be of a discrete type. The sequence of statements corresponding to a choice matching the value of the expression is executed. The choices must be static expressions of a discrete type or discrete ranges. A choice that is a discrete range is an abbreviation for a list of choices representing the values in the range. The choices must cover all possible values the expression in the *case* statement might have and must be mutually exclusive. The choice **others** may be given for the last alternative as a shorthand for the remaining possible values of the expression.

4.5 Loops [5.5]

The *loop* statement has three forms:

```
while boolean_expression loop
   sequence_of_statements
end loop;
```

```
for loop_parameter in [reverse] discrete_range loop
   sequence_of_statements
end loop;
```

```
loop
   sequence_of_statements
end loop;
```

The first loop, called the *while* loop, is executed repeatedly as long as the boolean_expression is TRUE. In the second form, called the *for* loop, the loop is executed once for each value in the discrete range with the loop parameter being equal to that value. The values are assigned to the loop parameter in increasing order when the keyword **reverse** is absent and in decreasing order when **reverse** is present. The loop parameter is not declared explicitly. It is implicitly declared by its presence in the loop and has the type of the specified discrete range. The third form of the loop is used when neither the *for* loop nor the *while* loop can be conveniently used. In this form, the loop iterates until it is exited explicitly, e.g., by executing an *exit*, a *return* or a *goto* statement, or implicitly when an exception is raised. The third loop form is also used to express infinite cycles that occur in *tasks* (concurrent programs) that are designed to never stop.

4.5.1 Naming Loops: A loop may be named by prefixing it with an identifier, for example,

```
L: loop ... end loop L;
```

A named loop must be terminated by its name.

4.6 Blocks [5.6]

A *block* statement is a sequence of statements preceded optionally by a set of local declarations and followed optionally by a sequence of exception handlers. A block can be named just as a loop can be named.

```
[ declare
    declarative_part ]
  begin
    sequence_of_statements
[ exception
    exception handlers ]
  end;
```

Blocks are used to confine the scope of declarations and exception handlers to the statements with which they are logically associated.

4.7 Exit Statement [5.7]

An *exit* statement is used to exit from a loop, either unconditionally (when no boolean expression has been specified) or conditionally (when a boolean expression is present).

    exit [loop_name] [when boolean_expression];

Unless a loop name is specified, the innermost loop surrounding the *exit* statement is the one exited.

4.8 Return [5.8]

A *return* statement is used to return from a function, a procedure or an *accept* statement. In case of a function, the *return* statement is also used to return the value computed by the function. A *return* statement of the form

    return expression;

must be used to return from a function. The value returned by the function is the value of *expression*. To return from a procedure, the form

    return;

is used.

4.9 Goto [5.9]

Each statement can be prefixed by a label of the form

    << identifier >>

Labels identify the statements they are associated with and are used in *goto* statements. The *goto* statement is used for explicitly transferring control to a statement whose label has been specified. The *goto* statement has the form

    goto label;

5. Subprograms [6]

Subprograms can be compiled *separately* and are called *compilation units*. Subprograms in Ada come in two varieties—procedures and functions. A procedure is executed for its effect (e.g., changing the values of the **in out** parameters, supplying values to **out** parameters or updating global variables) and functions are used to return values.

Subprograms are invoked (executed) by means of subprogram calls. A procedure call is a statement, while a function call is an operand in an expression. Execution of a procedure terminates upon reaching the end of the procedure or by executing a *return* statement. Execution of a function must terminate by executing a *return* statement that returns the function result. Subprograms in Ada may be recursive and reentrant.

A subprogram consists of two parts:

- a subprogram specification and

- a subprogram body.

A subprogram specification consists of the name of the subprogram, the names and types of its parameters, and, in case of a function, the type of the result. Subprogram specifications are of the form

    procedure name [(formal parameters)] ;

    function name [(formal parameters)] **return** T;

where *name* is an identifier (or alternatively, in case of a function, an operator symbol surrounded by double quotes) and T is the result type or subtype name.

Subprogram bodies have the form

    procedure name [(formal parameters)] **is**
       declarations
    begin
       sequence_of_statements
    [**exception**
       exception handlers]
    end name;

and

```
function name [ (formal parameters) ] return T is
   declarations
begin
   sequence_of_statements
[ exception
   exception handlers ]
end name;
```

In the *declarations* part of a subprogram body, declarations of all objects, types, subtypes, representation specifications and exceptions must come before the bodies of subprograms, packages and tasks.

A subprogram specification can be omitted only if the subprogram will be called after its body has been given (assuming it has not been declared in the visible part of a package). In this case the body of the subprogram acts as its own specification.

5.1 Formal Parameters

Formal parameters of a subprogram are local to the subprogram. They can have one of three modes — **in**, **out** and **in out**:

formal parameter mode	formal parameter behavior
in	The formal parameter acts like a constant in the subprogram with its value being supplied by the corresponding actual parameter. **in** is the default mode if no mode is explicitly specified.
out	The formal parameter acts like a local variable. Its value is assigned to the corresponding actual parameter on normal termination of the subprogram.
in out	The formal parameter behaves like an initialized local variable. Its initial value is that of the corresponding actual parameter. On normal termination of a subprogram, the value of a formal parameter is assigned to the corresponding actual parameter.

All the formal parameters of a function must have the mode **in**.

5.2 Subprogram Calls, Actual Parameters and Parameter Matching [6.4]

Subprogram calls have the form

procedure_name [(actual parameter list)] ;

function_name (actual parameter list) | function_name

Actual parameters may be specified in positional or named notation. Actual parameters may be given default initial values by associating the default initial values with the corresponding formal parameters. Such actual parameters may be omitted, but the named notation must then be used for the rest of the actual parameters in the subprogram call.

A procedure call is a statement by itself. A function call, on the other hand, can be used only as part of an expression, since functions return values.

5.3 Subprogram Overloading [6.6]

Subprogram overloading is the use of the same subprogram name for *different* subprograms. Ada allows the user to overload subprogram names. Overloading a subprogram hides the subprogram being overloaded if it and the new subprogram have *identical* specifications.

6. Visibility Rules [8]

The discussion of the visibility of entities in this section refers mainly to identifiers (variable names, subprogram names and so on), but also to literals, enumeration values and other entities.

A *declaration* associates an identifier with a program entity such as a variable, type definition, subprogram or formal parameter. An entity can be declared in several ways, such as in

- the declarative part of a subprogram, block or a package,
- a package specification,
- a record as one of its components,
- a subprogram formal parameter or
- a loop implicitly as a loop parameter (simply by the occurrence of an identifier in the loop heading).

6.1 Scope of Entities [8.2]

The *scope* of an entity is the region of the program text where its declaration is in effect. The scope of

1. an entity declared in a block, subprogram or task extends from the declaration to the end of the block, subprogram or task.

2. an entity declared in the visible part of a package declaration extends to the scope of the package declaration, which includes the rest of the

package specification and the package body. On the other hand, the scope of an entity declared in the *private part* of a package extends to the end of the package specification and the package body.

3. an entry in a task declaration extends from its declaration to the end of the scope of the task declaration. It includes the task body.

4. a record component extends from its declaration to the end of the scope of the record definition.

5. a loop parameter extends from its first occurrence to the end of the associated loop.

6. a parameter (including a generic parameter) extends from its declaration to the end of the scope it is declared in.

6.2 Visibility of Entities

The scope of entities with the same identifier can overlap as a result of overloading of subprograms and enumeration literals, nesting and so on. Ada *program units* such as subprograms, tasks and packages along with statements and blocks can be nested. Ada's visibility rules for entities are similar to those of Algol 60. In addition, Ada provides the user with a mechanism to control visibility to some degree.

An entity is said to be *directly visible* if it can be referred to directly by using the identifier associated with it. If the entity is not directly visible, then context can sometimes be added to make it directly visible. For example, a component C of a package P can be made visible in the context in which the package P is visible by using the *selected component notation* P.C for it.

An identifier associated with an entity for which overloading is not possible (e.g., variables, constants, loop parameters and labels) is *hidden* in an inner construct if the inner construct contains an entity with the same identifier. Within the inner construct, the hidden outer entity is not directly visible. An entity that can be overloaded is said to be *hidden* in an inner construct when the inner construct contains a declaration for another entity with the same identifier and with identical specifications. For example, a subprogram, which can be overloaded, is hidden in an inner construct only when a subprogram with an identical specification is declared in the inner construct.

6.3 Making Package Components Directly Visible

If a package is visible at a given point in a program, then its components are also visible at that point, using the selected component notation. The *use* clause can be used to make the components of such a package directly visible.

A *use* clause does not hide an identifier, although it may overload the identifier. If an entity cannot be made visible by a *use* clause (because a similar entity is already directly visible), then the selected component notation must be used. In case of overloading, identifiers made visible are considered only if a valid interpretation of the program cannot be found without them.

7. Input/Output [14]

General high-level input and output facilities are provided by the predefined packages SEQUENTIAL_IO, DIRECT_IO and TEXT_IO. They define the file types, file *modes* and file operations. SEQUENTIAL_IO and DIRECT_IO, which are generic, are used to interface with files in binary format. TEXT_IO is used to read from or write to a text file, i.e., a file represented as a sequences of characters. (Text files, unlike binary files, are human readable.) A package, named LOW_LEVEL_IO, is also provided for controlling peripheral devices directly.

An *external* [14.1] file is anything external to a program that can produce or receive a value. It is identified by a *name*, which is a string. System-dependent characteristics of a file, such as its *access rights* and its physical organization, are given by a second string, called the *form*. An external file cannot be operated upon directly. An *internal* file object (called simply a file unless there is an ambiguity) must first be created and then associated with an external file. It is this internal file which is used in performing file operations, such as reading from or writing to the associated external file. Files, both internal and external, are homogeneous objects, i.e., they contain only elements of the same type.

7.1 Using Text Files

The use and manipulation of text files is now summarized. TEXT_IO is made available to subprograms and packages compiled separately by prefixing them with

with TEXT_IO;

Text file operations and objects need not be qualified by TEXT_IO provided the following *use* clause has been given (assuming there is no ambiguity):

use TEXT_IO;

Text files are used in a manner similar to direct and sequential files. Package TEXT_IO, unlike DIRECT_IO and SEQUENTIAL_IO, is not generic and is therefore not instantiated. After internal files have been declared, they are associated with external files by creating a new external file or opening an existing one. Text files are sequential files; consequently, only two modes are applicable to them—read only (IN_FILE) and write only (OUT_FILE).

TEXT_IO provides operations GET and PUT, instead of READ and WRITE. GET and PUT for character and string values are directly available, while for integers, reals and enumeration (including boolean) types, they are got by appropriately instantiating the generic packages INTEGER_IO, FLOAT_IO, FIXED_IO, and ENUMERATION_IO.

Assuming the above *use* clause has been given, GET and PUT for INTEGER and COLOR types are made available by the declarations

> **package** IO_INTEGER **is new** INTEGER_IO(INTEGER);
> **package** IO_COLOR **is new** ENUMERATION_IO(COLOR);

The *use* clause

> **use** IO_INTEGER, IO_COLOR;

obviates the need to prefix GET and PUT for types INTEGER and COLOR by IO_INTEGER and IO_COLOR.

8. Main Programs and Compilation Units

Any complete subprogram can be a *main program* in Ada. A main program is executed from the command line in the environment, provided by an operating system, to support the development and execution of Ada programs. The main program must of course be prefixed by all the contextual information, such as the names of *compilation units*, necessary for its execution.

A program in Ada is a collection of one or more compilation units. A compilation unit is a declaration or a body of a subprogram or a package prefixed by any necessary *contextual information*. The contextual information consists of *with* and *use* clauses. The *with* clauses specify the compilation units required for the successful compilation of the declaration or body of the subprogram or the package. These compilation units must have been compiled before (or be predefined), since the *with* clauses specify dependencies between compilation units. The *use* clauses make the entities inside the specified compilation units directly visible inside the declaration or body that is being compiled.

9. Pragmas [2.8]

Pragmas are instructions (suggestions in some cases) to the compiler. For example, an Ada compiler can be instructed to pack arrays or records as densely as possible. A pragma can usually appear after a semicolon and wherever a statement, a declaration, a clause such as *use* and *with* clause, an *alternative*, a *variant* or an *exception handler* is allowed. Pragmas may be language-defined or implementation-defined.

10. More on Types

Ada allows a user to specify constraints on types and to define types that have the same set of values and operations as existing types, but which are still distinct from the existing types; It specifies when two types can be considered equivalent and imposes restrictions on type conversions.

10.1 Subtypes [3.3]

The set of values of a type T can be restricted by associating a constraint with it. The set of operations, except for assignment, is not affected. The new set of values plus the old set of operations is said to constitute a *subtype*; T is its *base* type. Subtype declarations do not introduce a new type. Every type T is a subtype of itself. Subtypes are declared as

> **subtype** identifier **is** subtype_indication;

where *subtype_indication* is a type or subtype name followed by an optional constraint. Constraints can be of four kinds—*range*, *index*, *accuracy* and *discriminant*. For example, the range constraint **range** 1..8 is used in the declaration of subtype STORIES

> **subtype** STORIES **is** INTEGER **range** 1..8;

to restrict the legal values of all objects of the subtype STORIES to be the integers between 1 and 8.

Certain characteristics of types and subtypes, such as specific values and operations, are available to the user and are called *attributes* of the types and the subtypes. The base type of any subtype (or type) T is given by the attribute T′BASE. This attribute can be used only to form other attributes, e.g., T′BASE′FIRST, which denotes the smallest element of the base type of T.

10.2 Derived Types [3.4]

A *derived* type is a new and distinct type derived from an existing type, called the *parent* type. The values and operations of the derived type are copies of the values and operations of its parent type. Derived types are declared as

> **type** NEW_TYPE **is new** OLD_TYPE [constraint];

The constraint specified in the declaration of the derived type NEW_TYPE must be compatible with any constraints imposed by the parent type OLD_TYPE. As with subtypes, constraints can be of four kinds—*range*, *index*, *accuracy* and *discriminant*.

Conversion is possible between a derived type and its parent type. The derived type uses the same notation for the literals and aggregates as the parent type. Such literals and aggregates are termed *overloaded*, since they designate values for more than one type. The type of the literal or the aggregate must be determinable from the context; otherwise it must be supplied explicitly by the programmer.

Some examples of derived types are

> **type** PRIMARY_COLOR **is new** COLOR; −−no new constraint imposed
> **type** AGE **is new** INTEGER **range** 0..150; −−range constraint imposed
> **type** CARD **is new** LINE(1..80); −−index constraint imposed

10.3 Type Equivalence

Type equivalence has been classified into two broad classes—*name* and *structural*. When are two types equivalent in Ada? Ada uses the concept of name equivalence to decide when two types are equivalent. Two objects have *equivalent types* if and only if they are declared using the same type identifier.

10.4 Type Conversions [4.6]

An expression E may be converted to another type or subtype by qualifying it with the type or subtype name T; this is written as

> T(E)

Type conversions are allowed only among numeric types, among derived types and among array types. Whenever a type conversion is allowed, the reverse conversion is also allowed.

10.5 Qualifying Expressions with Their Types

The type of an expression is determined from its operand types and the types of values returned by the operators. A *qualified expression* is used to state explicitly the type of an expression or an aggregate. Qualification of an expression or an aggregate with the type is necessary in situations where the type cannot be determined from the context. A *qualified expression* has the form

> T'(expression) | T'aggregate

where T is a type or subtype name. The expression or the aggregate must have the same type as the base type of T.

11. Packages

Packages, subprograms, tasks and generic units constitute the four forms of program units from which Ada programs are composed. Packages, like subprograms, can be compiled separately, thus allowing partitioning of large programs into smaller and more manageable parts. Packages are generally defined in two parts—the package specification and the package body. The specification specifies the facilities provided by the package. The body implements the facilities. Package specifications and package bodies can be compiled separately. However, the compilation of a package specification must precede the compilation of the corresponding package body.

Packages are an information hiding and data encapsulation mechanism. They can be used to group logically related entities such as constants, variables, types and subprograms. The user of a package can see only the package specification and not the implementation details supplied in the package body. Moreover, only the entities specified in the *visible* part of a package specification can be referred to by the package user.

11.1 Package Specifications [7.2]

The specification of a package has the form

```
package identifier is
    basic declarative items
[ private
    basic declarative items]
end identifier;
```

A *basic declarative item* is either a *basic declaration*, a *use* clause or a *representation* clause. A *basic declaration* is any declaration except the body of a subprogram, package or task, or a *body stub*.

The body of a subprogram, package (if there is one), task or a generic unit declared in a package specification must be given in the package body. Alternatively, a body stub or an INTERFACE pragma[39] may be given.

Two sets of declarations can appear in a package specification. The first set constitutes the *visible* part of the package. Objects declared here can be accessed using the selected component notation (i.e., by prefixing the object with the name of the package and a period) or directly by means of the *use* clause.

The second set of declarations follows the keyword **private**; it is not visible outside the package. These declarations contain structural or implementation details of private types that were declared in the visible part of the package. These details, which do not concern the user of the package, are provided in the package specification only to help the compiler in implementing the visible part of the package.

Nothing declared in the body of the package is visible outside the body. This restriction on visibility along with the restriction provided by the private part of

---

39. The INTERFACE pragma is used when calling subprograms written in other languages.

a package specification supports the information hiding provided by packages.

As an example, consider the package ORDERED_SET that implements a set whose elements are ordered by the time value associated with them. The elements are of a discrete type ID and the time values of the predefined type DURATION. The elements represent job identification numbers and the time value represents job execution time in seconds. Type ID is declared as

> **type** ID **is range** 1..100;

and this declaration is directly visible in the context in which ORDERED_SET is being declared. The specification of ORDERED_SET is

> **package** ORDERED_SET **is**
>   **procedure** INSERT(JOB: **in** ID; T: **in** DURATION);
>   ——add JOB to the set; JOB is a job that requires
>   ——T seconds of execution time
>   **procedure** SMALLEST(JOB: **out** ID);
>   ——Store in JOB, a job from the ordered set with the
>   ——smallest execution time; this job is deleted from the
>   ——set; SMALLEST should be called after ensuring
>   ——that the set is not empty.
>   **function** EMPTY **return** BOOLEAN;
> **end** ORDERED_SET;

Declarations given in a package specification are visible outside the package at points in a program only if the package name is visible at these points. Identifiers in the visible part of the package specification can be referred to using selected component notation—the name of the item prefixed with the name of the package and a period. For example,

> ORDERED_SET.EMPTY

The items can be made directly visible by means of the *use* clause. If the *use* clause

> **use** ORDERED_SET;

has appeared, then the function EMPTY can be referred to directly as

> EMPTY

provided no parameterless BOOLEAN function with the same name already exists, in which case EMPTY will refer to the existing function. Also, if two identical identifiers are made visible with the aid of *use* clauses then an ambiguity may result. To avoid the ambiguity, these identifiers must be qualified.

11.2 Package Bodies [7.3]

A package body has the form

> **package body** identifier **is**
>   declarations
> **[begin**
>   sequence_of_statements
> **[exception**
>   exception handlers **]]**
> **end** identifier;

The body of a package constitutes the implementation of a package. It contains local declarations and the bodies of the subprograms, packages and tasks whose specifications were given in the package specification. All items declared in a package specification are visible in the corresponding package body. However, the implementations of these items, given in the package body, are not visible outside. Items declared locally in a package body are likewise not visible outside the package body.

A package body can also contain a sequence of statements that are executed when the package body is processed. These statements can be used to initialize the objects declared in the specification and body of the package.

As an example, the body of package ORDERED_SET, which implements the ordered set specified earlier, is declared. It uses a BOOLEAN array IN_SET to indicate the jobs that are present in the set along with an array RANK that contains their execution times. IN_SET(I) is TRUE if job I is present in the set and FALSE otherwise. RANK(I) contains the execution time associated with job I (when it is present in the set). The set is empty when all elements of IN_SET are FALSE.

The package ORDERED_SET is implemented as

```
--type ID is visible in this environment
package body ORDERED_SET is
    IN_SET: array(ID) of BOOLEAN := (ID => FALSE);
    RANK: array(ID) of DURATION;

    procedure INSERT(JOB: in ID; T: in DURATION) is
    begin
        IN_SET(JOB) := TRUE; RANK(JOB) := T;
    end INSERT;

    procedure SMALLEST(JOB: out ID) is
                    --call only when the set is not empty
        T: DURATION := DURATION'LAST;
        SMALL: ID;
    begin
        for I in ID loop    --searching for the smallest rank job
            if IN_SET(I) and then RANK(I) <= T then
                SMALL := I; T := RANK(I);
            end if;
        end loop;
        IN_SET(SMALL) := FALSE;    --delete the job from the set
        JOB := SMALL;
    end SMALLEST;

    function EMPTY return BOOLEAN is
    begin
        for I in ID loop
            if IN_SET(I) then return FALSE; end if;
        end loop;
        return TRUE;
    end EMPTY;
end ORDERED_SET;
```

As an exercise for the reader, the package body may be reimplemented using ordered lists to store the elements of the set.

11.3 Private Types [7.4]

The implementation details of types declared in a package specification may be hidden from the user of the package by designating the types to be *private*. A type is designated as private by associating with it either the attribute **private** or the attribute **limited private**. A *limited private* type is also called a *limited* type. A private type is declared using a *private type declaration* given in the visible part of a package specification. For example,

type SET **is private**;
type ORD_SET **is limited private**;
type QUEUE **is limited private**;

The full type declaration is given later in the private part of a package specification instead of the package body. The full type declaration is given in the package specification itself to ensure that the specification contains sufficient information to allow the compilation of a unit using the package.

Objects of private types can be declared, passed as parameters, compared for equality and inequality, and assigned values of other objects of the same type. Limited private type objects, however, can be declared and passed only as parameters.

The private type declaration and the corresponding full type declarations offer two different views of a private type—one each for the outside and the inside worlds. Outside the package in which a private type is declared, objects of this private type can be manipulated and operated upon only in a restricted manner; inside this package, on the other hand, private type objects are like objects of any ordinary (i.e., nonprivate) types.

The implementation of a private type is visible inside the corresponding package body, so that the implementor of a private type can define operations on objects of the private type. This implementation is hidden from the users of a private type; this forces them to manipulate private type objects using only the operations automatically provided with the private type and those provided by the implementor of the private type.

12. Exceptions

An *exception* is an event that occurs unexpectedly or infrequently, for example, an error or exhaustion of data. The occurrence of an exception results in suspension of execution of the *normal* part of a program. Bringing the exception to the attention of the appropriate program statements that must respond to this unusual situation is called *raising* the exception. These statements, which are specified in an *exception handler*, are then executed to *handle* the exception. Exception handlers are specified at the end of a block, a subprogram, a package or a task. Execution of an exception handler completes execution of the block, subprogram, package and task. After the exception has been handled, execution is not resumed at or near the point where the exception was raised.

If no exception handlers are provided, then execution of the program segment (which may be a block, subprogram, package or task) in which the exception was raised is abandoned and the responsibility of responding to the exception is transferred to another part of the program. This transferring of responsibility is called *propagating* the exception.

12.1 Declaring Exceptions [11.1]

Exceptions are declared using declarations of the form

>   list of exception names: **exception**;

Some examples of exception declarations are

>   TEMP_OUTSIDE_LIMITS: **exception**;
>   FIRE, BREAK_IN: **exception**;

All user-defined exceptions must be raised explicitly when conditions warrant. Ada provides some *predefined exceptions* defined in the package STANDARD. The predefined exceptions provided are CONSTRAINT_ERROR, NUMERIC_ERROR, PROGRAM_ERROR, STORAGE_ERROR and TASKING_ERROR.

12.2 Raising Exceptions [11.3]

Exceptions are raised explicitly by means of the *raise* statement, which has the form

>   **raise** [exception_name];

Some examples are

>   **raise** TEMP_OUTSIDE_LIMITS;
>   **raise** NUMERIC_ERROR;   −−predefined exception is raised
>   **raise** STACK_OVERFLOW;
>   **raise**;   −−reraise the exception in question

A *raise* statement without an exception name can appear only in an exception handler. It reraises the exception that caused the exception handler containing the *raise* statement to be activated.

12.3 Specifying Exception Handlers [11.2]

An exception handler can occur only in a *frame* which can be a *block* statement, or the body of a subprogram, package, task or generic program unit. They are specified at the frame following the key word **exception**. Each exception handler contains a sequence of one or more statements to handle the associated exceptions. Exception handlers have the form

>   **when** exception_choice {| exception_choice} => sequence_of_statements

where *exception_choice* is the name of an exception or the keyword **others**.

If the exception choice **others** appears, it must appear by itself in an exception handler and this handler must be the last one specified in the block, subprogram, package or task. The choice **others** stands for all exceptions that may be raised in the block, subprogram, package or task, but for which an exception handler has not been explicitly specified. It also represents exceptions that are not visible, that is, those defined, raised and propagated from other parts of a program, but for which no handlers were provided.

If an exception is to be reraised in an exception handler associated with the choice **others**, so that the exception is propagated to some other part of the program and the execution of the handler terminated, then the abbreviated *raise* statement

    raise;

must be used. Using this form of the *raise* statement is necessary, because the name of the exception activating the handler is not known in the handler—it is anonymous.

When an exception is raised, the remainder of the statements in the block, subprogram, package or task are not executed. Instead execution of the appropriate exception handler, if any, is initiated. If no exception handler is provided for an exception (explicitly or implicitly using the choice **others**), execution of the block, subprogram, package or task is abandoned and the exception is propagated. If an exception cannot be handled in the main program, then the program is terminated.

The exception handler has the same rights and capabilities as the block, subprogram, package or task in which the exception is raised. For example, an exception handler associated with a subprogram has access to the local variables and parameters of the subprogram, and can contain the *return* statement.

An example of an exception handler is

```
when TEMP_OUTSIDE_LIMITS =>
    if T < T_MIN then
        PUT("SHUT DOWN => Vessel OVERCOOLING");
    else
        PUT("SHUT DOWN => Vessel OVERHEATING");
    end if;
```

12.4 Activation of Exception Handlers [11.4]

The specific exception handler activated to take care of an exception depends upon the execution path of the program and not the textual layout of the program—the association of a handler with an exception is dynamic and not static. Suppose no exception handler is provided in a subprogram S for an exception E. Exception E, when raised, will be propagated to the caller of S and handled there instead of being handled in the part of the program containing the declaration of S.

13. Generic Facilities

Subprograms and packages in Ada can be generic, that is, they can be templates of ordinary subprograms and packages. Generic subprograms and packages are often parameterized and can accept, in addition to normal parameters, types and subprograms as parameters. Generic subprograms and packages constitute the fourth form of a program unit from which programs are composed—the others being subprograms, packages and tasks.

Generic subprograms and packages have two parts—a generic specification and a body. They are specified by means of a generic declaration. A generic declaration consists of a generic part, where the generic formal parameters are declared, followed by the specification of the subprogram or the package. The body of a generic subprogram or a package has the same form as the body of an ordinary subprogram or a package.

Generic subprograms and packages cannot be used directly, since they are templates from which usable subprograms and packages are created. A generic subprogram or a package must first be instantiated (by means of a declaration) for some set of generic actual parameters. The instantiation creates a new subprogram or package, which can then be used just like any other subprogram or package. Many such instantiations can be created.

14. Program Structure and Separate Compilation

Ada provides several facilities that support the construction and management of large software projects. It supports both *programming-in-the-small* and *programming-in-the-large*. For example, program components can be compiled *separately* and programs can be developed either *bottom up* or *top down*.

14.1 Separate Compilation

The ability to compile components of a program independently is important for constructing large programs and creating libraries of precompiled programs. However, in *independent compilation* no checking is performed to determine whether the program component being compiled is consistent with the program components that have been already compiled.

Independent compilation is a practical necessity, but the lack of consistency checking is a serious problem. The solution adopted in Ada, called *separate compilation*, incorporates consistency checking into independent compilation.

14.2 Program Development [10.1.1, 10.2]

Bottom-up program development is the construction of a program by first building and testing its components. Such an approach is appropriate to making good use of software tools [KER76] and program libraries available at an implementation. The *with* clause supports the construction of a program using components available as *library units*.

Top-down program development is the same as program development by stepwise refinement. By providing facilities in a programming language to support stepwise refinement, the language allows the preservation of the some of the structure of the program development process. Ada supports top down programming in a limited way through the use of body stubs. The bodies of subprograms, packages and tasks in the outermost level of a compilation unit may be compiled separately as subunits by giving body stubs for them. Body stubs have the form

> subprogram_specification **is separate**;
>
> | **package body** identifier **is separate**;
>
> | **task body** identifier **is separate**;

Bodies corresponding to the stubs are compiled as *subunits*, which have the form

> **separate**(parent_unit_name) body

Each body being compiled in a subunit must be preceded by the name of the *parent* compilation unit *parent_unit_name* in which its body stub was given. If the parent is a subunit itself, then the name must include the name of its parent and so on. The name must be given in full as a selected component starting with the first ancestor that is not a subunit.

Everything visible at a body stub is visible in the corresponding subunit along with any additional context that is specified in the subunit.

15. Representation Clauses/Implementation-Dependent Features

Ada provides facilities that allow a programmer to access the underlying hardware and to control the data type representations. These facilities are essential for writing systems programs such as device drivers, process control systems, interrupt handlers and storage allocators.

15.1 Length Clause [13.2]

The amount of storage to be associated with an entity is specified by means of a length clause. It has the form

> **for** attribute **use** amount;

where *amount* is an integer expression specifying the maximum amount of storage to be associated with the entity specified in the *attribute*. The term *storage unit* will be used to refer to the basic unit of storage allocation for the Ada implementation, e.g, byte or word. Some attributes that can be specified are object size, total storage to be allocated for objects of an access type and the storage to be allocated for an activation of a task.

15.2 Record Representation Clause [13.4]

The alignment of a record, and the order, position and size of its components can be specified by means of the *record representation clause*. The allocation of each record can be forced to a starting address that is a multiple of a specified value by using the *alignment clause*. The location of each record component is specified as an offset from the beginning of the first storage unit (numbered zero) allocated to the record. The ordering of the bits, i.e., left to right or right to left, is machine dependent. The number of bits occupied by a component is specified by identifying the first and last bits. The number of bits in a storage unit of a machine is given by the implementation-dependent constant SYSTEM.STORAGE_UNIT.

As an example, consider the representation of program status words in an IBM 360-like computer [DOD83]. The program status word occupies two words (each word consists of four bytes) and is used to keep the status of the program with which it is associated. The program status word must be allocated at a double word boundary (i.e., starting at an even word address).

Objects representing program status words are declared to have type PROGRAM_STATUS_WORD, which is declared below, along with some related declarations:

```
WORD: constant := 4;    ——4 bytes per word

type STATE is (A, M, W, P);
type MODE is (FIX, DEC, EXP, SIGNIF);
type BYTE_MASK is array(0..7) of BOOLEAN;
type STATE_MASK is array(STATE) of BOOLEAN;
type MODE_MASK is array(MODE) of BOOLEAN;

type PROGRAM_STATUS_WORD is
    record
        SYSTEM_MASK: BYTE_MASK;
        PROTECTION_KEY: INTEGER range 0..3;
        MACHINE_STATE: STATE_MASK;
        INTERRUPT_CAUSE: INTERRUPTION_CODE;
        ILC: INTEGER range 0..3;
        CC: INTEGER range 0..3;
        PROGRAM_MASK: MODE_MASK;
        INST_ADDRESS: ADDRESS;
    end record;
```

Objects of type PROGRAM_STATUS_WORD are mapped to the underlying machine according to the following record representation and length clauses:

for PROGRAM_STATUS_WORD **use**
    record at mod 8;   ——align at even (8 byte) addresses
       SYSTEM_MASK **at** 0∗WORD **range** 0..7;
               ——allocate the first 8 bits of the first word
       ——bits 8 and 9 not used
       PROTECTION_KEY **at** 0∗WORD **range** 10..11;
       MACHINE_STATE **at** 0∗WORD **range** 12..15;
       INTERRUPT_CAUSE **at** 0∗WORD **range** 16..31;
       ILC **at** 1∗WORD **range** 0..1;
               ——allocate the first 2 bits of the second word
       CC **at** 1∗WORD **range** 2..3;
       PROGRAM_MASK **at** 1∗WORD **range** 4..7;
       INST_ADDRESS **at** 1∗WORD **range** 8..31;
    end record;

for PROGRAM_STATUS_WORD'SIZE **use** 2 ∗ SYSTEM.STORAGE_UNIT;
    ——allocate exactly two words for each program status word

15.3 Address Clause [13.5]

An *address clause* is used to

1. specify the starting address of an object in memory. With this mechanism, program objects can be associated with hardware objects such as device registers and hardware buffers.

2. specify that a subprogram, package or task is to be allocated starting at a specific memory location.

3. associate a hardware interrupt with an entry (cannot be an entry family). The occurrence of an interrupt causes a call to the associated entry to be issued. The priority of such calls is higher than that of calls issued by any user-defined tasks.

The address clause has the form

    for name **use at** address;

where *name* is the program entity that is being associated with the memory location *address*. An example of the use of an address clause is

    for HARDWARE_BUFFER **use at** 8#177562#;
          ——location 8#177562# can now be accessed by
          ——using the program variable HARDWARE_BUFFER

Annotated Bibliography

AHO75   Aho, A. V., J. E. Hopcroft and J. D. Ullman. *The Design and Analysis of Computer Algorithms.* Addison-Wesley Publishing Company, 1975.

AND79   Andler, S. Predicate Path Expressions. Conference Record of the *Sixth Annual ACM Symposium on Principles of Programming Languages*, pp. 226-236, San Antonio, Texas, January 1979.

AND81   Andrews, G. R. Synchronizing Resources. *TOPLAS*, v3, no. 4, pp. 405-430, October 1981. The concept of *synchronizing resources* is proposed to allow the writing of efficient concurrent programs for both computers with shared memory and computers that communicate by using message passing. Synchronizing resources are somewhat similar to Ada's tasks. Processes within a synchronizing resource interact by means of operations (i.e., message passing) and shared variables, while those in different resources interact only by means of operations. Contains many illustrative examples.

AND83   Andrews, G. R. and F. B. Schneider. Concepts and Notations for Concurrent Programming. *ACM Computing Surveys*, pp. 3-43, March 1983. Detailed survey of the evolution of concurrent programming facilities. Facilities for concurrent programming languages such as Modula, Concurrent Pascal and Ada are summarized. Concurrent programming languages are classified into three categories—*procedure-oriented*, *message-oriented* and *operation-oriented*. In procedure-oriented languages, such as Modula, Mesa and Edison, process interaction occurs by modifying the environment such as shared variables. This category is also called the *monitor model.* In message-oriented languages, such as Ada, CSP, Gypsy and PLITS, process interaction occurs using messages; processes do not share variables. In operation-oriented languages, such as DP and StarMod (also in Preliminary Ada), process interaction uses the *remote procedure* call.

BAR80   Barnes, J. P. G. An Overview of Ada. *Software—Practice and Experience*, v10, pp. 851-887, 1980. Describes the development of Ada. Presents an informal description of the language. Points out the differences between the July 1980 and June 1979 versions of Ada.

BAR82   Barnes, J. P. G. *Programming in Ada.* Addison-Wesley Publishing Company, 1982. Contains a fairly complete description of pre-ANSI Ada.

BAU80   Bauner, J. D. and G. Svenson. An Implementation and Evaluation of the Real-Time Primitives in the Programming Language Ada. Report TRITA-CS-8001, Dept. of Telecommunications and Computer Systems, Royal Institute of Technology, Stockholm, April 1980.

BEN82   Ben-Ari, M. *Principles of Concurrent Programming.* Prentice-Hall, 1982. Discusses concurrent programming with an emphasis on topics such as mutual exclusion, semaphores, monitors and Ada's rendezvous. It contains the development of Dekker's algorithm to implement mutual exclusion without the aid of any special primitives. Several initial versions of Dekker's algorithm and the dining-philosophers problem, representing initial attempts to arrive at the correct solution, are given along with the final version. Correctness of concurrent programs is also discussed.

BLA80   Black, A. P. Exception Handling and Data Abstractions. Research Report RC 8059, IBM, T. J. Watson Research Center, Yorktown Heights, N.Y. 10598, 1980. Presents a simple treatment of exceptions in the context of formal (algebraic) specifications of abstract data types.

BLU82   Blum, E. K. Programming Parallel Numerical Algorithms in Ada. In *The Relationship between Numerical Computation and Programming Languages*, edited by J. K. Reid, pp. 297-304, North-Holland Publishing Company, 1982. The design of Ada's concurrent programming facilities has been motivated by the kind of concurrency that appears in operating systems problems rather than the concurrency found in numerical applications. Consequently, it is hard and circuitous to write parallel numerical computations, e.g., parallel vector operations.

BOO82   Booch, G. *Ada Letters*, vII, no. 3, November-December 1982.

BRI72   Brinch Hansen, P. A Comparison of Two Synchronizing Concepts. *Acta Informatica*, v1, pp. 190-199, 1972. The use of semaphores and conditional critical regions in synchronizing processes is compared with the use of conditional critical regions. Programs that use conditional critical regions are clearer and much easier to prove correct than those that use semaphores.

BRI73a   Brinch Hansen, P. *Operating System Principles.* Prentice-Hall, 1973.

BRI73b   Brinch Hansen, P. Concurrent Programming Concepts. *ACM Computing Surveys,* v6, no. 4, pp. 223-245, December 1973. A survey of concurrent programming features from the semaphore to monitors. Points out advantages of high-level features for concurrency in programming languages, e.g., easier understanding of concurrent programs and automatic checking of assertions. Features from event queues and semaphores to critical regions and monitors are discussed. Contains many examples.

BRI75   Brinch Hansen, P. The Programming Language Concurrent Pascal. *IEEE Transactions on Software Engineering,* v1, no. 2, pp. 199-207, June 1975. The programming language Pascal is extended for concurrency by adding processes and monitors that define the data shared by processes and synchronization procedures by which processes access this data.

BRI77   Brinch Hansen, P. *The Architecture of Concurrent Programs.* Prentice-Hall, 1977. Discusses how monitors can be used to systematically construct concurrent programs. The development of an operating system called Solo is described. The programming language Concurrent Pascal is used.

BRI78a   Brinch Hansen, P. Distributed Processes: A Concurrent Programming Concept. *CACM,* v21, no. 11, November 1978. Brinch Hansen proposes that processes communicate by calling procedures in other processes and synchronize by means of guarded regions. No shared variables are used. Contains many examples.

BRI78b   Brinch Hansen, P. Multiprocessor Architectures for Concurrent Programs. *ACM 78 Conf. Proc.,* pp. 317-323, Washington, D. C., December 1978. Computer architectures should be tailored to support programming languages. A hierarchical multiprocessor architecture is proposed for real-time programs written in a block structured concurrent programming language with monitors and processes.

BRI81a   Brinch Hansen, P. Edison—A Multiprocessor Language. *Software—Practice & Experience*, v11, no. 4, pp. 325-361, April 1981. This is the reference manual for Edison, a new language designed by Brinch Hansen based on his experience in designing and using Concurrent Pascal. Edison was designed for real-time applications on a multiprocessor architecture. Edison will influence the design of the multiprocessor architecture, a refreshing change from the tradition of hardware influencing language design but not vice versa. Edison incorporates existing ideas and is engineered to be simpler than Pascal or Concurrent Pascal, but more powerful than their combination.

BRI81b   Brinch Hansen, P. The Design of Edison. *Software—Practice & Experience*, v11, no. 4, pp. 363-396, April 1981. The rationale behind the design of Edison.

BRI81c   Brinch Hansen, P. Edison Programs. *Software—Practice & Experience*, v11, no. 4, pp. 397-414, April 1981. Programs illustrating the practical use of Edison.

BRO76   Bron, C., M. M. Fokkinga and A. C. M. De Haas. A Proposal for Dealing with Abnormal Termination of Programs. Mem. Nr. 150, November 1976, Twente University of Technology, The Netherlands.

BRY79   Bryant, R. E. and J. B. Dennis. Concurrent Programming. In *Research Directions in Software Technology*, edited by P. Wegner, MIT Press, 1979. Overview of research in concurrent programming. Concurrent programming is classified into three categories—communication by altering the environment (e.g., shared variables and monitors), communication using message passing and dataflow programming. Dataflow programs are viewed as a network of operators, each computing a new value on receiving its input and sending it on to the next operator in the network. The book containing this paper also contains reviews of and responses to this paper by S. Owicki, P. Brinch Hansen and others.

CAL82   Calingaert, P. *Operating System Elements*. Prentice-Hall, 1982.

CAM74   Campbell, R. H. and A. N. Habermann. The Specification of Process Synchronization by Path Expressions. *Lecture Notes in Computer Science*, v16, Springer-Verlag, 1974.

CAR81   Cargill, T. A. A Robust Distributed Solution to the Dining Philosophers Problem. *Software—Practice and*

Experience, v10, no. 10, October 1982. Presents an elegant solution, written in Ada, in which the philosophers do not deadlock or starve. The solution is distributed in that synchronization and communication is limited to adjacent philosophers and the impact of a faltering philosopher is limited to his immediate neighborhood.

CLA80   Clarke, L., J. C. Wileden and A. L. Wolf. Nesting in Ada Programs Is for the Birds. *Proceedings of the ACM-SIGPLAN Symposium on the Ada Programming Language, SIGPLAN Notices*, v15, no. 11, pp. 139-145, 1980. The authors argue that the package facility and the context specification clauses, not nesting of program components, should be used for controlling the visibility of program entities. Nesting has a negative impact on program organization and readability, and is not conducive to top-down programming.

COF71   Coffman, E. G., M. J. Elphick and A. Shoshani. System Deadlocks. *ACM Computing Surveys*, v3, no. 2, pp. 67-78, June 1971. A comprehensive survey of theoretical and practical analysis of the deadlock problem.

COH82   Cohen, N. C. Parallel Quicksort: An Exploration of Concurrent Programming in Ada. *Ada Letters*, vII, no. 2, September-October 1982.

COL80   Coleman, D. Concurrent Pascal—An Appraisal. In *On the Construction of Programs*, edited by R. M. McKeag and A. M. MacNaghten, Cambridge Press, England, 1980. Concurrent Pascal is a simple portable extension of a subset of Pascal. It is well suited to the design of simple single-user operating systems and encourages the systematic design and testing of modular programs.

COM81   Special issue on Ada of the IEEE *Computer*, June 1981. Contains introductory articles on Ada, the Ada Environment, an Ada Language System, Ada for the Intel 432 Microcomputer and the Ada Compiler Validation Capability.

CON63   Conway, M. E. Design of a Separable Transition Diagram Compiler. *CACM*, pp. 396-408, July 1963.

COU71   Courtois, P. J., F. Heymans and D. L. Parnas. Concurrent Control with "Readers" and "Writers". *CACM*, v14, no. 10, pp. 667-668, October 1971. The problem of mutual exclusion of independent *reader* and *writer* processes is posed and two solutions presented.

DAH72   Dahl, O. J., E. W. Dijkstra and C. A. R. Hoare.
             Structured Programming. Academic Press, 1972. A classic
             book on the disciplined and methodological approach to
             programming that has come to be known as *structured
             programming*.

DEB82   Debakker, J. W. and J. I. Zucker. Processes and a Fair
             Semantics for the Ada Rendezvous. Mathematisch
             Centrum, Amsterdam, Netherlands, November 1982.

DEN75   Dennis, Jack B. An Example of Programming with
             Abstract Data Types. *SIGPLAN Notices*, v10, July 1975.

DER76   DeRemer, F. and H. H. Kron. Programming-in-the-large
             Versus Programming-in-the-small. *IEEE Transactions on
             Software Engineering*, vSE-2, pp. 80-86, June 1976.
             Existing programming languages do not support the development
             of large programs. Large programs are systems that are
             composed of modules or small programs which are usually written
             by different people. A language for programming-in-the-large
             should support the definition of modules, support information
             hiding and allow the specification of the dependencies between
             the modules. The ideas presented in this paper are the
             forerunners of the concept of packages in Ada

DIG80   *Microcomputer Interfaces Handbook*. Digital, 1980.

DIJ68a   Dijkstra, E. W. Cooperating Sequential Processes. In
             Programming Languages, edited by F. Genuys, Academic
             Press, 1968. The concepts of concurrent statements,
             semaphores, and critical regions are introduced and mutual
             exclusion is discussed.

DIJ71   Dijkstra, E. W. Hierarchical Ordering of Sequential
             Processes. *Acta Informatica*, v1, pp. 115-138, 1971.
             Dijkstra, in this classic paper, states that concurrency in an
             operating system should be controlled in steps which will lead to
             a layered design of an operating system. Processes in each layer
             should harmoniously cooperate with each other. A key problem
             in implementing this cooperation is *mutual exclusion*. Mutual
             exclusion is discussed in detail with many examples. Correctness
             of these examples of concurrent programming is also discussed.
             It is in this paper that Dijkstra first posed the dining-philosophers
             problem.

DIJ76   Dijkstra, E. W. *A Discipline of Programming*. Prentice-
             Hall, 1976. A classic book in which Dijkstra explains a

programming methodology based on the idea of statements being considered as predicate or specification transformers. Programs are constructed side by side with proofs of their correctness.

DOD78   *Requirements for High Order Computer Programming Languages (Steelman)*. United States Department of Defense, June 1978. Also in *Tutorial: Programming Language Design* [WAS80]. Ada was designed to meet the specifications given in the this document.

DOD79a   *Preliminary Ada Reference Manual. SIGPLAN Notices*, v14, no. 6, part A, June 1979. The suitability of Ada was tested by using this definition to write many large and complex programs. Based on the experience gained by this testing and evaluation, Ada was modified, resulting in its pre-ANSI form [DOD80b].

DOD79b   *Rationale for the Design of the Ada Programming Language. SIGPLAN Notices*, v14, no. 6, part B, June 1979. A comprehensive document that provides justification for the design of the preliminary version of Ada. This document is a must for all those interested in language design and those who want to know more about Ada.

DOD80a   *Requirements for Ada Programming Support Environments (Stoneman)*. United States Department of Defense, February 1980. In addition to specifying the requirements for an Ada Programming Support Environment (APSE), it provides criteria for assessing and evaluating APSE designs and offers guidance to APSE designers and implementors.

DOD80b   *Reference Manual for the Ada Programming Language*. United States Department of Defense, July 1980. Also published by Springer-Verlag, 1981. This document is the official document defining pre-ANSI Ada. Differences between this version of Ada (as defined here) and the preliminary version of Ada [DOD79b] are informally summarized by Barnes [BAR80] and informally detailed by Winkler [WIN81].

DOD82   *Reference Manual for the Ada Programming Language*. United States Department of Defense, 1982. In July 1982, the United States Department of Defense released for editorial review a revised *Reference Manual for the Ada Programming Language*. The revised manual incorporates changes to Ada made in the process of getting it adopted as an ANSI standard. Although some editorial changes to the *Reference Manual for the Ada Programming Language* are likely, no further changes to

Ada itself are expected. In any case, if there are any changes to Ada, they are likely to be esoteric in nature, and will, in all probability, have no impact on the material presented in this book. (Ada was adopted as an ANSI standard in February 1983.)

DOD83 *Reference Manual for the Ada Programming Language.* United States Department of Defense, January 1983. ANSI standard Ada.

DOW82 Downes, V. A. and S. J. Goldsack. *Programming Embedded Systems with Ada.* Prentice-Hall International, 1982. Introduction to pre-ANSI Ada [DOD80b]. An *embedded system*, a hospital patient monitoring system, is used as the focus of the book to introduce Ada. An important application area considered while designing Ada was embedded systems, which are defined as computer systems that interact directly with electromechanical devices.

EVE80 Eventoff, W., D. Harvey and R. J. Price. The Rendezvous and Monitor Concepts: Is There an Efficiency Difference? (Concurrent Programming Language). *Proceedings of the ACM-SIGPLAN Symposium on the Ada Programming Language, SIGPLAN Notices,* v15, no 11, pp. 156-165, November 1980. Compares the concept of *rendezvous* in Ada to the *monitor* concept in Concurrent Pascal. Program style, semantics and implementation are compared. The authors conclude that a language should provide facilities for both monitors and rendezvous.

FEL79 Feldman, J. A. High Level Programming for Distributed Computing. *CACM,* v22. no. 6, pp. 353-368, June 1979. Discusses the design of loosely coupled distributed systems based on the concepts of message passing, modules and transactions.

FEU84 Feuer, A. R. and N. H. Gehani (editors). *Comparing and Assessing Programming Languages—Ada, C and Pascal* Prentice-Hall, 1984. Contains papers comparing and assessing the three languages. Also, there are papers that discuss how to compare and assess languages.

FIN82 Finkel, R. A. and J. P. Fishburn. Parallelism in Alpha-Beta Search. To appear in *Artificial Intelligence.*

FIS78 Fisher, D. A. DoD's Common Programming Language Effort. *Computer,* pp. 24-23, v11, no. 3, March 1978. Describes the background, scope and goals of the project that led to the design of Ada. Contains brief synopsis of the various versions of the requirements—Strawman, Woodenman, Tinman and Ironman. Discusses the philosophy underlying the technical requirements laid down for the design of Ada.

GEH81   Gehani, N. H. Program Development by Stepwise Refinement and Related Topics. *Bell System Technical Journal*, v60, no. 3, pp. 347-378, March 1981. Takes another look at stepwise refinement in the context of recent developments in programming languages and programming methodology such as abstract data types, formal specifications, and multiversion programs. Offers explicit suggestions for the refinement process.

GEH82   Gehani, N. H. Concurrency in Ada and Multicomputers. *Computer Languages*, v7, no. 1, pp. 21-23, 1982. Points out the problems that will arise in implementing Ada on a network of computers with no shared memory. The problems result from the fact that tasks can share data using global variables and pointers.

GEH83a   Gehani, Narain. *Ada: An Advanced Introduction.* Prentice-Hall, 1983. The author first gives a quick introduction to the conventional aspects of Ada—features found in existing programming languages such as Pascal, C, PL/I, Algol 60 or Fortran, and then focuses on the novel aspects of Ada—data encapsulation, concurrency, exception handling, generic facilities, program structure and representation clauses. Interesting differences between Ada and other languages are pointed out. The book contains many realistic examples including some large ones, all of which have been tested on an Ada compiler.

GEH83b   Gehani, N. H. and T. A. Cargill. Concurrent Programming in the Ada Language: The Polling Bias. To be published in *Software—Practice and Experience*. Ada's facilities that support concurrent programming lead to and encourage the design of programs that use polling rather than nonpolling paradigms.

GEH83c   Gehani, N. H. An Early Assessment of the Ada Programming Language. In *Comparing and Assessing Programming Languages: Ada, C and Pascal* edited by Alan Feuer and Narain Gehani, Prentice-Hall, 1984. Summarizes some important facilities in the Ada language and assesses their strengths and weaknesses. Although much of the discussion in this paper focuses on problems in two areas—derived types and some aspects of the concurrent programming facilities—the author emphasizes that he has found Ada to be a good programming language with advanced programming facilities for constructing reliable, modular and portable programs. Many of these facilities are not available in languages widely used today. The assessment of the Ada language is based on the author's experience in writing many Ada programs that span a wide spectrum of programming applications and that exercise most of facilities.

GEN81   Gentleman, W. M. Message Passing Between Sequential Processes: The Reply Primitive and the Administrator Concept. *Software—Practice and Experience*, v11, pp. 435-466, 1981. The issues in message passing as a means of communication and synchronization between processes are discussed. The use of the *administrator* concept as a concurrent programming style is advocated and illustrated with many examples.

GOO75   Goodenough, J. Exception Handling: Issues and a Proposed Notation. *CACM*, v18, no. 12, pp. 683-696, December 1976. Detailed discussion on how exception handling should be incorporated into programming languages.

GOO80   Goodenough, J. et al. Ada Compiler Validation Implementors' Guide. Softech, 460 Totten Pond Road, Waltham, MA 02154, 1980. Attempts to find all the holes, even the minute ones, in Ada. This guide is especially important for the implementor. Testing suggestions for the implementor are also provided.

GRI81   Gries, D. *The Science of Programming*. Springer-Verlag, 1981. Teaches the development of correct programs in conjunction with their correctness proofs. The program development approach used is based on Dijkstra's predicate transformers [DIJ76].

HAB72   Habermann, A. N. Synchronization of Communicating Processes. *CACM*, v15, no. 3, pp. 171-176, March 1972.

HAB80   Habermann, A. N. and I. H. Nassi. Efficient Implementation of Ada Tasks. Technical Report CMU-CS-80-103, Department of Computer Science, Carnegie-Mellon University, January 1980. An efficient implementation of *accept* statement bodies is described. The number of context switches required in the implementation of a rendezvous is reduced, in most cases, by implementing *accept* statement bodies as critical sections and using the flow of control of the calling task to execute them.

HAI82   Hailpern, B. Concurrent Processing. Technical Report
RC 9582 (#42314), IBM Thomas J. Watson Research
Center, Yorktown Heights, N.Y. 10598, September 1982.
Brief discussion of concurrent programming.

HAL80   Halloran, R. Pentagon Pins Its Hopes on Ada; Just ask
any Computer. *The New York Times*, p. 18E, November
30, 1980.

HAV68   Havender, J. W. Avoiding Deadlock in Multi-Tasking
Systems. *IBM Systems Journal*, v2, pp. 74-84, 1968.
Designers and users of concurrent programs must be aware of the
deadlock problem. Conditions that lead to deadlock and
techniques to avoid deadlock are discussed.

HEH80   Hehner, E. C. R. On the Design of Concurrent Programs.
INFOR, v18, no. 4, pp. 289-299, November 1980. The
author advocates the design of concurrent programs by starting
from sequential programs. Such an approach is advantageous
because the starting point is a well understood sequential
program. The resulting concurrent programs require less mutual
exclusion than those developed using other techniques. The
method is illustrated by introducing concurrency into two
sequential sorting programs.

HEN81   Henry, R. Real-Time Programming Languages. *Int. J.
Man-Machine Studies*, v14, no. 3, pp. 355-369, 1981.
Compares various languages such as Coral, Modula and Ada for
concurrent and real-time programming facilities.

HIB81   Hibbard, P., A. Higen, J. Rosenberg, M. Shaw and M.
Sherman. *Studies in Ada Style*. Springer-Verlag, 1981.
Contains a reprint of an article by M. Shaw on the impact of
ideas on abstraction in modern programming languages. This
article is followed by a set of five Ada program written by the
other four authors. The style of the solutions, represented by the
Ada programs, is said to be influenced by the facilities in Ada.

HIL82   Hilfinger, P. A.. Implementation Strategies for Ada
Tasking Idioms. *Proceedings of the AdaTec Conference on
Ada*, pp. 26-30. October 1982. Discusses uses of Ada tasking
idioms that do not require the full generality of the Ada tasking
mechanism. Suggests ways of implementing these idioms
efficiently.

HOA62   Hoare, C. A. R. Quicksort. *Computer Journal*, v5, no. 1, pp. 10-15, 1962.

HOA73   Hoare, C. A. R. A Structured Paging System. *Computer Journal*, v16, no. 3, pp. 209-214, August 1973. Hoare extends structured programming concepts to parallel programming and applies them to the design of a paging system.

HOA74   Hoare, C. A. R. Monitors: An Operating System Concept. *CACM*, v17, no. 10, pp. 549-557, October 1974. The monitor is proposed as a method of structuring an operating system. Contains several illustrative examples.

HOA78a   Hoare, C. A. R. Towards a Theory of Parallel Programming. In *Programming Methodology, a Collection of Articles by Members of WG2.3*, edited by D. Gries, Springer-Verlag, 1978. Proposes parallel programming constructs with objectives such as security from error, efficiency, simplicity and breadth of application. Introduces the idea of critical regions.

HOA78b   Hoare, C. A. R. Communicating Sequential Processes. *CACM*, v21, no. 8, pp. 666-677, August 1978. Ada's tasks are based on Hoare's proposal that parallel processes should communicate using input and output commands. Combined with Dijkstra's guarded commands, this idea becomes very powerful and versatile. Structuring programs as a composition of communicating sequential processes is advocated by Hoare as fundamental. Contains many excellent examples.

HOA81   Hoare, C. A. R. The Emperor's Old Clothes. *The 1980 ACM Turing Award Lecture*, CACM v24, no. 2, pp. 75-83, February 1981. The author recounts his experiences in the design, implementation and standardization of programming languages and issues a warning for the future. He urges that Ada, which is a large and complex language containing unnecessary and dangerous features (e.g., exception handling), not be used for applications where reliability is critical, e.g., nuclear reactors and cruise missiles. Hoare takes this view, because he believes that it will be hard to implement a reliable compiler for Ada and write reliable programs in Ada.

HOL72a   Holt, R. C. Some Deadlock Properties of Computer Systems. *ACM Computing Surveys*, v4, no. 3, pp. 179-196, September 1972. Discusses deadlock in the context of operating systems, although the discussion extends easily to programming languages with concurrency in them. Holt gives definition for the terms *processes* and *deadlock* and discusses deadlock in terms of a graph-theoretic model. Efficient algorithms for deadlock detection and prevention are given.

HOL72b   Holt, R. C. and R. Kinread. Teaching and Using High Level Concurrent Programming. *Canadian Information Processing Society—Canadian Computer Conference Session*, 1972. The authors claim that the main reason for teaching concurrency is the concurrent nature of operating systems and that this will help those who design and modify operating systems. The authors introduce the concurrent programming language TOPS.

HOL78   Holt R. C, G. S. Graham, E. D. Lazowska and M. A. Scott. *Structured Concurrent Programming with Operating Systems Applications.* Addison-Wesley Publishing Company, 1978. Concurrent programming is illustrated using Concurrent SP/k, which is a subset of PL/I extended by adding facilities for concurrency.

HON79   Set of Sample Problems for the DoD High Order Language Program. Honeywell, Inc., Systems and Research Center, 2600 Ridgway Parkway, Minneapolis, MN 55412, 1979. Solutions to some programming problems in the language GREEN (the name given to the preliminary version of Ada).

HOR83   Horowitz, E. and A. Zorat. Divide and Conquer for Parallel Processing. *IEEE Transactions on Computers*, vC-32, no. 6, pp. 582-585, June 1983. Discusses characteristics of multiprocessor computers that are necessary for the efficient implementations of parallel divide-and-conquer algorithms.

HUS80   Huskey, V. R. and H. D. Huskey. Lady Lovelace and Charles Babbage. *Annals of the History of Computing*, v2, no. 4, pp. 299-329, October 1980. This paper reports the correspondence between them.

ICH80   Ichbiah, J. View-graphs for Jean Ichbiah's Presentation. In *Proceedings of the Ada Debut*, Defense Advanced Research Projects Agency, Arlington, VA 22209, September 1980. Contains a set of view-graphs that give an overview of Ada.

JEN74   Jensen, K. and N. Wirth. *The Pascal User Manual and Report*. Springer-Verlag, 1974. The user manual includes details of the implementation of Pascal on the CDC 6000 by Wirth. The report contains the definition of Pascal and is considered to be the de facto Pascal standard. It is small (about 75 pages) and—perhaps because of this smallness—there are some ambiguities and several details are missing.

JOH80   Johnson, O. and J. Ramanathan. Recent Directions in Concurrent Programming Languages. IBM Technical Report RC 8378 (#36493), Yorktown Heights, N.Y. 10598. Comparison of the concurrent programming concepts in three languages—Ada, Modula and Concurrent Pascal. The producer-consumer example is used to illustrate the differences.

KAU81   Kaubisch, W. H., R. H. Perrot and C. A. R. Hoare. Quasiparallel Programming. *Software—Practice and Experience*, v6, pp. 341-356, 1976. A concurrent programming language Simone, an extension of Pascal, is described. Simone is designed primarily for programming simulation applications.

KER76   Kernighan, B. W. and P. J. Plauger. *Software Tools*. Addison-Wesley Publishing Company, 1976. The book explains how to write good programs that make good tools. These tools are intended for use in the construction of other programs. Real, nontrivial examples are given.

KER81   Kernighan, B. W. and P. J. Plauger. *Software Tools in Pascal*. Addison-Wesley Publishing Company, 1981. Same as KER76, but the language used is Pascal.

KES81   Kessels, J. L. W. The Soma: A Programming Language Construct for Distributed Processing. *IEEE Transactions on Software Engineering*, vSE-7, no. 5, September 1981. Discusses some limitations of monitors—programming a service as a process or a monitor is an arbitrary decision, monitors inhibit parallelism, and implementation of monitors requires shared memory. Proposes a programming construct called the *soma* (software machine) to eliminate these limitations. Like Ada tasks, somas are active program components, but they exchange messages using mailboxes.

KIE79   Kieburtz, R. B. and A. Silberschatz. Comments on "Communicating Sequential Processes". *TOPLAS*, v1, no. 2, pp. 218-225, 1979.

KRI81   Krieg-Brueckner, B. Ada and the German Pay Phone: An Illustrative Example of Parallel Processing. *Lecture Notes in Computer Science*, v123, Springer-Verlag, 1981. Tutorial illustration, by means of an example, of the concurrent programming facilities in Ada. Author (a member of the Ada language design team [DOD79a]) concludes by saying that the high-level concurrent facilities of Ada support program structuring and provide a degree of reliability if no shared (global) variables are used (the use of shared variables is strongly discouraged). These facilities do not prevent the conventional concurrent programming problems such as deadlock and starvation.

KNU75   Knuth, D. E. and R. W. Moore. An Analysis of Alpha-Beta Pruning. *Artificial Intelligence*, v6, no. 4, pp. 293-326, 1975.

LAM83   Lamb, D. A. and P. N. Hilfinger. Simulation of Procedure Variables Using Ada Tasks. *IEEE Transactions on Software Engineering*, vSE-9, no. 1, pp. 13-15, January 1983. Ada does not allow the declaration of objects of type procedure (similar to the declaration of objects of types integer, real, array, task and so on). Tasks, which are similar to procedures, syntactically more than semantically, are used to simulate procedure variables.

LEB82   LeBlanc, R. J. and J. J. Goda. Ada and Software Development Support: A New Concept in Language Design. *Computer*, pp. 75-81, May 1982. Ada has excellent facilities for the development of large scale software. Much of Ada's complexity is due to these features. Ada is unfairly criticized as being complex in comparison with other languages, such as Pascal, which have no facilities for large-scale software development.

LED81   Ledgard, H. *ADA: An Introduction*. Springer-Verlag, 1981. A brief introduction to a subset of pre-ANSI Ada. Also contains the full pre-ANSI Ada Reference Manual [DOD80b].

LED82   Ledgard, H. and A. Singer. Scaling Down Ada (or Towards a Standard Ada Subset). *CACM*, v25, no. 2, pp. 121-125, February 1982. Authors make suggestions for trimming and streamlining Ada with the intention of reducing its size and complexity which, they claim, is the most significant technical obstacle to its success.

LEV77   Levin, R. Programming Structures for Exception Condition Handling. Ph.D. Thesis, Computer Science Department, Carnegie Mellon University, 1977.

Programming methodologies have failed to address a crucial aspect of program construction—exceptions. Surveys exception-handling facilities in languages that preceded Ada, e.g., PL/I and Bliss. Proposes an exception-handling mechanism for programming languages that has been designed taking into account issues of verifiability, uniformity, adequacy and practicality.

LIS74   Liskov, B. H. and S. N. Zilles. Programming with Abstract Data Types. *SIGPLAN Notices*, v9, no. 4, April 1974.

LIS77   Liskov, B. H. et al. Abstraction Mechanisms in CLU. *CACM*, v20, pp. 564-576, August 1977.

LOV82   Loveman, S. B. Tutorial on Ada Exceptions. In *Using Selected Features of Ada: A Collection of Papers*. Software Technology Development Division, CENTACS, U. S. Army Communication—Electronics Command, Fort Monmouth, N.J., November 1982. Also in *The Ada Programming Language—A Tutorial*, edited by S. A. Saib and R. E. Fritz. IEEE Catalog No. EHO 202-2, IEEE Computer Society Press, 1983.

LUC80   Luckham, D. C. and W. Polak. Ada Exception Handling: An Axiomatic Approach. *ACM Transactions on Programming Languages and Systems*, v2, no. 2, April 1980. The exception handling of preliminary Ada is considered.

LUC81   Luckham, D. C., H. J. Larsen, D. R. Stevenson and F. W. von Henke. ADAM—An Ada based Language for Multi-Processing. Technical Report No. STAN-CS-81-867, Dept. of Computer Science, Stanford University, Stanford, CA 94305, 1981. Adam is an experimental programming language designed to facilitate the study of Ada implementation issues such as multitask scheduling and compilation of Ada tasks. Adam is derived from Ada and contains essentially all of sequential Ada plus some tasking facilities which are lower level than those of Ada. The authors could have used Ada, but they did not do so to avoid simulating low-level protection required for implementing critical regions by the high-level rendezvous concept. Moreover, although any scheduling policy can be simulated in Ada, the underlying scheduling algorithm, as implied by the task rendezvous, is very rigid.

MAH81   Mahjoub, A. Some Comments on Ada as a Real-Time Programming Language. *SIGPLAN Notices*, v16, no. 2, pp. 89-95, February 1981. Programmer control over scheduling, missing in Ada, is desirable because optimal scheduling is dependent on the real-time application.

MAO80   Mao, Y. W. and R. T. Yeh. Communication Port: A Language Concept for Concurrent Programming. *IEEE Transactions on Software Engineering*, vSE-6, no. 2, pp. 194-204, March 1980. Processes communicate using ports, which seems very similar to Ada's rendezvous. A port is owned by a *master* process and other processes called *servant* processes can use the port to communicate with the master processes. All servant processes are explicitly specified. A master process can disconnect communication at any time.

MAR82   Marsland, T. A. and M. Campbell. Parallel Search in Strongly Ordered Game Trees. *ACM Computing Surveys*, v14, no. 4, pp. 533-551, December 1982.

MAY80   Mayoh, B. Parallelism in Ada: Program Design and Meaning. In *Proceedings of the Fourth Colloque International sur la Programmation*, edited by B. Robinet, Springer-Verlag, 1980. (Also Report PB-103, Department of Computer Science, Aarhus University, Denmark, 1979.)

MCC79   McCorduck, P. *Machines Who Think*. W. H. Freeman and Company, 1979. A personal inquiry into the history and prospects of artificial intelligence.

MCD82   McDermid, J. A. Ada on Multiple Processors. Royal Signals and Radar Establishment, Malvern, England, March 1982. Techniques for implementing the Ada rendezvous on multicomputers.

MCG82a McGettrick, A. D. *Program Verification Using Ada*. Cambridge University Press, 1982.

MCG82b McGraw, J. C. The VAL Language: Description and Analysis. *ACM TOPLAS*, v4, no. 1, pp. 44-82, January 1982. Describes the dataflow language VAL. Concurrency in dataflow languages is implicit and, in case of VAL, concurrency is couched in its array operations. Dataflow languages are designed to encourage the development of programs on *dataflow machines*, which will consist of hundreds or thousands of cooperating processors.

MEL83a Mellichamp, D. A. The Structure of Real-Time Systems. In *Real-Time Computing*, edited by D. A. Mellichamp, pp. 12-32. Van Nostrand Reinhold, 1983.

MEL83b   Mellichamp, D. A. Real-Time Basic. In *Real-Time Computing*, edited by D. A. Mellichamp. Van Nostrand Reinhold, 1983.

MOO77   Moore, L. D. *Ada: Countess of Lovelace — Byron's Legitimate Daughter*. John Murray, 1977. The first full biography of Ada. I found it somewhat boring. The article titled *Lady Lovelace and Charles Babbage* [HUS80] is much shorter and more interesting.

NAB   Nabakov, V. *Ada*. Penguin Books. Much more interesting reading than the reference manual [WAN82].

NIS81   Nissen, J. C. D., P. Wallis, B. A. Wichmann and others. Ada Europe Guidelines for the Portability of Ada Programs. Technical Report, National Physical Laboratory, Teddington, Middlesex, TW11 0LW, UK. Guide to aid programmers in designing and coding portable programs.

NOT80   Notkin, D. S. An Experience with Parallelism in Ada. *Proceedings of the ACM-SIGPLAN Symposium on the Ada Programming Language, SIGPLAN Notices*, v15, no. 11, pp. 9-15, 1980. Detailed discussion of the implementation of a system with parallelism for use in project management. The author then discusses influence of the tasking facilities in Ada on the design of this system. The author concludes by saying that as users gain experience in using the concurrent programming facilities in Ada, they will design systems in a manner that exploits these facilities.

OWI76a   Owicki, S. S. and D. Gries. An Axiomatic Proof Technique for Parallel Programs. *Acta Informatica*, v6, pp. 319-340, 1976. Hoare's axiomatic technique for proving the partial correctness of sequential programs is extended for proving the partial correctness of concurrent programs. Proofs in the extended technique use auxiliary variables.

OWI76b   Owicki, S. S. and D. Gries. Verifying Properties of Parallel Programs: An Axiomatic Approach. *CACM*, v19, no. 5, pp. 279-285, May 1976. The dining-philosophers problem is used to illustrate the proof technique for concurrent programs [OWI76a], showing, in addition to partial correctness, mutual exclusion and freedom from blocking and termination.

PAR72   Parnas, D. On the Criteria to Be Used in Decomposing Systems into Modules. *CACM*, v15, pp. 1053-1058,

December 1972. The advantages of composing a system from modules are widely recognized. Suggests rules for decomposing a system into modules by comparing two decompositions of a software system—one composed of modules representing execution steps and the other representing logical functions. The second formulation uses the *principle of information hiding*, i.e., only information relevant to the user of the module should be available to the user and all other information should be hidden. The second formulation is easier to modify and understand than the first one.

PER80   Perrot, R. H. Languages for Parallel Computers. In *On the Construction of Programs*, edited by R. M. McKeag and A. M. MacNaghten, Cambridge Press, England, 1980. Discusses a particular type of parallel programming called *synchronous* or *lockstep* parallel programming in which a sequence of instructions can be applied to disjoint sets of data, e.g., vector and array processing. In this kind of parallelism there are no synchronization or mutual exclusion problems.

PER82   Perry, D. Low Level Language Features. In *Using Selected Features of Ada: A Collection of Papers*. Software Technology Development Division, CENTACS, U. S. Army Communication—Electronics Command, Fort Monmouth, N.J., November 1982. Also in *The Ada Programming Language—A Tutorial*, edited by S. A. Saib and R. E. Fritz. IEEE Catalog No. EHO 202-2, IEEE Computer Society Press, 1983. Discusses the use of the implementation-dependent low-level package LOW_LEVEL_IO to write device drivers. Contains a sample version of the package LOW_LEVEL_IO that is used to write an example card reader driver.

PRA75   Pratt, T. W. *Programming Languages: Design and Implementation*. Prentice-Hall, 1975.

PRA83   Pratt, V. Five Paradigm Shifts in Programming Language Design and Their Realization in Viron, a Dataflow Programming Environment. *Conference Record of the Tenth Annual ACM Symposium on Principles of Programming Languages*, Austin, Texas, January 1983.

PYL81   Pyle, I. C. *The Ada Programming Language*. Prentice-Hall International, 1981. This book is a fairly comprehensive introduction to Ada. It contains brief notes for Fortran and Pascal programmers interested in Ada.

RAM83   Ramakrishnan, I. V. and J. C. Browne. A Paradigm for the Design of Parallel Algorithms with Applications. *IEEE Transactions on Software Engineering*, vSE-9, no. 4, pp. 411-415, July 1983.

RIT78   D. M. Ritchie, S. C. Johnson, M. E. Lesk and B. W. Kernighan. The C Programming Language. *Bell System Technical Journal*, Part 2, v57, no. 6, pp. 1991-2019, July-August 1978.

ROB81   Roberts, E. S., E. M. Clarke, A. Evans, Jr. and C. R. Morgan. Task Management in Ada: A Critical Evaluation for Real-Time Multiprocessors. *Software—Practice & Experience*, v11, no. 10, pp. 1019-1052, October 1981. Preliminary Ada is used in the discussion.

ROU80   Roubine, O. and J. C. Heliard. Parallel Processing in Ada. In *On the Construction of Programs*, edited by R. M. McKeag and A. M. MacNaghten, Cambridge Press, England, 1980. Rationale behind the design of the tasking facilities in Preliminary Ada along with illustrative examples.

SAI83   Saib, S. A. and R. E. Fritz. *The Ada Programming Language—A Tutorial*. IEEE Catalog No. EHO 202-2, IEEE Computer Society Press, 1983. Contains reprints of articles on various aspects of Ada—history, environment, implementations, overview, real-time programming, criticisms and influences. Many of the papers included in this collection have been specifically listed in the bibliography.

SCH80   Schwartz, R. L. and P. M. Melliar-Smith. On the Suitability of Ada for Artificial Intelligence Applications. SRI International, 333 Ravenswood Avenue, Menlo Park, CA 94205, July 1980. The preliminary version of Ada is considered to analyze its suitability for programming artificial intelligence (AI) applications. Although a useful proportion of AI programs can be written in Ada, the authors do not feel that preliminary Ada is suitable as a general research programming language for AI.

SCH81   Schuman, S. A., E. M. Clarke Jr. and C. N. Nikolaou. Programming Distributed Applications in Ada: A First Approach. *Proceedings of the IEEE 1981 International Conference on Parallel Processing*, pp. 38-49, Columbus, Ohio, 1981.

SHU82   Shuman, S. Tutorial on Ada Tasking. In *Using Selected Features of Ada: A Collection of Papers.* Software Technology Development Division, CENTACS, U. S. Army Communication—Electronics Command, Fort Monmouth, N.J., November 1982. Also in *The Ada Programming Language—A Tutorial*, edited by S. A. Saib and R. E. Fritz. IEEE Catalog No. EHO 202-2, IEEE Computer Society Press, 1983.

STO82   Stotts, P. D., Jr. A Comparative Survey of Concurrent Programming Languages. *SIGPLAN Notices*, v17, no. 9, pp. 76-87, September 1982. Discusses issues in the design of concurrent programming languages such as communication and synchronization methods, process creation and topology, and real-time support. A table summarizing a comparison of several languages based on these issues is given.

TEO72   Teorey, T. J. and T. B. Pinkerton. A Comparative Analysis of Disk Scheduling Policies. *CACM*, v15, no. 3, pp. 177-184, March 1972.

THO74   Thompson, K. and D. M. Ritchie. The UNIX Time-Sharing System. *CACM*, v17, no. 7, 1974.

WAN82   Wand, I. C., J. Zalewski and R. P. Young. Ada Bibliography. To be published in *Ada Letters*. Comprehensive bibliography of articles and books related to Ada.

WAS80   Wasserman, A. I. *Tutorial: Programming Language Design.* IEEE Computer Society, 1980. Contains reprints of articles on various aspects of programming language design— design philosophy, control structures, data types, the designs of Pascal and Ada, exception handling and programming language design experience. In particular, it contains the document describing the final requirements (called *Steelman*) which formed the basis for the design of Ada.

WEG80   Wegner, P. *Programming with Ada: An Introduction by Means of Graduated Examples.* Prentice-Hall, 1980. Introduction to the preliminary version of Ada.

WEG81   Wegner, P. A Self-Assessment Procedure Dealing with the Programming Language Ada. *CACM*, v24, no. 10, pp. 647-677, October 1981. A set of short mechanisms to help readers assess and develop their knowledge of Ada.

WEG83   Wegner, P. and S. A. Smolka. Processes, Tasks, and Monitors: A   Comparative   Study   of   Concurrent

Programming Primitives. *IEEE Transactions on Software Engineering*, vSE-9, no. 4, pp. 446-462, July 1983. The concurrent programming models of CSP, Ada and monitors are compared. Ada's facilities are quite similar to those of CSP (not surprising since Ada's facilities are based on those proposed in CSP). Still, there are important differences in the task naming and nondeterministic task interaction.

Ada's concurrent programming model, the rendezvous, is quite different from the monitor concurrent programming model. For example, monitors are passive objects while Ada's tasks are active objects. An attempt to implement a monitor using Ada's tasks suggests that Ada packages (with encapsulated tasks) may be more appropriate than tasks as a user interface for concurrent programming.

WEL80   Welsh, J., A. Lister and E. J. Salzman. A Comparison of Two Notations for Process Communication. In *Language Design and Programming Methodology*, edited by J. Tobias, *Lecture Notes in Computer Science Series*, No. 79, Springer-Verlag 1980. Comparison of Hoare's "Communicating Sequential Processes" and Brinch Hansen's "Distributed Processes".

WEL81   Welsh, J. and A. Lister. A Comparative Study of Task Communication in Ada. *Software—Practice and Experience*, v11, pp. 257-290, 1981. Compares the mechanism for process communication in Ada with those in Hoare's "Communicating Sequential Processes" and Brinch Hansen's "Distributed Processes".

WET83   Wetherell, C. S. Private Communication. February 28 and March 18, 1983.

WIC81   Wichmann, B. A. Tutorial Material on the Real Data-Types in Ada. Technical Report, National Physical Laboratory, Teddington, Middlesex, TW11 0LW, UK, 1981. (Also in *Ada Letters*, v1, no. 2, pp. 15-33, 1981.) Introduces the novel features of Ada in the area of numerics to programmers familiar with numeric computations, but not with Ada.

WIC82   Wichmann, B. A. A Comparison of Pascal and Ada. *Computer Journal*, v25, no. 2, pp. 248-252, 1982.

WIR71   Wirth, N. Program Development by Stepwise Refinement. *CACM*, v14, no. 4, 1971. Classic paper on stepwise refinement. F. P. Brooks in his book *The Mythical Man-Month* calls stepwise refinement the most important programming formalization of the 1970s.

WIR73   Wirth, N. *Systematic Programming: An Introduction.* Prentice-Hall, 1973.

WIR76   Wirth, N. *Algorithms + Data Structures = Programs.* Prentice-Hall, 1976.

WIR77a   Wirth, N. Modula: A Language for Modular Multiprogramming. *Software—Practice and Experience*, v7, pp. 3-35, 1977. The high-level language Modula is an attempt to break one of the last holds of assembly language programming, viz., machine-dependent system programming such as device drivers. Modula is a Pascal descendant. It has facilities for multiprogramming and has been designed specifically for the PDP-11 computers. It introduces the concept of the module (similar to the Ada package) and has the concepts of processes, interface modules and signals.

WIR77b   Wirth, N. The Use of Modula. *Software—Practice and Experience*, v7, 1977.

WIR77c   Wirth, N. Design and Implementation of Modula. *Software—Practice and Experience*, v7, 1977.

WIR77d   Wirth, N. Towards a Discipline of Real-Time Programming. *CACM*, v20, no. 8, pp. 577-583, 1977. Divides programming into three increasingly more complicated categories—sequential programming, multiprogramming and real-time programming. Reasoning about real-time programs can only become manageable if a strict programming discipline is practiced.

WIR80   Wirth, N. Modula-2. Technical Report #36, Institüt fur Informatik, ETH, CH-8092 Zurich, Switzerland, 1980. Modula-2 is the result of experience gained by Wirth from designing, implementing and using Modula. The concept of processes has been replaced by the lower level notion of coroutines. The advantage is that now the programmer can write any desired scheduling algorithm and not be forced to use the one built into the language for the scheduling of processes as in Modula. Modula-2 also supports the notion of programming in the large by providing separate definition and implementation modules. The language is tailored to the PDP-11 series of computers (as was Modula).

WIR82   Wirth, N. *Programming in Modula-2*. Springer-Verlag, 1982.

WUL73   Wulf, W. A. and M. Shaw. Global Variable Considered Harmful. *SIGPLAN Notices*, v8, no. 2. pp. 28-34, February 1973.

YEM82   Yemini, S. On the Suitability of Ada Multitasking for Expressing Parallel Algorithms. *Proceedings of the AdaTec Conference on Ada*, pp. 91-97, October 1982. The Ada tasking facilities do not provide the ability to evaluate and distribute in parallel to the tasks at task creation time; lack of such an ability results in serialization and offsets some of the gains of parallelism. Constructs to remedy this problem are proposed.

YOU80a   Young, S. J. Trends in the Design of Real Time Languages. *The Australian Computer Bulletin*, v4, no. 5, pp. 5-7, June 1980. (Also in the March 1980 issue of *Computer Bulletin*).

YOU80b   Young, S. J. Low Level Device Programming from a High Level Language. *IEE Proceedings Part E.*, v127, no. 2, pp. 37-44, March 1980. A tutorial paper describing high-level programming language constructs that obviate the necessity of using assembly language for writing device drivers. The high-level constructs discussed are very similar to the representation clauses of Ada.

YOU82   Young, S. J. *Real Time Languages: Design and Development*. Halstead, 1982. Discussion of the design and development of programming languages with an emphasis on real-time programming. States characteristics of real-time programs and systems, requirements for and facilities desired in a real-time programming language. The discussion is illustrated examples from RTL/2, Modula and Ada—languages with facilities for real-time programming—and their synopses.

ZUC81   Zuckerman, S. L. Problems with the Multitasking Facilities in the Ada Programming Language. Technical Note, Defense Communications Engineering Center, Reston, Virginia, May 1981. Author claims that Ada's unconventional multitasking facilities do not provide capabilities equivalent to multitasking facilities in existing languages.

Index

J

L

M

N

O

P

Q

R

S

T

W